Praise for The Five Congregational Personality Types

In his latest book, *The Five Congregational Personality Types: An Ancient Pathway for Congregational Renewal in the 21st Century*, professor, pastor, and practitioner, Michael Adam Beck, offers a biblical understanding of congregational personality types, and how the embodiment of these "personality types" may help or hinder a congregation's future. According to Pastor Beck the pathway forward is for congregational leaders to begin the ancient and sacred journey of listening, learning, and loving, to ultimately take on the personality of Jesus.

–Bishop Daniel G. Beaudoin, *Northwestern Ohio Synod, Evangelical Lutheran Church in America*

Rev. Dr. Michael Beck has already proven he is one of our lead writers and practitioners when it comes to creating fresh expressions of ministry and igniting church renewal in the 21st century. Infused with practical experience and scholarly wisdom, this book offers new perspectives and helpful insights for understanding the multi-dimensional contexts of congregational life and leadership. Michael provides a pathway to help congregations get unstuck, to rebuild and reorient themselves towards greater vitality and renewal.

–Bishop Tracy S. Malone, *Resident Bishop of the Ohio East Episcopal Area of the United Methodist Church*

Michael Beck has once again delivered a navigation tool that enables congregations and pastors to find our way into, out of, and through this thing called "church." The matrix of church and pastor "personality types" provides a playground for relational adventuring that has the potential to bring everyone onto the same team. This essential resource is a GPS system enabling church teams to discover who they are, map out where to go, and provide multiple routes to get there. Every church needs to experience this process!

–Rev. Rob Hutchinson, *Director of Church Development, Western North Carolina Conference of the United Methodist Church*

Michael Beck is helping the church find its future. He knows how to lead congregations that care about the people in their community, lead them to Christ, and see the transformation everyone experiences when God is at work. He offers five congregational types rooted in scripture that will enable you to celebrate your church and help laity and clergy share both vital leadership and the joy of ministry. Michael Beck will give you new knowledge, insights, and offer you hope for the church and its ministry.

–**Bishop Tom Berlin**, *Resident Bishop of the Florida Conference of the United Methodist Church. His books include* Reckless Love: Jesus' Call to Love Our Neighbor, *and* Courage: Jesus and the Call to Brave Faith

Michael Beck is a disciple-maker, and his guidance in fresh-expression ways of doing this have blessed and benefitted many. In this book, he expands his work into the collective aspect of discipleship--that is, when individual Jesus followers come together, they form congregations that have a corporate personality. It is important to know this in order to maximize the strengths and minimize the weaknesses of common life. In this book, Michael shines a lot of light on our life together.

–**Dr. Steve Harper**, *retired UMC Elder and seminary professor, author of many books, including* Life in Christ

All followers of Jesus are called to make disciples, but how they carry out this calling will vary depending on their unique gifts, abilities, and calling. Similarly, each local church has its unique personality and assembly, and while they all share the general call to make disciples, the specific approach will differ. In *The Five Congregational Personality Types*, readers will gain a deeper understanding of their own church's culture and makeup and develop contextual intelligence regarding their local community. This book provides a valuable framework for understanding the diversity within the body of Christ and equips readers to make disciples in a way that is uniquely suited to their individual and corporate giftings.

–**Rev. Dr. Rosario Picardo**, *Co-Pastor Mosaic Church and Executive Pastor of Church Planting, Gem City Church Collective*

What if every congregation could flourish in their identity and be more reflective of the nature and character of the Triune God? Michael Adam Beck offers a life changing guidebook to help congregations flourish. Congregations and leaders will not want to pass up this resource.

–**Rev. Dr. Susan Arnold**, *Director of Congregational Development & Revitalization, Holston Conference, United Methodist Church*

The Five Congregational Personality Types clearly names what many have long suspected: congregations - just like the people who compromise them - have distinct personality traits that frame their strengths and their shadows. The same is true of the clergy and laity who lead them. Michael Beck offers insight and practical guidance for navigating the inherent tensions in these personality differences and encourages us all to live into our Spirit-inspired potential.

–Magrey R. deVega, *Hyde Park United Methodist Church, Tampa, FL, and author of* The Bible Year: A Journey Through Scripture in 365 Days *and* Questions Jesus Asked: A Six-Week Study in the Gospels

Congregations have unique histories, narratives and even personalities. It turns out these personalities are deeply connected to the way the body of Jesus Christ functions in the world. When so much is at stake in the local church—salvation, healing, mutual encouragement and accountability, growth as disciples, empowerment to bear witness—it is essential that we become more self-aware about who we are as congregations, what is good and what gets in the way. Michael Beck has taken a deep, deep dive into the personalities of our congregations. For those who lead, love and lament their present condition, this resource is a gift that we need, right now.

–Bishop Ken Carter, *Western North Carolina Conference, United Methodist Church*

Rev. Dr. Michael Beck has done it again! *The Five Congregational Personality Types* is a powerful piece of congregational development we didn't know was missing from our knowledge about the church. Each chapter contains both learnings and applications for all types of church leaders and their congregations. All churches and pastors have gifts and strengths. Beck gives language to how we can better understand this "arranged marriage" to become the church God is calling us to be. This book and the online assessment are tools for pastors to use with a team of people in their church/charge.

–Ken Willard, *PCC, Director of Congregational Vitality West Virginia United Methodist Church Conference*

**Scan the QR code to visit a
Facebook group for
The Five Congregational Personality Types**

THE FIVE
CONGREGATIONAL
PERSONALITY TYPES

MICHAEL ADAM BECK

THE FIVE
CONGREGATIONAL
PERSONALITY TYPES

AN ANCIENT PATHWAY FOR
CONGREGATIONAL RENEWAL IN THE 21ST CENTURY

 invite
PRESS

Plano, Texas

DEDICATION

To the faithful ones who have served alongside Jill and me at each congregation. We have known Christ and the power of his resurrection and the sharing of his sufferings by becoming like him in his death. Together we have experienced resurrection (Phil 3:10-11).

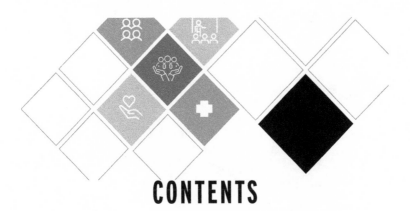

CONTENTS

Foreword   xv

Exploration: The Five Congregational Personality Types

1. Introduction   1
2. The Divine Love Triangle   16
3. The Five Congregational Personality Types   23
4. The Power of the Dark Side   36
5. The Seven Churches in Asia Minor   47

Application: The Five Congregational Personality Types

6. The Arranged Marriage   69
7. Applying the Five Congregational Personality Types   75
   1. Proclamation Centered   75
   2. Fellowship Centered   88
   3. Generosity Centered   98
   4. Outreach Centered   110
   5. Healing Centered   120
8. When the honeymoon is over   135
Conclusion: Love—The Final Word   141
References   145

FOREWORD

Jesus designed his church so that everyone has a part to play. As disciples, when we live together in community, we have the potential to grow into the fullness of Christ, activating kingdom potential within us both individually and collectively.

The letter to the Ephesians lists five distinct intelligences that Christ bestows upon the church: Apostles, Prophets, Evangelists, Shepherds, and Teachers, or APEST. Using the language of "given grace" according to the measure of "Christ's gift," these intelligences are to "build up" the "body of Christ" (Eph 4:1-13).

For over two decades now I have been calling for a recalibration of the church around the fivefold ministry from Ephesians 4. A return to the fivefold ministry is a return to the primordial form, one of the meta-ideas, essential for the multiplication of the church.

These gifts for the upbuilding of the church are actually five archetypes, already evident long before the earthly ministry of Jesus. The archetypes are the somewhat mysterious, recurrent symbols, values, or motifs that are deeply latent in all story, art, thought, and action. The fivefold typology is in some way a category universal to all humankind. When we become followers of Jesus, the Holy Spirit breathes on these traits, imbuing them with new life for the service of the kingdom. Michael will rightly refer to these as five distinct "personality types."

The five personality types were embodied fully by Jesus, the exemplary apostle, prophet, evangelist, shepherd, and teacher. Jesus is the fullness of these archetypes in one fully human, fully God being.

But it takes all of us collectively together to make one Jesus, one "body of Christ" in the world. Each of us is a kind of cell in the greater body. A healthy church needs all five APEST characteristics to mature to its fullest potential. The APEST provides a means for releasing the whole priesthood of all believers to be in ministry together.

It is the dream of every teacher to create a community of students that surpass them. If we are taking our cues from our Rabbi Jesus, we want to build disciples who are better than us. We want to create a community of learners who "will do greater things than these" (John 14:12). We want students who take our ideas deeper and further.

I am proud that Michael Beck calls me his Rabbi. He is one of the few people I know who has been able to revitalize a series of dying churches that, in his words, "no one else wants or sees." He is an active practitioner in the trenches of ministry, and his faithfulness to Jesus has produced fruitfulness for the kingdom. His commitment to the local church is admirable. How he can do that while teaching at seminaries, consistently providing thought leadership, and writing books like the one you hold in your hands is a mystery to me. He brings what I have called elsewhere a prophetic intelligence. His pioneering work in *contextual intelligence*—the ability to read the signs of the times and know what to do—is a gift to the church.

In a Christendom iteration of the church that has largely exiled the APE's, Michael has found a way to be an apostolic reformer from within the inherited system of The United Methodist Church, the church that saved him from the gutters and nurtured him in the faith his entire life.

As a student of movements that shift the tracks of history, I have documented how every historical renewal movement recovers to some degree the following elements: priesthood of believers, kingdom of God over church, prophetic protest, church planting, and mission on the fringes and among the poor. Early Methodism included each of these elements in a strong way. Michael is that kind of Methodist for the 21st century, and he is now the most influential voice in his tribe.

In *The Five Congregational Types*, Michael shows how the fivefold gifting of Ephesians 4 has deep resonance with the Five Factor Model in trait psychology. He shows the APEST typologies are another way to understand how personalities become embodied in community. His insight informs how the gifting and personality of a leader can shape a culture. People who innately possess certain personality traits are drawn to leaders with similar traits. Over time congregations begin to reflect the archetypes of the founders and leaders of the community—for better or for worse. Sometime this can lead to one-dimensional congregations that lack the full diversity of the APEST.

Practices are the embodiment of values. This is the living out of a culture's assumptions in such a way that they can be observed and experienced by others. Michael will describe what he calls the five personality types of congregations and how these communities, often subconsciously, embody these five central values. He does this through providing deep Biblical theology in conversation with church history and emerging learnings from fields of study like sociology and psychology.

I truly believe that it is only through growing in each dimension of the APEST that congregations can fully grow toward "the measure of the full stature of Christ" (Eph 4:13). This book is a practical tool in guiding us toward that end. It is indeed an ancient pathway for church renewal in a new age.

May we see the body of Christ grow up in the likeness of our founder Jesus in the 21st century.

- Alan Hirsch, award-winning author on missional leadership, organizations, and spirituality. Founder of *Movement Leaders Collective* and *Forge Missional Training Network*.

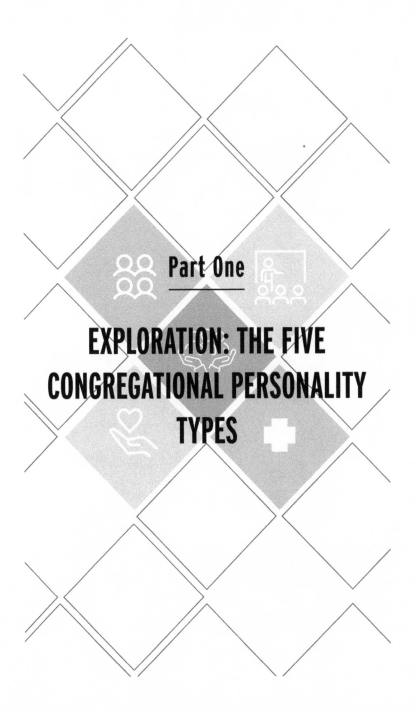

Part One

EXPLORATION: THE FIVE CONGREGATIONAL PERSONALITY TYPES

INTRODUCTION

We drove for miles along old US Route 301 through the sprawling tangled underbrush, swamps, and forests of the North Florida heartland. We passed the little community of Cross Creek beyond the secluded cracker-style farm now made famous by Pulitzer Prize–winning novelist Marjorie Kinnan Rawlings in *The Yearling*. It felt like the space had been somehow unaltered by time and "progress." We journeyed deeper into the backwoods, wild beauty untouched by suburban sprawl. My wife and children, urbanites all, found themselves seemingly in the middle of nowhere. No post office. No stop lights. No gas station. And most certainly no Walmart!

After miles of scenic scape with an occasional unpaved road crossing the highway, we came across an expansive lake shoreline bordered by old-growth cypress trees, knotgrass, and spatterdock. The lake was both the major landmark and center of life for which this community was named: Lochloosa. We turned onto a winding dirt path, the only marker being a hand-painted church sign partially overgrown with vines. At the fork in the road, we came across the familiar site of a cross on a white, wooden-frame church.

The building was the old-fashioned, one-room church design that was all the rage back in the 1880s. A sanctuary served multiple duty as worship space, Sunday school classroom, and pastor's office. A tangle of underbrush now marked the spot where the outhouse once stood. Later, the congregation added a small kitchen, a few Sunday school classrooms, and a bathroom with indoor plumbing! Then came the fellowship hall addition, a single room, lined with long tables for the potluck. The architecture was communicating something about the congregation inside, but my wife and I were too young to discern what exactly that was just yet.

We entered the sanctuary for the first time late on a Sunday afternoon at the invitation of the congregation. A special guest musical group was playing that day, a group of local celebrity acclaim called the Overall Gang. They played harps, banjos, a kick drum, and an odd instrument we had never seen before called an autoharp (which is a string instrument belonging to the zither family).

Then I noticed it. They were barefoot. Not just the musicians but the dozen or so members of the congregation. Most of them had taken off their shoes and slid them under the pew.

Now I need to confess here. I'm a city boy. I was born in Gainesville and raised in a poverty-stricken neighborhood in Ocala, Florida, known to the locals as the "white ghetto." I grew up with a corner store, basketball park, baseball field, recreation center, restaurants, and of course several churches, all within walking distance. In some ways I felt like I had crossed into a different reality. My wife, Jill, and our blended family of eight children felt like all eyes were on us, not only because we arrived late, getting lost on the treacherous back roads with no street signs and no GPS, but because we were the new pastoral family to this congregation.

What does one do in a situation that feels foreign, strange, and intimidating? Well, you join in with the locals. Instinctively and (looking back now) with probably a whisper from the Holy Spirit, I took off my shoes as well. Jill and each of our children, like a row of little ducklings, followed in kind. Thus began our journey of listening, learning, and loving.

The council chair, a distinguished white-haired gentleman, and the only one in the group who didn't speak with a distinct Southern, North Florida drawl, stood up to address the group. "We would like to welcome our new pastoral family. They will be joining us this July." He smiled. The people clapped briefly. A couple said "amen." Then they went back to their music, interspersed with people standing to give testimony of what God had done in their lives.

The "sing" concluded after several hours, but church was just getting started. Adjacent to the original 1882 sanctuary was a more recently constructed aluminum building. The one-room edifice was called the fellowship hall. It was a place where plentiful covered dishes lined long plastic pop-up tables.

We sat as guests and strangers to our hosts. Surely, we were an odd group in their eyes. But as we began to eat together, something sacred started to happen. I guessed that this was why Jesus was so into breaking bread at tables. This is where the magic of community happens. Folks began to share their names and stories, letting us know which of the two families they came from and how their ancestral line traced back. They encouraged us to try their dishes, legendary in these parts, they assured us. It seemed as if they had perfected how to fry every meat imaginable, and even some of the vegetables! A whole table dedicated to desserts loomed before us, promising simultaneously both momentary delight and an early death.

One of the great matriarchs through whom each person present was somehow related was seated at the head of the table. She glowed with an air of holiness. Her descendants could trace their legacy of faith directly back to her, and she was imbued with a kind of royal demeanor. She was expecting my approach as I took an empty chair beside her. I paid my homage to her majesty, introducing myself and telling her about the wonderful things I had heard. She began to explain to me who each person was and how they were related to her.

Many people expressed concerns as they spoke with us. They told us about a time when they could remember the church being so full it was standing room only, a time when some of their favorite pastors held revivals. They reminisced about the days when the place was crawling with youth and kids and they had young pastors with families. Some expressed sheer delight that we came with a built-in youth group. After all, we doubled the worship attendance of the congregation, just us Becks! They talked about how for decades, fewer and fewer people were coming to church. The kids were gone now. They had a wide variety of theories for why this was but similar strands in each storyline.

Cautiously but hopefully, they were inviting us into their world. They knew that our relationship was just beginning and that in a few weeks' time, we would return officially as the clergy family. Their apprehension centered around how frequently their pastors came and went. "They won't let you stay here long" was a frequent comment. This caused them to feel like they were a kind of stepping stone for young pastors climbing the ladder of success or a rest home for retired clergy making their last stop as a pastor.

This was our first appointment as a pastoral family: Lochloosa United Methodist Church. In Methodist speak I was what was called a "supply pastor," a kind of almost-pastor but without formal seminary education or credentials. I was in for quite an education indeed. In the span of one year, from 2011 to 2012, our little congregation of twelve grew to almost one hundred! This was miraculous. We had the highest percentage increase in attendance in the whole state of Florida! But then again, we did double the congregation on our first Sunday—with just our family.

Those folks taught me how to be a pastor. It wasn't really a great challenge for them because I had no idea how to be a pastor and had no seminary education. But they had what we call in the recovery community some good old G.O.D.: the Gift Of Desperation. They just didn't want their little church to close, and they were willing to try new stuff—within a range of acceptability. As long as we could keep gathering together for fellowship as a top priority, we could explore other new and creative ways to be the church as well.

Now I am first and foremost a *preacher*. I've had a lifelong love affair with the Bible. Reading it, studying it, inwardly digesting it, and figuring out the most creative ways to share it with others—that has been one of the great obsessions of my life.

I experienced a supernatural encounter with Jesus Christ by picking up a jailhouse edition of the Gideons Bible my mother left from one of her many stays as a guest in the local jail. I read Paul's short second letter to Timothy, and by the third chapter, somewhere between inheriting the faith from Grandma and "godlessness in the last days," my heart experienced a convulsion. Before I knew it, I was on my face in the shower with the lights out, where I met the Savior and Lord of the universe. I love the Bible. It was the instrument Jesus used to reach into my hellish life as a ninth-grade dropout and repeat felon. The Word of God introduced me to the living Word of God: Jesus Christ.

I love to read the Bible. I love to memorize the Bible. I love to preach the Bible. And I love to teach the Bible. Today, fifteen years later we have a team of preachers at our network of churches, and rule number one is "preach the passage." Rule number two is "preach the passage." Rule number three is "preach the passage." When we exegete our community well and preach the passage faithfully, God always has a relevant message for the real social situations of our context.

The Bible has more fascinating, challenging, crazy, infuriating, life-giving things to say than any preacher could ever come up with. It's all in there: rape, genocide, incest, patriarchy, kick-ass female warriors, revolts, and lots of grace, love, redemption. Every single word of it points toward and is fulfilled in Jesus of Nazareth.

For me the Bible is not just something to read, memorize, and preach; it needs ultimately to be expressed through our hands. My primary ministry focus is outreach. The Word comes alive most when we embody it through acts of service. This includes feeding the hungry, providing drink for the thirsty, welcoming strangers, clothing the naked, caring for the sick, and visiting the incarcerated (Matt 25:34–36). It is in the face of the marginalized, oppressed, and suffering that we see the face of Jesus most clearly.

The problem was that this little congregation, Lochloosa, didn't really care much about sermons or give a whole lot of thought to outreach. I mean, they knew that was a part of all the churchy stuff, but that wasn't what got their spiritual juices flowing. They knew that sermons would happen at church, of course, but they didn't want too much sermonizing, especially as we were coming up on the 12:00 hour on Sunday morning. That was stop time. Pull the rip cord. Shut it down. We are done. Hallelujah. Praise God. Now let's fellowship! Most of the time, fellowship included fried food, an overflowing table, and lots of desserts.

I often wonder how these people put up with this young Bible-philiac with those long-winded sermons that I enjoyed preparing and delivering. Why in the world did they keep coming back when I would go over that magical one-hour mark week after week? I mean, I thought the sermons were great, a tour de force in biblical exegesis and proclamation, but it seemed I was the only one among the congregation who felt that way.

What probably saved me were the words of a wise old mentor: "Just love the folks."

"But they do this, and they do that. I can see huge possibilities. We could have real revival. If we did this, people would come for miles to little old Lochloosa just to see!" I protested.

But she repeated again, "Just love the folks. Remember the three L's: listen … learn … love." I took her words to heart, and that's what I tried to do.

Another mentor told me, "Win the LOLs," by whom he meant "little old ladies," the matriarchs of the church who held all the power, the true leaders of the church. So, I started visiting them in their homes, listening to their stories, and trying to discover their pain, their hopes, and their dreams. Word got around that this young preacher (whose sermons were way too long) was making home visits. My first stop? You guessed it, the matriarch herself, "bishop" of these lands called Lochloosa.

It seems they would tolerate my too-long sermons as long as I kept up the visits, along with some other things.

"We need to bring back those sings," one told me. While at first, they were foreign to me, I grew to love those song gatherings. The music, the instruments, the testifying, they were acts of faithful subversion, defying the powers that be and the economic machine that pillaged rural places like this one. I learned about the pain these people carried, how they often felt overlooked and stripped of young leaders and resources by the urban centers nearby. They sang and danced their faith as a way to hold on to hope and their unique personality type as a congregation.[1]

"We need to have those potlucks once a month . . . at least!" said another. I agreed! It was the best food I had ever had in my life, attested by the fact I gained twenty pounds while being the pastor there.

"Why did we ever stop those yard sales that brought the whole community to our church?" asked another. I had never really thought of a yard sale as an outreach event, but they really were in this context.

---

1. Michael Adam Beck and Tyler Kleeberger, *Fresh Expressions of the Rural Church* (Nashville: Abingdon Press, 2022).

"Preacher, can you shorten your sermons a bit? They are fine and all, but you know what really gets in my craw?" croaked little old Mrs. Louise, direct descendant to the Matriarch Bishop: "When we don't sing every verse of a song. A song tells a story. We don't need to be dicing those up. They're written like that for a reason you know . . . in order."

Got it. More potlucks. More stories. More songs sung together, and every single verse. More gatherings at the church that were not a *church service*. Looking back now, I realize that this congregation had a unique way of living out their identity. They had a distinct "personality type" that infused everything they did. Their personality type manifested as *fellowship*. This is a culture that is built around the New Testament value of κοινωνία (*koinonia*), which can mean partnership, social intercourse, financial benefaction, or communion. It is a community defined by intimate relationships and the enjoyment of being together. We will explore this more fully later. They would put up with this long-winded, wet-behind-the-ears preacher if I would make sure that they could *be together as much as possible.*

Now that was all fine and dandy, and people actually started coming back to church. But as far as outsiders go, no new people entered into the congregation. This is what I call the *dark side* of this congregation's personality type, a blind spot that if not dealt with can keep a congregation unhealthy. A fellowship-centered congregation can be very inwardly focused, even exclusive toward outsiders, and as beautiful and biblical as fellowship is, it can't be the only way a congregation lives out its identity. To be a church of Jesus by definition means we need to reach new people and make disciples that multiply. The church is "missionary by its very nature," after all.[2] This is where I stumbled into a lesson that I've carried with me ever since. It's captured by this phrase:

Grow the center, experiment on the edge.

What do I mean by that? Well, as an outreach-oriented preacher at heart pastoring a fellowship congregation, I had to make some adjustments. But as I remembered to "just love the folks" and "listen,

---

2. Vatican Council II, *Ad Gentes (Decree on the Missionary Activity of the Church)*, Vatican Archive, https://www.vatican.va/archive/hist_councils/ii_vatican_council/documents/vat-ii_decree_19651207_ad-gentes_en.html.

learn, and love," I discovered that if you do that long enough, what you are actually doing is *leading*. Yes, *the best leaders are those who listen, learn, and love well*. Because then people begin to see that you genuinely care for them. And when the people begin to trust you as their leader, you can journey together with them to a new place, even a place you or they have never been to before.

As a community we had to face the fact that we had a dark side. We could not simply keep the gift of this wonderful fellowship to ourselves. We had to invite others in to experience it. So, there is a fourth *L* as you continue listening, learning, and loving . . . *leading*. You can think of the fourth *L* as a kind of fulcrum, a handle or pivot point from which we can move together in a new direction.

In that one-room church house hidden among the old-growth cypress trees, knotgrass, and spatterdock, I stumbled into a discovery that has proved true with each revitalization I have served as pastor and with each congregation I've interacted with as a coach and consultant. Congregations, while incredibly unique in a diversity of ways, have a central value that is definitive of the culture. This manifests as a kind of collective *personality type*, the communal embodiment of a core value. Sometimes this value exists at a subconscious level within the congregation, although it becomes obvious when you know what to look for.

A *personality* is a set of relatively enduring behavioral and cognitive characteristics, traits, or predispositions that people take with them to different situations and interactions with others. One way to assess the differences among individuals is to understand the collection of qualities, or the mental and behavioral features, that make up their personalities. Psychologists widely agree that personality is relatively stable across time and consistent across contexts, situations, and interactions.[3]

A *culture* can be defined as a unique meaning and information system shared by a group and transmitted across generations that allows the group to meet basic needs of survival, pursue happiness and well-being, and derive meaning from life.[4] Anthropologists in their

3. David Matsumoto and Linda Juang, *Culture and Psychology*, 4th ed. (Belmont, CA: Wadsworth/Thomson, 2008), 258.
4. Matsumoto and Juang, *Culture and Psychology*, 27.

ethnographic fieldwork began to identify the ways that collections of individuals form distinct group cultures. Their work formed the basis for the idea of *national character*, which refers to the perception that each culture has a modal personality type and that most persons in that culture share aspects of it. The work of cultural psychologists and sociologists helps us understand the interplay between *personality* and *culture*.[5]

Sociologist Manuel Castells reflects on how *identity*, people's source of meaning and experience, is shaped by collective actors and contextual factors. While personality is, at some level, biologically determined, it is also communally determined. Castells comments at length about how powerfully, smaller, local expressions of collective identity can challenge and resist larger trends like globalization and cosmopolitanism, which move toward cultural singularity. He defines a *social movement* as the purposive collective actions whose outcome transforms the values and institutions of society.[6]

Resistance identity, Castells notes, is generated by actors who are in devalued conditions within the dominant structures but who embody values opposed to those permeating the institutions of society. The identity of resistance leads to the formation of *communes* or *communities*, which are collective resistance against oppression or the dominant culture defined by history, geography, or biology.[7]

This is exactly what Christian congregations are: communities that share features of social movements and resistance identity. They are communities who order their lives by a different set of values than the dominant culture. Within every congregation is a culture of resistance of some form. It can be around worshiping one God in a polytheistic environment, giving money to help others in a self-serving consumeristic culture, caring for the victims of injustice wounded by corrupt systems, or fidelity to biblical truth over other ideologies. Unfortunately, congregations can become so syncretistic with national culture that they are unaware of the core values around which their life was organized. Thankfully, these can be awakened.

---

5. Matsumoto and Juang, *Culture and Psychology*, 259.
6. Manuel Castells, *The Power of Identity*, 2nd ed., vol. 2 of The Information Age: Economy, Society, and Culture (Malden, MA: Wiley-Blackwell, 2010), 3.
7. Castells, *Power of Identity*, 8–9.

The dominant approach to understanding personality today is known as trait psychology. As we will explore more fully throughout the book, the hundreds of distinct traits have been summarized within five dominant personality dimensions (extroversion, agreeableness, openness, conscientiousness, and neuroticism), which are universal to all human beings. This is called the Five Factor Model (FFM).[8] These aspects of our individuality find embodiment in community.

While every congregation is different in the same way no two human beings are the same, there are also five dominant personality dimensions universal to all congregations. The congregational types are the communal embodiment of the five personality dimensions: extroversion, agreeableness, openness, conscientiousness, and neuroticism:

1. Extroversion finds communal embodiment as an "outreach-centered" congregation.

2. Agreeableness finds communal embodiment as a "fellowship-centered" congregation.

3. Openness finds communal embodiment as a "healing-centered" congregation.

4. Conscientiousness finds communal embodiment as a "proclamation-centered" congregation.

5. Neuroticism: finds communal embodiment as a "generosity-centered" congregation. Unlike the first four personality dimensions, a lower score in neuroticism is preferred. Low neuroticism leads to a more generous congregation because they trust God's provision.

Each of these personalities has a strength and a weakness. People often naturally group themselves unconsciously with others who share similar traits and values. Being in relationship with others can enhance or diminish the individual traits of our personality. A healthy community can help us fulfill some of our most noble traits. We can

---

8. Matsumoto and Juang, *Culture and Psychology*, 258.

hear that in the relational sentiment when we say that person or group "brings out the best in me."

Likewise, a toxic community can facilitate negative aspects of personality coming out in harmful ways. Good people will follow the will of a group or obey authority figures who instruct them to perform acts conflicting with their personal conscience. We often refer to this as "peer pressure" or the direct or indirect influence on members of social groups with similar interests, experiences, or social statuses. A peer group can significantly influence a person's beliefs, values, and behavior, for better or for worse.

Alan Hirsch, a prominent Australian missiologist, author, and thought leader in the missional church movement, shows how the gifts Jesus bestows for the upbuilding of the church in Ephesians 4:7–13, called the APEST typology (Apostle, Prophet, Evangelist, Shepherd, Teacher), are actually five archetypes already evident long before the earthly ministry of Jesus. Hirsch understands archetypes as those "somewhat mysterious, recurrent symbols, values, or motifs that are deeply latent in all story, art, thought, and action."[9] He believes that the fivefold typology is in some way a category universal to all humankind. When we become Christians, the Holy Spirit breathes on these preexisting personality traits, imbuing them with new life for the service of the kingdom.

We will go more in-depth later. For now, these APEST typologies are another way to understand how personalities become embodied in community. In particular, this informs how the gifting and personality of a leader can shape a culture. People who innately possess certain personality traits are drawn to leaders with similar traits. Over time congregations begin to reflect the archetypes of the founders and leaders of the community—for better or for worse.

There is a direct connection between the Big Five Personality Traits, the APEST, and the Five Congregational Types, which we will explore in depth in the next chapter.[10] For now, I simply want to describe the five types of congregations and their central values:

9. Alan Hirsch, *5Q: Reactivating the Original Intelligence and Capacity of the Body of Christ* (100 Movements Publishing, 2017), 33.

10. S. Roccas, L. Sagiv, S. H. Schwartz, and A. Knafo, "The Big Five Person-

1. **Proclamation Centered:** This congregation values *truth* (ἀλήθεια) and loves growing and sharing in quality teaching and preaching.

2. **Outreach Centered:** This congregation values *service* (διακονέω) and embodying the good news in word and deed. They live to serve those outside the community.

3. **Healing Centered:** This congregation values *wholeness* (ἰάομαι) and the manifestation of Jesus' life in the world, seeking to be a community where people experience healing.

4. **Generosity Centered:** This congregation values *singleness/ generosity* (ἁπλότης) and uses its resources to invest in ministries that make a kingdom impact.

5. **Fellowship Centered:** This congregation values *community* (κοινωνία) and loves to be together and nurture one another.

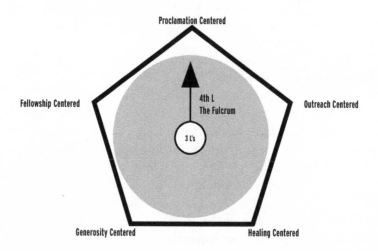

ality Factors and Personal Values," *Personality and Social Psychology Bulletin* 28, vol. 6 (2002): 789–801. https://doi.org/10.1177/0146167202289008.

The most compelling aspect of the five congregational personality types is how we see them clearly embedded in the early life of the church. In Acts 2:43–47 we see that those first believers shared in deep relationships (fellowship centered); devoted themselves to the apostles' teaching (proclamation centered); broke bread together, shared all things in common, and gave to those experiencing poverty (generosity centered); prayed and pointed to "signs and wonders" (healing centered); and had outsiders added to their numbers daily (outreach). A healthy, growing ancient church in Acts expressed all these characteristics at some level, and we should seek to embody them in our congregational life today.

To summarize, congregations are more than an aggregate of individuals. They each have a distinct cultural personality. This personality can be profoundly shaped by its founders. Consider, for example, Ignatius of Loyola and the Jesuit order, John Wesley and the people called Methodists, Mother Teresa and her Missionaries of Charity, and Martin Luther King Jr. and the civil rights movement. Those expressions bear the traits of their founder's core ideas and personalities— again—for better or for worse.

Congregational culture can also be shaped (and reshaped) by leaders. Every leader brings a distinct personality to the congregation. In fact, the "stronger the personality of the leaders, the more their influence will be reflected throughout the organization, especially in highly centralized organizations."[11] Understanding the interaction between these personalities (congregation and leader) is essential to a fruitful ministry.

The problem here is that congregations should *not* take on the personality of their leaders. We have seen how devastating this has been for the church across the ages. Certainly, today we are inundated with one breaking headline after another in which a large influential church pastor is caught in some kind of moral failure, scandal, or abuse of their power. In each situation those leaders have big personalities, and the congregations to some extent took on the personality of the leader.

---

11. Roger Heuser and Norman Shawchuck, *Leading the Congregation: Caring for Yourself While Serving Others*, rev. ed. (Nashville: Abingdon Press, 2010), 93.

The five congregational types offer us a way to avoid this dilemma. Congregations should take on the personality of Jesus. In fact, every congregation can at some level take on the five distinct personality traits of Jesus noted in Ephesians 4:1–16: apostle, prophet, evangelist, shepherd, and teacher. Jesus is the fullness of what each of those types can be. Every congregation should flourish in their own unique personality but seek to grow in the other four dimensions as well.

Am I saying your congregation should have a case of multiple personality disorder? No, I'm saying every congregation should have a case of Jesus' personality dimension. We should be maturing in healing (apostle), generosity (prophet), outreach (evangelist), fellowship (shepherd), and proclamation (teacher).

The unending collapse of congregations driven by a big-personality leader exposes how we have mis-structured the church itself in the West. A single centralized leader exerting great influence over the entire congregation is not faithful to Jesus' design. The way we can avoid this scenario and all the abuses that come with it is through a distributed, polycentric, team-based, and shared leadership approach.[12]

For our purposes the simplest way to understand this is that a congregation is made up of many personalities. Some will score high on openness, extroversion, conscientiousness, agreeableness, or some high/low on neuroticism. Some will be gifted apostles or prophets or evangelists or shepherds or teachers. We can equip and empower them to lead teams in their areas of gifting, flowing from the unique wiring of their personality. This enables them to feel fulfilled in their life and ministry.

Imagine teams of laity set free to grow in each of the five areas. The leadership is shared among the people, and a more mature expression of Jesus is embodied in the world. The five congregational personality types give us a framework to mature toward the "full stature of Christ" (Eph 4:13). As the body of Christ, we find ourselves therefore in a *divine love triangle* among pastor(s), congregation, and community, which we will now explore together.

---

12. For an extensive treatment of this idea, see Michael Adam Beck, *Deep and Wild: Remissioning Your Church from the Outside In* (Franklin, TN: Seedbed Publishing, 2021).

Team Exercise One

Have everyone take the Five Congregational Personality Types (FCPT) Assessment.

1. Review your FCPT Assessment. Do you agree with the results? Why or why not?

2. What are the pastor's top scores on the assessment? Does this make sense with what you know about his or her personality?

3. How many on your team scored high on the same FCPT assessment typology? What does this say about your team or congregation?

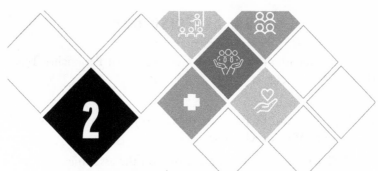

THE DIVINE LOVE TRIANGLE

At Lochloosa we brought back those monthly potlucks and yard sales and started singing every verse of every song with our shoes off. But we also did something else. A couple of us started going to lunch down at Diane's Diner, a little BBQ joint in a small town just north of us called Hawthorne.

Every Sunday after church we would gather in that space and do what we loved to do: fellowship and eat. But we also engaged strangers at our table, the folks eating good BBQ, and our servers. The servers were like the "persons of peace" that Jesus tells us to find and do life within his missional blueprint (Luke 10:6). These are people who exchanged peace with us, welcomed us, and invited us into the community. They were the natives who showed us how things worked in that environment. They knew everybody and knew everybody's business. They were the connectors of people, gateways to relationships, and keepers of knowledge.

As we learned our servers' names and stories, we ultimately popped the question: "Why don't y'all come to church sometime?" To which they responded, "Because we are here taking care of y'all every Sunday . . . dummy!" Then, in a flash of inspiration, the lights came on.

"Okay, so what would church look like for you? When would it happen? Where would it happen?" Now that was the million-dollar question, and it would produce a kingdom gold rush.

This led us to start what I would call today a "fresh expression of church" with those Diane's Diner servers and their patrons. This is a form of church for people who don't now go to church: Bible study, worship, and prayer, right there over BBQ-laden tables. This led to the growth of the inherited church. The Diane's Diner servers connected us with lots of outsiders all over the area surrounding Lochloosa. We started a new Sunday evening worship experience at the church just for them. The rest is history. We had the highest percentage increase in attendance in the Florida Conference—boom!

AVERAGE WORSHIP ATTENDANCE

Total attendance at primary worship services

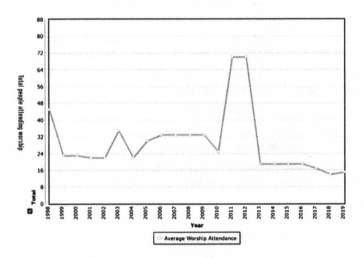

Disappointingly, after our large blended family moved on to the next appointment and there was a change of leadership, many of the exciting new things ceased, and the congregation spiraled into decline again. They collapsed, subconsciously, back into the embodiment of a single trait: the one-dimensional nature of a fellowship-centered congregation.

If we could diagram what happened, it would look like this: We listened, learned, and loved together by leaning into the unique personality type of the congregation (fellowship). But we also began to journey together into a form of outreach that folded new people into our sweet fellowship.

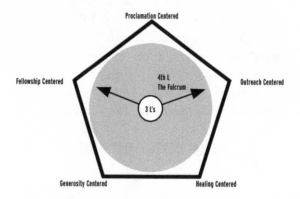

Through the little experiment in the diner, we learned how to connect relationally in ways that offered the kind of "food" that our community was desperately desiring. We became an overall healthier congregation. We realized that the strength of our unique personality also cast a shadow, a "dark side" that we will explore in a coming chapter.

Those people made a pastor out of me. And yes, I still preach shoeless every Sunday and sing every verse because a song tells a story. But more importantly, they were teaching me this:

1. Every congregation has a unique personality type, which has a bright side and a dark side.

2. Every pastor has a unique personality type that has a bright side and a dark side.

3. When we learn one another's unique personality types and love one another through differences, we can build trust.

4. When we trust one another, we can journey together from the center to experiment on the edge.

5. Every community needs a healthy congregation reaching out in love.

6. New life can burst forth in this love triangle of congregation, pastor, and community!

You've heard of being in a "love triangle," right? Typically, this is not a good thing! One person is in love with two people, or two people are competing for the affections of a single person. No congregation should look like that! Let me reframe what I mean by a love triangle.

Most people I know who have great marriages are those who say there are really three people in the relationship: their spouse, themselves, and God in the center holding it all together!

Historically, we think of God as existing in a kind of love triangle. We have called this the Trinity. God is One in the deepest sense of the word and yet three persons. This is a great mystery of our faith. God the Father, God the Son, and God the Spirit live in a divine community, a relational matrix, a loving dance. In the missional church movement, we think of God sending the Son and the Father and Son sending the Spirit, but we include another sending movement in the dance: the Trinity sending the church.[13] The church is an extension of God's own divine relational dance on the earth.

Now consider this love triangle. God has sent the church, our life is derived from the life of the Triune God, but most churches consist of three primary relationships:

1. The Congregation
2. The Pastor(s)
3. The Larger Community

Obviously, we have an additional connecting relationship to the wider church, but depending on a church's polity, that relationship can take different forms. For our purposes we will focus on these three key relationships, each flowing from the life of God.

---

13.   David J. Bosch, *Transforming Mission: Paradigm Shifts in Theology of Mission*, American Society of Missiology Series, No. 16 (Maryknoll, NY: Orbis Books, 1991), 390.

Maybe your team is saying, "Our church is in serious trouble. Why are we talking about love triangles?" The late family systems theorist and leadership consultant Edwin Friedman wrote, "To reorient oneself away from a focus on technology toward a focus on emotional process requires that, like Columbus, we think in ways that not only are different from traditional routes but that also sometimes go in the opposite direction."[14] It's easier to jump to the quick-fix solutions of the emerging gurus of the day with their "three easy steps to make your church grow again" than to do the actual relational work of loving one another through differences.

Friedman's revolutionary work emphasized the power of "presence" in the leader of a family, organization, or congregation and the ability of leaders to self-differentiate. Self-differentiation means the capacity to be an "I" while remaining connected to a "we." This is the ability to be true to one's own values and life vision while valuing and sustaining relationships with those around you. This enables the leader to be less reactionary and focus on emotional barriers and nurturing relationships with others. The ideal here is to remain engaged in the system but in a nonreactive manner, or what Friedman called being a "nonanxious presence."[15] The love triangle gives us a framework to help us do this.

In healthy churches a divine dance of love flows from God through the pastor, and then the people, into the community, and often back again. If there is a "love blockage" between any of these relationships, it diminishes the health of the congregation. If a congregation dislikes their pastor or a pastor resents their congregation, nothing healthy will flow out or into the community.

---

14. Edwin H. Friedman, *A Failure of Nerve: Leadership in the Age of the Quick Fix* (New York: Seabury Press, 2007), 54.

15. Edwin H. Friedman, *Generation to Generation: Family Process in Church and Synagogue* (New York: Guilford Press, 2011), 27.

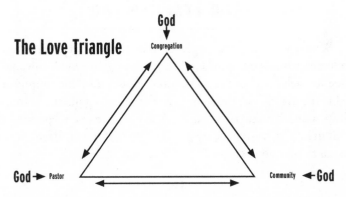

The Love Triangle

God
Congregation
God ▶ Pastor
Community ◀ God

In this book I hope to share some practical ways we can use the five congregational types so that congregations, pastors, and communities can overcome these blockages and love one another back to health.

Congregations can find new forms of vitality when they gain awareness of their personality type and seek to grow in their area of weakness. They own the strength of their dominant trait but then seek to grow in the other personality dimensions. It takes a team of committed leaders to confront the shadow, to move the leadership fulcrum, to grow the congregation in these new areas, often one at a time. This helps congregations become a more robust, fuller expression of the body of Christ as they explore growth in the five core dimensions. This journey of love is the ancient way of congregational renewal. Let's awaken it for the twenty-first century.

Team Exercise Two

With your team pray together and then consider the love triangle diagram. The love of God flows through a series of primarily three key relationships: congregation, pastor, and community. Examine the diagram together and use the following questions to have an open and honest conversation. Make sure to keep "speaking the truth in love" as your primary guide (Eph. 4:15)! Ask, "Is my contribution to the conversation 1. TRUE and 2. LOVING?"

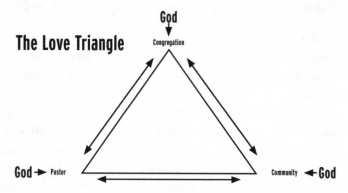

1. Do you feel a "love blockage" anywhere among the three key relationships?

2. What makes you feel that way? Give some practical examples that illustrate these feelings.

THE FIVE CONGREGATIONAL PERSONALITY TYPES

*But I have this against you, that you have abandoned the love
you had at first.*

—Revelation 2:4

I finally became a "real pastor" one day, institutionally speaking. I went to seminary, got a stole from the bishop, and got a T-shirt to tell the tale. Additionally, my wife, the Reverend Jill Beck, also became a "real pastor." She is now my copastor and partner in missional mischief. More importantly, the congregations we've served have allowed us to earn the title of pastor. Turns out it's not a position that an institution can grant but rather a role one is invited to play in the lives of people who know you care about them.

Collectively, we have guided six congregations in a row through revitalization processes, but we carry Lochloosa in our hearts wherever we go.

The churches we were sent to had seen better days. Some were on the brink of closure; others were already dead inside but unaware of it. Jill and I actively pray, "Lord, send us to the churches no one else wants or sees." We are called to be interventionists and triage unit pastors who in God's power try to love congregations back to life.

The Lord has blessed me to serve on an international scale as a professor, coach, consultant, and author. I've coached many pastors, leaders, and innovators across the ecclesial spectrum, and I've led workshops, trainings, and consultations with hundreds of congregations across the country. Within those relationships I've been able to learn and test these ideas. My own doctoral research was focused on semiotics, the study of signs and symbols that constitute human culture and their use or interpretation,[16] and I'm especially passionate about helping my seminary students grow in the area of contextual intelligence, "the ability to accurately diagnose a context and make the correct decisions regarding what to do."[17]

However, first and foremost, I am writing this book as an active pastor serving the local church in the twenty-first century. Jill and I serve two congregations and a network of fresh expressions. Again, Fresh Expressions are forms of church for people who don't go to conventional churches. They gather in tattoo parlors, dog parks, burrito joints, running tracks, yoga studios, and digital spaces. A blended ecology of church refers to inherited and fresh forms of church living together in a symbiotic relationship.[18] Shepherding these communities is our day job. As I write these words, I'm doing so between committee meetings and praying about what I'm going to preach this Sunday. I'm not writing as some theorist, far removed from frontline ministry. I'm writing as a pastor, failing forward, learning, adapting, and trying to figure out what ministry looks like in a massively changed landscape.

Jill and I don't only live together, we work together. She puts up with me essentially twenty-four hours a day, seven days a week! And for this she has been sainted by people who know us well. In our marriage Jill and I have benefited greatly from understanding our own personality types. Through knowing what makes each other tick (and even explode sometimes), we can love each other more deeply

---

16. M. Gottdiener, K. Boklund-Lagopoulou, and A. P. Lagopoulos (eds.). *Semiotics.* (London SAGE Publications Ltd, 2003), https://dx.doi.org/10.4135/9781446263419.

17. Leonard Sweet and Michael Adam Beck, *Contextual Intelligence: Unlocking the Ancient Secrets to Mission on the Front Lines* (Oviedo, FL: HigherLife, 2020).

18. Michael Adam Beck with Jorge Acevedo, *A Field Guide to Methodist Fresh Expressions* (Nashville: Abingdon Press, 2020), xxix.

as we continue in the fifteen-year dance of our marriage. Navigating these personality differences started when we began dating.

Dating can be understood as the early stage of romantic relationships in which two people meet and engage in activities together. Typically, the intent is for each party to evaluate the other's suitability as a partner in an ongoing intimate relationship.

In the dating world we've all heard the phrase, "They're just not my type." This is often a statement of incompatibility. *Type* is a loaded word. What do we mean when we use it? Are we talking about physical characteristics, personality, culture, mannerisms, intelligence, or social capabilities? It can be one of those things or a combination of all or some of them.

Dating apps have been proved successful in matching people in meaningful relationships because they've been programmed to understand these compatibility factors. While it may seem like mysterious algorithms based on lines of code that might pick our future spouse, much of it is merely a search tool that makes match recommendations by using our data. Some apps track our swipes and who swipes on us. Often these decisions are made in a split second and based primarily on physical appearance. Simple logic would indicate that the more you use the app, the more data you provide, which in theory helps the algorithm get more of your preferences to work with. This is a superficial way to find a lifelong partner.

Yet other apps employ more advanced algorithms using extensive questionnaires. They collect as much personal information on each user as possible. People are matched based on location and age, education and employment, as well as the multitude of preferences you feed into the app. Users with similar search preferences and responses to questions who are looking for the same things, relationally speaking, are paired with a higher match percentage.

It's easy to see that a mixture of factors combines to help someone find their "type." What these algorithms are really picking up on are distinct personality *traits*. A trait is simply a characteristic or quality distinguishing a person. Understanding how different personalities interact can help effectively pair and sustain people in vital relationships.

Jill and I have several close clergy friends who have found their lifelong partners using dating apps. For us, dating apps were a little before our time, and we did not have access to these benefits. We had to figure things out, as some would say, "the old-fashioned way" through the trial-and-error process of a dating relationship. But we have both benefited from the Enneagram (Jill is a Two, the Helper/ Giver, and I'm an Eight, the Challenger/Protector) and multiple other personality assessments like Myers-Briggs, Strength Finders, and spiritual gift inventories.

However, we have found the Revised NEO Personality Inventory (NEO-PI-R) based on the Five Factor Model (FFM) most helpful in understanding each other in our ongoing relationship. The NEO-PI-R, more commonly called the "Big Five Assessment," is a 240-item instrument, scientifically validated through hundreds of studies across many different cultures. It produces scores on the five major personality traits and six subscores for each of those major traits.[19]

The trait approach in modern psychology has a long history dating back to the work of Gordon Allport in 1936.[20] Yet these ideas have a much deeper history. It was Hippocrates (460–370 BC), Greek physician of the classical period, who first suggested four types of temperament: sanguine, phlegmatic, choleric, and melancholic. Remarkably, the letter to Ephesians lists five personality types, using the language of "given grace" according to the measure of "Christ's gift" to "build up" the "body of Christ" (Eph 4:7–12).

Hirsch demonstrates that these five personality types were embodied fully by Jesus, the exemplary apostle, prophet, evangelist, shepherd, and teacher.[21] Jesus is the fullness of these personality types in one fully human, fully God being. But it takes all of us collectively together to make one Jesus, one "body of Christ" in the world. Each of us is a kind of cell in the greater body. I will show that the fivefold

---

19. David Matsumoto and Linda Juang, *Culture and Psychology*, 4th ed. (Belmont, CA: Wadsworth/Thomson, 2008), 265.

20. Matsumoto and Juang, *Culture and Psychology*, 263.

21. Alan Hirsch, *5Q: Reactivating the Original Intelligence and Capacity of the Body of Christ* (100 Movements Publishing, 2017), 74.

gifting of Ephesians 4 has deep connections with the FFM in trait psychology.

In 1884 English Victorian-era polymath, statistician, sociologist, psychologist, and anthropologist Sir Francis Galton was first to investigate the hypothesis that it is possible to derive a comprehensive taxonomy of human personality traits by sampling language: the lexical hypothesis. Hundreds of traits were explored by various researchers across time.[22]

It's important to distinguish the Five Factor Model from the Five Factor Theory (FFT). The latter is a theory about the origin of the traits, which is a continual source of controversy. However, the FFM is widely accepted and built upon decades of research that confirm there are five distinct basic personality dimensions that appear universal for all humans across all cultures.[23]

Contemporary personality psychologists have accepted that the multitude of various traits can be organized into these "big five" basic dimensions of personality: extroversion, agreeableness, openness, conscientiousness, and neuroticism.[24] Longitudinal and cross-sectional studies of men and women in many countries across cultural traditions reveal that personality traits are highly stable and change in consistent ways in various stages of aging.[25] In essence, the Big Five personality traits are used to describe the broad traits that serve as building blocks of personality. One way to think about each trait is on a kind of spectrum, as described below:

Extroversion (outgoing/energetic vs. solitary/reserved)

Agreeableness (friendly/compassionate vs. critical/rational)

Openness to experience (inventive/curious vs. consistent/cautious)

22. Laura E. Berk, *Exploring Lifespan Development*, 1st ed. (Boston: Pearson/Allyn and Bacon, 2008), 424.

23. Matsumoto and Juang, *Culture and Psychology*, 264.

24. Robert A. Power and Michael Pluess, "Heritability Estimates of the Big Five Personality Traits Based on Common Genetic Variants," *Translational Psychiatry* 5, no. 7 (2015): 604, doi:10.1038/tp.2015.96.

25. Berk, *Exploring Lifespan Development*, 425.

Conscientiousness (efficient/organized vs. extravagant/careless)

Neuroticism (sensitive/nervous vs. resilient/confident)

Extroversion has been understood as sociability, the quality of being social with others. Extroverts are typically talkative, active, and assertive, and they exhibit high amounts of emotional expressiveness. Introverts, on the other hand, are typically quiet, passive, and sober; they prefer solitude; and they have less energy in social situations. Extroverts can be characterized by a breadth of activities (as opposed to depth). The trait is marked by extended engagement with the external world. Extroverts enjoy interacting with people and are often perceived as full of energy. Again, every person exists on a spectrum. It is false to assume there is a pure extrovert or introvert since people are often able to adapt in social settings.

Agreeableness refers to kindness, the quality of being friendly, generous, and considerate of others. The agreeableness trait reflects a general concern for social harmony. Agreeable individuals value getting along with others and making things work. They are generally considerate, soft-hearted, kind, generous, trustworthy, helpful, and willing to compromise their interests to help others. Agreeable people also have an optimistic view of human nature. They show genuine concern for others and their development. Disagreeable individuals can place self-interest above getting along with others and seem unconcerned with others' well-being. Individuals low on agreeableness can be ruthless, suspicious, stingy, antagonistic, and critical.

Openness refers to creativity and intrigue, the quality of being imaginative and sometimes artistic. People who are open to experience are intellectually curious, open to emotion, sensitive to beauty, and willing to experiment with new things. They tend to be liberal and open-handed, with a focus on originality. Conversely, those with low openness are characterized as pragmatic and data-driven, uncreative, conventional, and conservative, and they can be perceived to be dogmatic and closed-minded.

Conscientiousness refers to thoughtfulness, the habit of being attentive to the needs of others. It includes a tendency to display self-discipline, act dutifully, and strive for achievement against measures or outside expectations. They tend to be well-organized, punctual, hardworking, and ambitious. High conscientiousness can be perceived as being stubborn, overly focused, and indicating a preference for planned rather than spontaneous behavior. People low on this trait can seem negligent, lazy, disorganized, late, and aimless.

Neuroticism often involves sadness and heightened emotionality. It is sometimes called emotional instability or is reversed and referred to as emotional stability. Neuroticism is a classic temperament trait that was studied in temperament research for decades. It was later adapted by the Five Factors Model. People high on this trait are vulnerable, temperamental, worry-prone, self-pitying, and self-conscious. Conversely, individuals who score low in neuroticism are less easily upset and are less emotionally reactive. They tend to be calm, emotionally stable, even-tempered, self-content, and free from persistent negative feelings.[26]

Jill's highest score on the Big Five Assessment is agreeableness with conscientiousness being a close second. She is kind, generous, and always caring toward others. She wants to see social harmony in our family and in our churches. She values people and leads through forming deep relationships. She sees the best in others and tries to nurture them into their fullest potential. She also likes to have structure, rules, and an order to things. She posts expectations and chore charts on the walls of our home. She likes to have an agenda for meetings and shows up with her *Book of Discipline* in hand! People describe her as genuine, loving, and organized. They will follow her because they know she cares. In ministry she is pastoral and admin-

---

26. Berk, 425.

istrative. She tends to focus more on the people already in the community, caring for them, helping them to become healthier versions of themselves.

My highest score on the Big Five is openness with extroversion being a close second. I spend a good deal of time wandering around in my own imagination. I'm always asking why things can't be done differently. I'm constantly on a treasure hunt for goodness, beauty, and truth. I appreciate art in all its forms. I love to experiment with new ideas, take risks, and innovate new ways. As an entrepreneur I've started and run businesses since I was a teenager. I like to be around people, especially new people. It gives me energy. I see every person as a bundle of complexities that I want to unravel and understand. I notice the potential in people that sometimes they don't see in themselves, and I try to empower and activate them to reach it. In ministry I tend to be more apostolic and focused on outsiders.

There is a good deal of debate around nature vs. nurture in the personality traits conversation. Cultural psychologists see culture and psychology not as separate entities but as a mutually constituted system in which each creates and sustains the other.[27] Jill and I both come from traumatic childhoods. We both survived abandonment and abuse. Those scars show up sometimes in our relationship. Jill comes from a large Southern family with dozens of relatives. I was adopted by grandparents who died when I was young and have gone through life with no relatives.

I'm also a "fixer," meaning when someone presents a problem, I'm automatically searching for solutions. But I've learned over time that Jill doesn't want me to "fix" things in most situations. She is simply sharing what's going on in her day. She values it when I take off my "fixer" hat and put on my "listener" hat. She is a nurturing, stable, let's-do-it-by-the-book kind of person. I tend to be a visionary, wild, and rules-are-meant-to-be-broken person.

We also have brought together a large blended family from two failed marriages. We have combined a small country of children, all

---

27. Matsumoto and Juang, *Culture and Psychology*, 260.

with their own unique personality types. Our personalities come out in our parenting styles. Jill likes order, lists, rules, and consequences when those rules are broken. I connect with our kids primarily through imagination, play, adventurous unplanned trips, and unending grace for mistakes. These personality traits put us in conflict sometimes, and Jill needs me to be a dad who lays down the law. I compromise and cooperate, adjusting my own personality to make it work, and she does likewise in many ways.

The main idea of this book is that each congregation also has a distinct "personality type" that typically manifests as one or more of the five mentioned above: Proclamation Centered, Fellowship Centered, Generosity Centered, Outreach Centered, or Healing Centered. These types are really the communal embodiments of shared traits and values.

The strong correlation with the Big Five, the five congregational types, and fivefold APEST typology from Ephesians 4 is not a coincidence. Leaders shape cultures. As noted earlier, communal personality types can take on the characteristics of founding leaders. Further, "like attracts like" can be true as certain personality types are attracted to certain leadership gifts.

Consider these correlations:

1. Teacher: "the preacher" and "educator." Proclamation and teaching are primary giftings. Teachers cultivate proclamation-centered congregations where biblical truth is rightly taught and transmitted generationally. Conscientiousness is a primary trait of teachers. They thrive in the orderly study and passionate proclamation of Scripture.

2. Evangelist: the "recruiter" and "promoter." Proclamation, networking, and connecter of people are primary giftings. Evangelists cultivate outreach-centered congregations that embody the gospel in word and deed with people outside the church. Extroversion is a classic trait of the evangelist. They turn strangers into friends easily and often.

3. Apostle: the "sent one" and "healer." Innovating, moving to the edge, connecting outsiders, and expecting the supernatural are primary giftings. Apostles cultivate healing-centered congregations, in which God's shalom is extended across new boundaries. Openness is a main trait of their personality.

4. Prophet: the "activist" and "truth teller." A heart for justice and allegiance to God are primary giftings. Prophets cultivate generosity-centered cultures where idolatry is confronted and fidelity to God is a core value. Neuroticism can be an obvious trait of prophets (simply read Isaiah to Malachi in the Old Testament), but when healthy, they are a stable force for good.

5. Shepherd/Pastor: the "nurturer" and "shepherd." Creating fellowship, care giving, and cultivating others are primary giftings. Pastors cultivate fellowship-centered congregations where people can be nurtured to their fullest potential in Christ. Agreeableness is a primary trait of pastors.

Consider these correlations:

1. Extroversion: finds communal embodiment as an outreach-centered congregation where infectious evangelists thrive.

2. Agreeableness: finds communal embodiment as a fellowship-centered congregation where kind pastors thrive.

3. Openness: finds communal embodiment as a healing-centered congregation where creative apostles thrive.

4. Conscientiousness: finds communal embodiment as a proclamation-centered congregation where thoughtful teachers thrive.

5. Neuroticism: finds communal embodiment as a generosity-centered congregation where emotive prophets thrive. (Interestingly, many biblical prophets were known for sadness or emotional instability but called upon God's people for

generous fidelity. Jesus is the fullest expression of a healthy prophet.) Emotionally stable congregations (low in neuroticism) trust in God's provision; they are not anxiety-prone (Matt 6:34), thus becoming a channel of God's generosity.

We find another interesting correlation with the five congregational types and the work of Dr. Gary Chapman and the five love languages.[28] Chapman posits that we all have a primary love language through which we give and receive love: Words of Affirmation, Acts of Service, Receiving Gifts, Quality Time, or Physical Touch. I believe it's possible that those five love languages find embodiment communally within the five distinct congregational types. While not a perfect correlation, consider the following:

1. Words of Affirmation: finds communal embodiment as a proclamation-centered congregation.

2. Acts of Service: finds communal embodiment as an outreach-centered congregation.

3. Receiving Gifts: finds communal embodiment as a generosity-centered congregation.

4. Quality Time: finds communal embodiment as a fellowship-centered congregation.

5. Physical Touch: finds communal embodiment as a healing-centered congregation.

In short, we can find a wealth of biblical, sociological, and psychological support for the five congregational types. Each of these angles on personality traits points to something that is perhaps universally true: the five congregational types are the communal embodiment of these archetypal personality traits. What if they provide a framework to help people have healthier relationships with God, each other, and the world? What if the five congregational personal-

---

28. See Gary D. Chapman, *The Five Love Languages: How to Express Heartfelt Commitment to Your Mate* (Chicago: Northfield Publishing, 1995).

ity types can serve as the building blocks of healthy, thriving, and robust congregations? What if they offer a way that congregations can find healing and new life?

Team Exercise Three

Gather your team. Make sure everyone has read the chapter. Open in prayer. Use these questions to guide your conversation. Based on what you've learned so far, choose which of the five congregational personality types you believe most resonates with your church so far. For each type let every person on the team answer: (a) Why do you believe that type best describes your congregation? (b) What indicators do you see that make you think this?

1. Proclamation Centered: This congregation values truth (ἀλήθεια) and loves growing and sharing in quality teaching and preaching.

2. Outreach Centered: This congregation values service (διακονέω) and embodying the good news in word and deed; they live to serve those outside the community.

3. Generosity Centered: This congregation values singleness/generosity (ἁπλότης) and uses its resources to invest in ministries that make a kingdom impact.

4. Fellowship Centered: This congregation values community (κοινωνία) and loves to be together and nurture one another.

5. Healing Centered: This congregation values wholeness (ἰάομαι) and the manifestation of Jesus' life in the world, seeking to be a community where people experience healing.

THE POWER OF THE DARK SIDE

Being in people-helping professions these days is not easy. Even before the pandemic, the phenomenon of burnout was prevalent. This is true of all people but is glaringly obvious in the context of congregational life. Leaders are quitting the ministry in droves. The last several years have amplified that reality.

One aspect of burnout is *compassion fatigue.*[29] Our ability to feel empathy is diminished. We are running on fumes and feel like we are about to crash and burn. Every meeting on our calendar feels heavy. We start to hope our next appointment doesn't show up. We go through the motions of ministry, but our hearts feel cold and dead. People whose company we once enjoyed start to feel like a nuisance. Congregations collectively can fall into this loveless state as well.

Is Jesus knocking on our front door like he did the church in Ephesus? Asking us to rekindle "the love you had at first"? How can leaders find passion for ministry again? How can congregations get excited about serving local communities amid what seems like a chain of unending losses?

I believe the answer lies in the ability of a congregation to understand their own unique personality and how they best can connect with those around them. Pastors and laity can spend an inordinate amount of time doing a lot of the wrong things. The world has shifted into a post-Christendom scenario. The largest growing

---

29. Bethany Dearborn Hiser, *From Burned Out to Beloved: Soul Care for Wounded Healers* (Downers Grove, IL: InterVarsity Press, 2020).

group of people is the tribe called "nones," those who indicate "no religious affiliation" in surveys. The flocks of already-Christians are dwindling in the pens. Yet the expectations of congregations remain largely unchanged.

Many congregations have little awareness of their personality type or what motivates them to do what they do. Clergy also can lack awareness of their congregation's type and their own. All the activity with little results leads to fatigue. Relationships are strained, and a toxic spiral of decline continues. Meanwhile, the larger community outside of the congregations' walls goes neglected, often suspicious of this museum-like institution occupying space in the neighborhood, like a relic from ages past.

Typically, a pastor can make one of two big but opposite mistakes:

1. We spring into action, leaning on our strengths and straining to lead the congregation without doing the work of learning their congregational type.

2. We learn our congregation's type and dedicate ourselves wholly to serving the area of strength to please them, oblivious to the dark side it creates.

Typically, a congregation can make one of two big but opposite mistakes:

1. We think the pastor's full-time job is to be our personal spiritual butler. We pay them to serve us in a way that suits our unique personality type as a congregation.

2. We codependently seek to please the pastor(s), bending around their unique personality while perhaps never getting around to serving the community surrounding us.

Every single community on earth (rural, urban, digital, etc.) needs a healthy, loving pastor and congregation to love them toward the fullness of God's kingdom. We should be constantly involved in God's love triangle, more effectively loving each other and the community that cradles the life of our congregation. But notice how the love flows back and forth through the triangle from the community back into the congregation and from the congregation into the community. It's not a one-way street. The flow of God's love is not sequential in the sense that we need to get everything together internally before we start to engage the community.

Congregations do not get healthy and then *do mission*; congregations get healthy in the process of *being on mission*. If we are constantly focused on internal squabbles or simply apathetic toward our community, we are not effectively being the church of Jesus Christ.

A love blockage in one of these areas is almost always the deciding factor in a congregation's health.

As we will see in Jesus' assessment of the churches in Asia Minor in the next chapter, he celebrates the good and challenges the bad. In his assessment he names their strengths but also exposes their weaknesses. It's in the shadows, the areas of weakness, where if the pastor and congregation change, the most explosive new creation potential is unleashed!

Carl Jung (1875–1961) was a Swiss psychiatrist and psychoanalyst who founded analytical psychology. He identified "archetypes," which are the inherited tendencies within the collective unconscious that dispose a person to behave similarly to ancestors who confronted similar experiences. He suggested that we have a "collective unconscious," which he understood as the deepest level of the psyche, which contains inherited experiences of human and prehuman species. These unconscious elements swirl beneath the surface of our conscious mind and are held in balance by the "self." The *self* is constantly balancing and integrating these aspects of the unconscious to provide unity and stability.[30]

Jung believed also in a darker self, the "shadow" archetype, which is the animalistic part of the personality. He saw the *shadow* as containing our immoral, passionate, and unacceptable desires and activities. In essence, the shadow, the primitive part of our nature, can drive us

---

30. Duane P. Schultz and Sydney Ellen Schultz, *A History of Modern Psychology*, 9th ed. (Belmont, CA: Thomson/Wadsworth, 2008), 457.

to do things we would not ordinarily do. Some aspects of the shadow can be positivity, spontaneity, creativity, insight, and deep emotion, for instance. However, it is also the place where our actions can cause harm to ourselves and others.[31]

Like Jung's concept of the shadow, the "dark side" of a congregation is actually the shadow of its strength. While we seek, often at a subconscious level, to embody a core value, the overemphasis of a single trait creates a blind spot. Biblically speaking, the congregation is one-dimensional.

This is what Paul is getting at as he describes that nature of the body of Christ: "Are all apostles? Are all prophets? Are all teachers? Do all work powerful deeds?" (1 Cor 12:29). If a community consisted only of teachers, who would be an apostle to the edges to expand into new spaces? If the community consisted entirely of apostles, who would care for those already in the community? Likewise, if a community focused only on outreach, who would nurture fellowship among the existing congregation? If a congregation focused only on proclamation but never called people to a life of generosity, what impact would they really make on the world? If a congregation prioritized fellowship but never reached out to serve those outside, how would they grow?

Unfortunately, this is exactly the condition of most churches today: they become content with embodying a single personality trait, and so they atrophy and collapse. It would be like Paul's comical debacle, "The eye cannot say to the hand, 'I have no need of you,' nor again the head to the feet, 'I have no need of you'" (1 Cor 12:21). This would create an immobilized and impaired body. A healthy congregation understands, "For just as the body is one and has many members, and all the members of the body, though many, are one body, so it is with Christ" (12:12). They seek to grow in all five dimensions "until all of us come to the unity of the faith and of the knowledge of the Son of God, to maturity, to the measure of the full stature of Christ" (Eph 4:13).

Again, we call those blind spots that every congregation has their "dark side." The light of our greatest strength usually casts a shadow. God's transformative power is most evident in the wounds that we try

31. Schultz and Schultz, *History of Modern Psychology*, 458.

to conceal. That's the very place where what I call "(re)missioning" can take place.

(Re)missioning is not the same as revitalization. Revitalization usually involves some process of making internal changes that will help a congregation be restored to some former state of vitality. Usually, the indicators have to do with numbers, and more specifically nickels and noses, or how many people show up and how much they give.

(Re)missioning is the process through which people and congregations reorganize their life around the central principle of God's mission. It is a process through which a congregation rediscovers their *why*. It involves recentering on the great commandment (love God, love neighbor) and the great commission (go into all the world and make disciples) in a church's local context. A key assumption in the (re)missioning approach is that we are in a mostly post-Christendom scenario in much of the West.[32] This means that the church is no longer at the center of society and life. Not only do we have challenges within the congregation, but we are also faced with massive challenges in connecting with our communities.

(Re)missioning has less to do with revitalization from the inside out and more to do with renewal that flows from the outside in. When we join what God is already doing in our communities, we can feed that energy back into the congregation. This requires the simultaneous process I mentioned earlier: caring for the center, nurturing the existing congregation, *and* experimenting on the edge with people outside the church. We don't get everything worked out internally and then begin small iterative experiments in the community. That is a fatal mistake. Most likely, things will never be all worked out internally, at least in the way we think they should. At the same time, we have to cultivate a congregation healthy enough that outsiders can come in without being further wounded by a toxic church culture.

The five congregational types give us a framework to see our weaknesses and grow in all five dimensions, to more fully think, act, and love like Jesus.

---

32.   Michael Adam Beck, *Deep and Wild: Remissioning Your Church from the Outside In* (Franklin, TN: Seedbed Publishing, 2021).

What if it is exactly in our greatest weaknesses and challenges that we may discover the power of resurrection? What if Darth Vader was right: "You don't know the power of the dark side"! This idea very much aligns with Paul's concept of a "thorn in the flesh."

In 2 Corinthians 12 Paul describes surpassingly great gifts, revelations, and visions that were given to him. Paul claims that to keep him in check, God gave him a thorn, or "a messenger of Satan to torment me, to keep me from being too elated" (2 Cor 12:7). Biblical scholars have speculated for almost two thousand years what that thorn might be (a medical condition, an addiction, a struggle with sin), but for our purposes we will simply call it what Paul does: a "weakness." Paul goes on to say that he pleaded with God to remove this weakness three times, but the Lord replied, "My grace is sufficient for you, for power is made perfect in weakness" (2 Cor 12:9). Did you catch that? "Power" is made perfect in "weakness."

This is the heart of what I've argued in my autobiographical book, *Painting with Ashes*: that "our weakness is our superpower" in Christ.[33] Life is a disabled event. We are all *dis*abled in some way, physically, emotionally, or spiritually. It's from the ashes of our wounds, struggles, and failures that God can paint beautiful portraits of healing for others. This is true not only on an individual level but a communal one as well. What is the "thorn in the flesh" of your congregation? That's your dark side. We all have one!

It's in our weakness, our need to lean into God's grace, our utter dependence upon God's love, that Jesus' power is made perfect. And it is in acknowledging, naming, and turning that weakness over to God as a community that we may find new creation potential.

If a pastor and congregation can become aware of that weakness, that thorn, they can enter into a graceful process of transfiguration together. They will find their "superpower" and be able to perceive and join in what God is doing in the world.

Pastors, have you ever felt like you are working so hard, putting in so many hours, and seeing no fruit? If you're honest, have you even at

---

33. Michael Adam Beck, *Painting with Ashes: When Your Weakness Becomes Your Superpower* (Plano, TX: Invite Resources, 2022).

times felt resentment toward the congregation? Have you ever felt like you were spending a lot of time doing the wrong things?

Congregations, have you ever felt like you're spinning your wheels? Jumping onto the next big idea only to find more decline, or maybe even feeling like you're moving backwards? Honestly, have you even begun to feel resentment toward your pastor? Or notice that you're cycling through them fast, one after another?

Pastors, it's easy to get locked into stereotypes about the congregation. "This church is so unhealthy, all they ever want to do is complain," or "This congregation doesn't care about the Word, they just want to get together and eat!" or "More people show up to serve at the food pantry than participate in the worship service! God, why have you done this to me?" Suddenly, we pastors find ourselves as a new Moses, leading these hard-hearted and stubborn people through the wilderness, when all they want to do is go back to Egypt. Now this might be true of some congregations, but what if there's a different possible fate than rebellions, poisonous snakes, orgies, and golden bulls? (See Exodus.)

Congregations, can't we also get locked into stereotypes about our pastors? "That preacher doesn't know when to land the plane. By the times he's done, the food is cold," or "Why is she always out there with those drug addicts and homeless folks? She hasn't visited me one time," or "I love that our pastor does so many visits, but boy, I wish he would spend some more time preparing for his sermons. Talk about boooooooring!" Resentment grows. Suddenly, the congregation finds themselves as following a mad Saul, someone who has lost the favor and anointing of God but still has the position. (See First and Second Samuel.)

In this scenario everyone loses: the pastor(s), the congregation, and the larger community we are called to serve and share the gospel. A choice must be made. What's more important, holding on to the stereotypes or hitting the reset button on the relationship?

If your congregation is in the critical care unit, we must be able to assess the patient's condition and make correct decisions regarding their care. Knowing your congregation's personality type is critical in this assessment.

Congregations on their deathbed don't need the next quick-fix strategy or a heroic solo leader who can turn it all around. Churches are motivated to enter into a journey of transformation and lasting fruitfulness through a single force: love. People must be loved into loving. When a congregation discovers their own inner resources and are awakened to love their community, (re)missioning can occur.

Every congregation has a distinct heart, which is a unique expression of Christ. The heart can be either healthy or sick. A truly healthy congregation could have fairly balanced aspects of various personality traits, but these congregations are a kind of white rhino in the world today—functionally extinct. The ultimate state of health for a congregation is to mature "to the measure of the full stature of Christ" (Eph 4:13). This would include embodying at some level each of the five personality types. However, this is more a lifelong journey of grace than a destination at which we arrive. Once we understand the five types and see our growth areas (dark side), we have a spiritual framework for growing more fully toward maturity and flourishing.

Many congregations are in decline because they don't know who they are. A minister can waste a great deal of time and energy expending effort that is rejected by the congregation. Even if they are highly effective in one area, if their gifts don't align with dominant congregational traits, it will have little impact.

(Re)missioning can occur when a team of leaders learns a congregation's personality type and then utilizes this knowledge to form a discipleship process around their weaknesses. Just as in the corrective measures of Jesus in Revelation, as a church we should be encouraged in what we are doing right but always redirected to the greater work of our mission in the world. This is the ancient way of revitalization for the twenty-first century.

So then, let's enter into a journey together using the *power of imagination* to help your congregation experience (re)missioning.

Edwin Friedman speaks of the "imaginative gridlock" that can take place in sick and declining relational systems. The ability to imagine different possibilities is seemingly lost. You can tell you are in such a system when we are always trying harder, looking for answers rather than reframing questions, and engaging in either/or thinking that creates false dichotomies.[34] Friedman writes:

> When any relationship system is imaginatively gridlocked, it cannot get free simply through more thinking about the problem. Conceptually stuck systems cannot become unstuck simply by trying harder. For a fundamental reorientation to occur, that spirit of adventure which optimizes serendipity and which enables new perceptions beyond the control of our thinking processes must happen first. This is equally true regarding families, institutions, whole nations, and entire civilizations.[35]

Friedman goes on to suggest that one major criterion for judging the anxiety level of any community is its capacity to be playful. In the following pages I want to invite your team to explore a posture of wonder and play.

Next, we will examine Jesus' assessment of seven real congregations in Asia Minor. Jesus will expose their dark sides and show them the places where they have room for growth. If they repent and make the course correction, Jesus suggests, the treasures of resurrection await.

This is not an exercise in inductive Bible study. Let this be a time of adventure and imagination for your team. Can you find yourselves in the seven churches? Can you begin to consider that the hope for a thriving congregational life is not about the next new strategy but how you know and love one another and the larger community? Can you begin to locate yourselves within the five types of congregations? Our playful exploration of Revelation is a way for you to break free from imaginative gridlock. Within this fascinating masterpiece that ends the Bible, we will find a framework for (re)missioning. Before we move on, as a team, pause to check in with one another by completing the exercise on the next page.

---

34.   Edwin H. Friedman, *A Failure of Nerve: Leadership in the Age of the Quick Fix*, 10th anniversary rev. ed., ed. Margaret M. Treadwell and Edward W. Beal (New York: Church Publishing, 2017), 34.

35.   Friedman, *Failure of Nerve*, 35.

Team Exercise Four

Relational Fulfillment Meters

With your team fill out the relational fulfillment meters.

1. As a congregation, on a scale of 1 to 10, with one being empty and ten being full, what is the current level of your relational fulfillment? At what level do you feel seen, known, and loved by your pastor?

2. Pastor or pastoral team, on a scale of 1 to 10, with one being empty and ten being full, what is the current level of your relational fulfillment? How seen, known, and loved do you feel by your congregation?

3. Together as pastor and congregation, on a scale of 1 to 10, with one being empty and ten being full, what is the current relational fulfillment level of your community? How seen, known, and loved do you think your community feels by your church?

Relational Fulfillment Meters

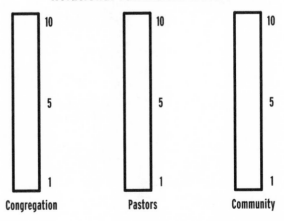

| Congregation | Pastors | Community |

4. Look at the responses together and talk about why you feel the way you do about each one.

5. To prepare for the next chapter, read Revelation 1–3. Take notes of any observations you have about the seven churches in Asia Minor.

THE SEVEN CHURCHES IN ASIA MINOR

I know where you live!
Revelation 2:13 (NIV)

The church of Pergamum receives a postcard directly from the throne room. The Risen Lord then begins to evaluate the congregation and its leadership. He celebrates some good fruit and calls out some rotten fruit. Imagine how utterly terrifying this assessment is for the folks in Pergamum. They know they have some putrid fruit, and suddenly Jesus shows up on the front porch saying, "I know where you live!"

If Jesus were to knock on the front door of your congregation, would you be ready for his evaluation? Would you have some things you would need to clean up quickly before you invited him in? What would he celebrate? What would he condemn?

Pergamum was just one of seven real churches in Asia Minor. In the book of Revelation, Jesus is kicking the tires and examining the hearts of each of these congregations. In most cases he affirms good things, condemns bad things, and provides a corrective. Even to the churches that are significantly unhealthy, Jesus offers a graceful opportunity to repent and change course. What are the personality types of the seven churches? Jesus' consultation with these churches provides a potential framework for (re)missioning congregations today.

Perhaps the first couple of chapters of Revelation can be a guide to help us think about the health of our own congregation. Biblical scholar Ben Witherington III suggests strong evidence that Revelation chapters 2–3 are exhortations addressed to particular congregations on the western edge of the province of Asia, with whom the author John had direct contact.[36] In Revelation 2–3 Jesus is speaking to these seven real churches, in seven real locations, made up of communities of real people. In the next chapters John the revelator launches into a visionary panorama that moves from the past to the future to the present and back to the future again. We see all kinds of metaphors and images that describe deeper spiritual realities. John's visions are saturated in scriptural allusions. Almost every verse drips with connections to other parts of the Bible. We might feel like we need a decoder ring to figure out what's going on!

But chapters 2 and 3 are straightforward. Dr. David deSilva, distinguished professor of New Testament and Greek with an expertise in Revelation, suggests that these chapters are "the most transparent and explicit in terms of referring to local conditions and challenges" within the historical and rhetorical setting.[37] They contain a series of oracles meant to encourage and exhort the congregations to do some deep inner reflection and repentance. Jesus' assessment of these congregations can reveal both the heart of Christ and what he hopes to see in the congregations that bear his name. Each pronouncement to a church has a kind of formula, an address to a specific church, a statement about the multifaceted aspects of Jesus' personhood and lordship, an evaluation of what the congregation is doing right, followed by a callout of something the congregation is doing wrong. Most receive a call to repentance and a warning, followed by a promise that if they make a course correction and allow Jesus to heal whatever has grown sick, they will receive a specific reward. Only two of the congregations receive a fully positive inspection!

36. Ben Witherington III, *Revelation*, The New Cambridge Bible Commentary (Cambridge, UK: Cambridge University Press, 2003), 7.

37. David A. deSilva, *Seeing Things John's Way: The Rhetoric of the Book of Revelation*, 1st ed. (Louisville: Westminster John Knox Press, 2009), 30.

We could break down the structure of each congregational assessment like this:

1. Addressee: a particular pastor and their congregation

2. A "thus sayeth" statement indicating a direct word from Jesus through the revelator

3. Identity statements about Jesus drawn from Revelation 1

4. Celebration of fruit (a commendation for six of the congregations)

5. Confrontation of unfaithfulness (except in Smyrna and Philadelphia!)

6. Warning to repent or expect consequences (except in Smyrna and Philadelphia!)

7. A "who has ears" statement that indicates broader application to the wider church

8. Promise of reward

That each evaluation is addressed to an "angel" could mean an actual angelic being of God who is assigned to each church. But more likely the ἄγγελος (*angelos*) simply means "a messenger," or more specifically by implication, *the bishop or pastor* of that congregation. As Dr. Colin J. Hemer, the late research fellow at Tyndale House in Cambridge, England, noted, "It is difficult to think of a human writer being instructed to write the words of Christ to supernatural beings."[38] Angelic beings could not be held responsible for the faults of their human churches. Many scholars favor the latter translation. That's right, pastors: Jesus is talking to you and through you!

But Jesus is not speaking to the pastor *alone*. He is speaking to communities of believers. These small epistles must be understood as an evaluation of the entire congregation, not merely the shepherd of the flock. That's right, church: Jesus is talking to you too! There is

---

38. Colin J. Hemer, *The Letters to the Seven Churches of Asia in Their Local Setting* (Grand Rapids: William B. Eerdmans, 2001), 33.

no scapegoating. There's no room for congregations to say, "Well, if we only had a better pastor" and conversely no room for pastors to say, "If I only had a better congregation." We are all in this together.

Finally, it's important to note that Revelation is Jewish apocalyptic literature designed to be read in community by a powerless, marginalized, and oppressed group of people. Western congregations, particularly in the US context, are worlds away from the social, religious, and political milieu of these early Christians. For them, following Jesus was a matter of life or death. They had little to no governmental protection for the practice of their religion. In fact, they were considered a subversive sect, actively arrested, and sometimes executed for their faith. It's important to notice that the problems these congregations faced were both internal and external. In some cases the greatest challenges were arising from within the church. In other cases their engagement with the larger community attracted opposition and attack.

I'm going to playfully suggest that the seven congregations in Asia Minor in varying degrees can provide a helpful framework for how we use the five congregational types. These short oracles provide a window into the dark side of each kind of congregation and suggest an appropriate corrective measure. Would the church at Sardis almost two thousand years ago say, "We are a generosity-centered congregation"? That's unlikely, but a careful reading of the text suggests that they would fit that category to some extent. Later, we will dig into what each type of congregation looks like today, but let's begin with this imaginative biblical exploration from which we will draw a framework later.

1. Ephesus

The pastor and the church of Ephesus need to remember that Jesus is the one who holds the seven stars in his right hand and walks among the seven golden lampstands (Rev 2:1). Jesus holds these seven churches in the palm of his hand. They are like lampstands lighting up their communities, but some are burning brighter than others. Jesus first celebrates Ephesus, which is known for their deeds, hard work, and perseverance. They could represent what we would call an outreach-centered congregation.

This congregation focuses on humble deeds offered in service to others. They also don't let victimizers and charlatans prey upon their people, as we will see in some of the other congregations. They keep pressing on under adverse circumstances, which for them means violent persecution (Rev 2:3).

Ephesus was by far the largest and most important city of the region. It was a harbor city that served as both a religious and commercial hub. The archaeological evidence testifies to the marvelous architecture of the city. Two temples to Augustus were built here, and Emperor Domitian named Ephesus the guardian of the imperial cult. It was also the site of the Temple of Artemis, considered one of the seven wonders of the ancient world. The city was the location for the Olympic Games. The Ephesus congregation was the oldest of the seven churches addressed in the letter, perhaps over forty years old at the time John was writing. This was no brand-new church plant but a congregation with an overall impressive track record.[39]

Yet they do not get a clean bill of health! Jesus tells them: "You have forsaken the love you had at first." Ouch! Have you had times in your own life and your own church when you could say the same? This is a congregation with a dark side. They are working hard, but their love has grown cold. They are possibly doing the right things for the wrong reasons. This is a typical default for exhausted outreach-centered congregations who experience compassion fatigue. Jesus encourages them to rekindle their love, or he will serve them an eviction notice (Rev 2:5)!

Jesus, however, celebrates that they have done a good job protecting the congregation from particularly contentious doctrines or groups. The Nicolaitans, mentioned both here and at the church in Pergamum, are thought to be an early heretical sect. While heavily debated, multiple early church fathers including Irenaeus, Hippolytus, Epiphanius, and Theodoret identify the founder of the sect as Nicolaus the Deacon, one of the seven chosen deacons in Acts 6:5.[40]

---

39. Hemer, *Letters to the Seven Churches*, 35–56.

40. Steven J. Friesen, *Imperial Cults and the Apocalypse of John: Reading Revelation in the Ruins* (New York: Oxford University Press, 2006), 193.

There the διακονέω deacons were chosen by the first disciples to be "table servants" so the apostles could dedicate themselves to the prayers and proclamation of the word. The first deacons were dedicated to what we would call the outreach ministries of the church.

There is evidence in the name Νικολαϊτῶν (a combination of *nike* and *laos,* meaning "victory people") that it was a rogue theological movement that took "Christian freedom" to mean they were "free to sin" because they had victory in Christ.[41] If the early church fathers are correct and Nicolaus was the author of the heresy and the sect, it is an early biblical example of authority and leadership gone very wrong. They apparently rejected or contorted the apostolic kerygma and emerging structural hierarchies. More alarming was their encouragement of an antinomian (Latin, *anti* = against, *nomos* = law) form of the faith. This meant Christians were released by grace from the obligation of observing moral laws.

The Ephesians were on guard against this very real danger, something they had obviously had firsthand experience with. Typically, outreach-centered congregations will function in a flattened rather than a hierarchical leadership structure. They emphasize a shared leadership way, a "priesthood of all believers," who focus together on serving their communities. They truly believe that many hands make light work. But this is also a breeding ground for unhealthy individuals to cause damage.

One person, fully empowered and unleashed to be involved in the ministry of outreach, can either be a force for great good or cause a lot of problems. When an unhealthy person assumes a position of power too quickly, he or she can use that authority in harmful ways. This can cause a lot of fallout within a congregation.

When compassion fatigue sets in, a common dark side in outreach congregations, they can become particularly vulnerable to this type of scenario. Worn-out volunteers and pastors keep doing the right things but with the wrong motivation. People get involved with toxic conversations, and the negativity spreads like a virus among the people. The infection must be identified and removed, and this is something the Ephesus congregation did at least partly right, being that Jesus celebrates them for containing it (Rev 2:2).

---

41. Friesen, *Imperial Cults,*193.

If they repent and overcome their shortcomings, they will be fully restored and find themselves back in the garden of Eden we learn more about later in the book (Rev 21–22). Jesus is graceful, giving them another chance to hit the reset button and start over. This is a defining characteristic of each of Jesus' congregational assessments.

2. Smyrna

For the messenger in the church in Smyrna, we get one of the two fully positive reports among the seven churches. If we would like to hold up a model church that Jesus celebrates as the ideal, this is the one.

To this congregation Jesus wants them to know he is the First and the Last, the crucified and Risen One, the one who conquered death itself, which is particularly meaningful for this congregation. This is a church experiencing a significant level of challenge and persecution. The city of Smyrna, thirty-five miles north of Ephesus, was prosperous with an excellent harbor. They enjoyed both deep political connections with the Roman empire (like Ephesus, they hosted the imperial cult) and a flourishing Jewish population. This is a double whammy for the Christian congregation at Smyrna, for apparently certain members of both groups are actively persecuting them.[42]

Jesus sees their "affliction and poverty" but holds this in tension with "even though you are rich" (Rev 2:9). This sounds like a generosity-centered church but with seemingly little resources. They give what resources they have to make a kingdom impact in the world. Essentially, they are the opposite of what we will see in Laodicea, a congregation with lots of resources but in whom the flow of generosity has run dry.[43] Against incredible odds, the Smyrna church is faithfully proclaiming the word, shared in a deep sustaining fellowship; healing is normative, and they are actively reaching out into the

---

42. Hemer, *Letters to the Seven Churches*, 57–77.

43. N. T. Wright and Michael F. Bird, *The New Testament in Its World: An Introduction to the History, Literature and Theology of the First Christians* (London: Society for Promoting Christian Knowledge, 2019), 819.

community. Their activity, however, has attracted some opposition. They are actively being slandered and attacked for their faithfulness (Rev 2:9).

Yet Jesus assures them that he knows their situation intimately. A greater test is coming. The devil is actively persecuting them and using people as puppets to do so. Some of them will be incarcerated and even killed for their faith. Can you imagine being this church? Essentially, "You are doing everything right, but get ready to be imprisoned and die for your faith!" May we all seek to have the impact and fruitfulness of Smyrna! Jesus promises them that if they are faithful "until death," they will receive a crown in the new creation (Rev 2:10). Their victory will result in a resurrection life that can never be overcome by death again. Jesus' promises to them are directly linked with their situation.

The call to be "faithful until death" is a major theme of Revelation. The churches are experiencing persecution and crisis, but if they hold fast, don't fall into idolatry, and keep serving Christ, they have a great reward in store. When we think about the magnitude of the challenges facing Smyrna, hopefully it makes the beer bottle fights in our church committee meetings over minor things seem petty and even silly.

I indicated earlier that congregations who embody all five personality types are a kind of white rhino, very rare in the world today, maybe even extinct. Congregations who want to grow toward the "full stature of Christ" in which all five APEST types are present at some level (Eph 4:7–13) can focus on Smyrna as a spiritual goal to grow toward. Like the ongoing adventure of grace in our individual lives, communally maturing into all five personality types is more of a journey than a destination.

3. Pergamum

To the pastor and congregation at Pergamum, we get the potent "I know where you live" greeting referenced earlier. Jesus wants them to remember that he is the one whose Word is like a sharp two-edged sword (Rev 2:12). Even though Satan's throne is in their neighborhood, this is a congregation that has remained faithful and true. They too have seen persecution and even the martyrdom of some of their own. They live deep in enemy territory, but somehow through the thick relationships they share, they've been able to persevere. This sounds like a fellowship-centered congregation!

Pergamum was once the capital city of the region. It had parallels with Athens and Corinth, and like those cities it boasted a huge acropolis with various temples, including those to Zeus and Athena. The legendary temple to Asclepius, the god of healing, was located on the plain below the acropolis. Furthermore, a temple dedicated to Augustus and Rome made the city the seat of emperor worship. This is likely what merits its description as Satan's throne, which made a mere mortal into a god, the deepest form of idolatry. Many Christians were executed by refusing to engage in emperor worship or suffered economic disadvantages by not participating in the corrupt imperial trade guilds. This is a major theme throughout Revelation. The congregation is somehow bearing fruit amid these challenges.[44]

However, they do not get a clean bill of health. Some of the people in this congregation have bought into false teaching, and that false teaching has led to some sinful behaviors being accepted in the community. This can be the dark side of a fellowship-centered congregation. They have deep abiding relationships with one another, but they are lite or ambivalent toward sound teaching and preaching. When lacking a clear commitment to the faithful proclamation of the word, all kinds of weird behaviors can sneak in (Rev 2:14–15).

It is possible that a false teacher arose from within, infiltrated their fellowship, or led them astray. This makes Jesus' description as the one with the double-edged sword in his mouth all the more potent. If they don't remove whatever toxic behaviors have been spreading through their community, Jesus will come and cut them out himself. This is a dark side in congregations whose primary trait is agreeableness in which a concern for social harmony trumps all. The biblical concept of fellowship (κοινωνία, *koinonia*) is essential to any healthy church, but these congregations must move toward obedience to Scripture and outreach to the community. Inwardly fo-

---

44. Hemer, *Lettes to the Seven Churches*, 78–105.

cused congregations can be a breeding ground for heresy, selfishness, and lack of engagement in the mission of God, as we will see later.

The ever-graceful Jesus gives them an opportunity to do a 180-degree turn in the other direction, to repent of their sins, and to get back on track. If they fail to do this, Jesus will unleash the literal "double-edged sword" of his Word, a word that brings hope and healing but also a word that brings conviction for our thoughts and behaviors that miss the mark (Rev 2:16). Having a deep and abiding fellowship must also include faithfulness to his Word. It must also lead to missional engagement with outsiders. Fellowship congregations can become gated communities where only the insiders know the secret code.

If they can overcome these challenges, they are given a massive promise! They will receive the "hidden manna," the bread of eternal life, the "white stone with a new name" (Rev 2:17). They will be forgiven, receive a new identity, and be bearers of a new name, given not by mortals but by God. God will wipe the slate clean and make his dwelling among them for all eternity.

4. Thyatira

To the pastor and congregation of Thyatira, Jesus wants to demonstrate his all-powerful and glorious risen self. He shows up to their house with eyes of blazing fire and feet of burnished bronze. He has walked through flames and blazed a path of new creation for them. Among the seven cities who receive a letter, Thyatira was the smallest and least significant. It was a city of mostly trade guilds, many of which participated in allegiance to Caesar and the empire cult. This would not work in the favor of Christians in this city.[45]

Jesus mentions that he knows specifically of their "deeds" and "service," as well as their perseverance. Unlike with Ephesus, Thyatira's "deeds" are increasing, becoming greater than they were at first (Rev 2:19, NIV). Those deeds are described as being anchored in "love and faith." Deeds of love and faith are easily connected to healing. As we will explore later, openness, healing, and the apostolic are

---

45. Hemer, *Letters to the Seven Churches*, 106–28.

inextricably linked together. We will see how the apostles contin-ued, through touch, the healing ministry of Jesus. We are embodied beings, and one of the most intimate forms of communion is to be touched in a healing way. Let's imagine Thyatira as a healing-centered congregation.

Nevertheless, there is an issue in Thyatira. A false prophetess is stirring up trouble with some form of antinomian teaching. Who-ever this woman is, whether she's a person or a figuration, she has been given the opportunity to repent and reset, and she has refused. She is misguiding people, leading them into sinful patterns of be-havior that include some forms of sexual immorality, which is also a biblical way to refer to idolatry (Rev 2:21–23).[46] As we will explore later, idolatry is a heart condition (Matt 6:21) that often involves a generosity blockage and lack of concern for the marginalized.

Perhaps the idolatry in Thyatira is associated with participation in the local trade guilds, which could include immoral rituals. In congregations that focus on healing and the full expression of the su-pernatural gifts of the Spirit, this is a common dark side. Certain so-called remarkably gifted persons can go off track and use their gifts in exploitive and harmful ways. In communities where the culture is built around a single big-personality leader, there is massive potential for harm. This is why shared, distributed, team-based leadership is so essential in becoming a mature expression of the body of Christ.

Jesus informs the church at Thyatira that their acts of "love and faith" must be grounded in the right motivation and centered in the Word. Laying on of hands, healing, prophesying, and other mani-festations of the Spirit should be expected in congregations, but the power dynamics can easily go astray. The motivation for these gifts to manifest must be well intentioned. We are accountable for our actions, but Jesus reminds Thyatira that he also "searches hearts and minds" (Rev 2:23, NIV). He sees our motivations.

The double-edged sword of congregations that value healing can be the perverse and abusive ways touch can be used to cause great

---

46.   Leon L. Morris, *Revelation: An Introduction and Commentary*, Tyndale New Testament Commentaries, vol. 20 (Downers Grove, IL: InterVarsity Press, 2009), 74–75.

harm. By faith the disciples laid their hands on the sick, and they were healed. But throughout history many have used their hands to bring harm. For the false prophetess at Thyatira, she has taken physical touch too far. Christians, known to live a holy and chaste life, so much so that they greet each other with a "holy kiss" (2 Cor 13:12), have fallen into acts of sexual immorality in Thyatira.

Apparently, the "Jezebel, who calls herself a prophet," has turned some in the congregation fully toward the dark side. However, her own actions will swing back and destroy her. When a situation like this happens in a congregation, usually many are harmed in the process. This is why the Thyatirans are instructed not to tolerate this (Rev 2:21–23). For those who have not gotten caught up in the craziness and fallout, Jesus says simply, "I will not impose any other burden on you, except to hold on to what you have until I come" (Rev 2:24–25, NIV). The best thing to do for people in a congregation like this is confront the dysfunction, root it out, and seek to create an ecosystem of healing rather than harm.

The promise that Jesus makes to them if they overcome is almost an inverted power dynamic. They have been known as the little church of humble acts of faith and healing, but if they do the Lord's will "to the end," they will be given authority over the nations and rule in the power of Christ. They will taste true spiritual power and rise like the morning star (Rev 2:27–29). In other words, the least will be great, the last shall be first, the meek will inherit the earth, and the humble servants will rule beside Jesus.

5. Sardis

To the pastor and the church of Sardis, the tone of Jesus' assessment turns to mostly a scathing rebuke. He starts by enlightening them to the reality that he is the one who holds the seven spirits of God and the seven stars in his hand. In other words, he is the true power source of the congregation. He can cut the electricity and turn the lights out.

Essentially, this is a church that mostly failed the health test. The city of Sardis was among the oldest and most important cities in Asia

Minor. It served as the capital of the kingdom of Lydia up until 549 BC. It was located on the northern slope of Mount Tmolus, and its acropolis straddled the spurs of the mountain. Sardis was a major trade city. The most important of these trades was the manufacture and dyeing of delicate woolen stuffs and carpets. The Pactolus stream flowed through the marketplace carrying "golden sands" (i.e., the gold dust of Mount Tmolus). The metallurgists of Sardis invented purification processes for gold and silver. This was a wealthy city with a strong Jewish presence and featured one of the largest synagogues of the time.[47]

The church at Sardis is a generosity-centered congregation gone wrong. Jesus starts by saying, "I know your deeds; you have a reputation of being alive, but you are dead. Wake up!" (Rev 3:2, NIV). This is not a friendly message. This is Jesus throwing down the gauntlet, embodying the role of prophet. This congregation looks good on the outside, most likely consisting of wealthy and powerful members, probably gathering in a nicer home or structure in the affluent city.[48] But inside they are dead. As we will learn later, generosity-centered congregations understand stewardship and can use their resources to make a tremendous kingdom impact in their communities. But the dark side of these congregations can render them with a shallow faith. They throw money at problems, but most members never get their hands dirty. They can more reflect the values of the world around them than the Jesus inside of them.

Jesus, the ever graceful one, gives them the opportunity for a reset. They need to strengthen the little light they have left before it flickers out and finish the good work that they started. He issues a direct call to repentance, *metanoia*: have a change of heart and mind, turn around, and move in a new direction. They need to remember what they "received and heard." Somehow the proclamation aspect of their identity has become watered down (Rev 3:3). They have gone astray. Another dark side of generosity-centered congregations is that the preacher(s) must be a kind of politician. They try not to upset big donors, so they can feel like they must play to their base

---

47. Hemer, *Letters to the Seven Churches*, 129–52.
48. Wright and Bird, *The New Testament in its World*, 819.

and end up delivering watered-down sermons with no prophetic direction that would lead to conviction. We could say light on "truth" but heavy on "love." This creates a church a mile wide and an inch deep. People become apathetic and shallow in their faith.

Jesus lets them know that if they continue like this, if they don't wake up from their spiritual slumber, he will abruptly remove their light from its stand. Communicating in a metaphor they will understand, a city known for its textile industry, he celebrates that there are a few who have not "soiled their clothes" (Rev 3:4). Those faithful ones will be given a new outfit, washed white in the blood of the Lamb, and they will walk with Jesus in the new creation. If others repent, they too will have their soiled clothing replaced. Interestingly, the passage indicates that one can have one's name written in the "book of life," but one can also have one's name blotted out (Rev 3:5). Those who repent will not be blotted out.

6. Philadelphia

To the pastor and congregation in Philadelphia, Jesus wants to reveal that he is the holy and true one, the one who holds the keys of David. He is the one who defines holiness and truth, and he is the fulfillment of the prophecy of a coming Messiah-Priest-King, the one from the lineage of David, who will rule on an eternal throne over a peaceable kingdom. Jesus is the one who can open the doors of the fullness of God's kingdom and the only one who can close them too (Rev 3:7). This is yet another Old Testament connection to a person who would be "the key to the house of David; what he opens no one can shut, and what he shuts no one can open" (Isaiah 22:22, NIV). Notice this opener is particularly loaded with biblical allusions.

Philadelphia is another one of the two churches who receives an all-A+ report card. While Jesus sees their "deeds" and that they have "little strength," yet the shining value of this community remains that they have "kept my word and have not denied my name" (Rev 3:8, NIV). The key to an open door could be a reference to a wide-open opportunity to engage in evangelistic activity and preach the gospel. This is not a one-dimensional congregation. We can see openness, an apostolic function, and an extroverted tendency toward outreach. Yet this is a proclamation-centered congregation; their primary value is *truth*, faithfulness to the Word of God. Because of that faithfulness, Jesus has opened a door of connection to his presence that no one can shut.

This church is also known for generous love and faithful acts of service. But the recurring theme of their assessment is, "You have kept my command to endure patiently" (Rev 3:10, NIV). Proclamation-centered congregations value the preaching and teaching of the Word of God and fidelity to that word above all things. This is a community with a primary strength in the conscientious trait, where thoughtful teachers pass down the truth of Jesus from generation to generation.

The ancient city of Philadelphia sat near the Cogamus River, twenty-seven miles from Sardis and forty-eight miles from Laodicea. It was sometimes referred to as "Little Athens" because of the pagan temples and other public buildings that were spread across the city. It was a place of religious power, also known as a seat of learning. There is another reference to a "synagogue of Satan," which is interesting being that there is no early record of a Jewish community in Philadelphia (Rev 3:9). Hemer suggests potentially a community of ethnic Jews who rejected the Christians' claim as a spiritual Israel.[49] Most likely, active persecution against Christians in the city is alive and well. Thus, Jesus encourages them to hold on to their own identity as descendants of Israel through Christ. They are receiving encouragement directly from Jesus and spreading that word in their place. Their fidelity to God in the face of these competing ideologies is all the more impressive when we understand their context.[50]

This lowly, powerless, but faithful congregation is promised that in their humility, they will be exalted. As servants of all, Jesus will

---

49. Hemer, *Letters to the Seven Churches*, 175. The language of "synagogue of Satan" is perhaps a metaphor. We need to be cautious about anti-Semitic statements here while also acknowledging that some Jewish communities actively joined in the persecution of Christians.

50. Hemer, *Letters to the Seven Churches*, 153–77.

make their persecutors come, fall down at their feet, "and acknowledge that I have loved you" (Rev 3:9, NIV). Their only directive is to endure, hold on to what they already have, and keep pressing on. Jesus promises they will be spared from the coming tribulation (Rev 3:10). They also will receive the crown of glory and become a permanent fixture in the new temple in the new Jerusalem, with a new name in a restored and renewed cosmos, a reality which is "coming down out of heaven from my God" (Rev 3:11–12, NIV). These rich metaphors are once again filled with scriptural references that this congregation would know well.

Oh, that we might all become a Philadelphia kind of congregation!

7. Laodicea

To the pastor and the church in Laodicea, Jesus unveils to them that he is the "Amen," the final word, the faithful and true witness. He emphasizes his lordship as the cosmic ruler over all God's creation.

Laodicea is another church that gets a less than stellar review. The city was located in the Lycus River Valley together with Hierapolis and Colossae. The valley itself served as a natural route of travel from east to west. The Seleucid king Antiochus II founded the city and named it after his wife Laodice about 260 BC. Archaeological remains of the city display an ingenious aqueduct system through which water was piped into the city. The water was rich with calcium, which over time would cause the pipes to clog. The aqueduct was designed with vents covered with stone lids that could be removed periodically for cleaning.[51]

So, when Jesus starts to chastise the church for being neither "cold nor hot"—"because you are lukewarm—neither hot nor cold—I am about to spit you out of my mouth" (Rev 3:16, NIV)—he is most likely referring to a known geographic feature of the city. The water supply was lukewarm, in contrast to the hot springs at nearby Hierapolis and the cold, pure waters of Colossae. It would

---

51. Hemer, *Letters to the Seven Churches*, 178–209.

not be exaggerative to paraphrase what Jesus is saying as "You make me want to vomit." But it is unlikely he is encouraging one of two extremes, hot fervor or cold apathy. Archaeology confirms that the water carried from hot mineral springs some five miles south would have become tepid before entering the city. Perhaps a good way to describe this congregation is that they are simply ineffective and disengaged in the work of ministry.

This is a congregation whose generosity has run dry. Apparently, they have amassed a good deal of financial security. They are wealthy in their own eyes (Rev 3:17). An interesting contrast to Smyrna, who had little material wealth but were profusely generous, this city was technologically advanced. Both the aqueduct and stadium ruins are still present. They traded in cloth, particularly the black wool produced in the area. A medical school in the city housed a famous ophthalmologist, and reportedly eye lotions, "Phrygian powder," originated from the area. Members of the congregation were likely involved in some of these lucrative trades and industries.[52]

Despite the apparent advantageous economic position, Jesus evaluates them as unaware of their true condition: "You are wretched, pitiful, poor, blind, and naked" (Rev 3:17). He advises them "to buy from me gold refined in the fire, so you can become rich; and white clothes to wear, so you can cover your shameful nakedness; and salve to put on your eyes, so you can see" (Rev 3:18). All of these metaphors are based in the urban and historical features of their actual context.

One of the saddest congregations in the world is a church that has great resources but doesn't use them to bring healing and provision to those in the community who stand in need. It is the antithesis of generosity. God's primary nature is revealed in how God gives, "For God so loved the world that he gave" (John 3:16), as we will see in detail later. How sad is it when we receive good gifts from God but then we hoard them away for ourselves. The potential for the Laodicean congregation to share the Word, serve others, and fund systemic transformation in the community is huge, but it is a blessing squandered. This is the dark side of generosity and fellowship

---

52. Hemer, *Letters to the Seven Churches*, 178–209.

congregations who exist in a state of relative comfort for a time; they become internally focused, disengaged in the mission of God.

Jesus, ever graceful and patient, reminds the church that his rebuke and discipline comes in love. Now is the opportunity to repent and reset. The time is now! "Here I am! I stand at the door and knock. If anyone hears my voice and opens the door, I will come in and eat with that person, and they with me" (Rev 3:20, NIV). Somehow in their diminished and noninclusive life, they have even shut out Jesus himself. He's been waiting patiently for them to invite him in. Is it possible to shut Jesus out of his own church? Somehow it seems Laodicea did.

However, if they can turn it all around and overcome their current state, Jesus will give them victory, like the athletes in their stadium. They will even be given "the right to sit with me on my throne, just as I was victorious and sat down with my Father on his throne" (Rev 3:21, NIV).

Can you imagine sitting on the throne of the cosmos next to Jesus? This is exactly the magnitude of potential impact that Laodicea could have. But what if that promise is not only for them? What if all these promises are available to us? What if Jesus is kicking the tires of our congregations, evaluating us, encouraging the good and calling out the bad? Is there a way that we can come back from the brink of our dark side and find health? If our church is already a specimen of health, can we grow even more healthy? I believe every congregation can. This will be the practical focus of the rest of the book.

Like most good stories, it starts with an arranged marriage.

Team Exercise Five

Imagine Jesus showed up on the front porch of your congregation. Using a similar structure of congregational examinations from Revelation 2–3, create a one-page "letter to your church." Use historical and geographical features of your own congregation and community. Brainstorm ideas and let one person be the note taker and letter drafter.

Include each of these key features:

1. Addressee: "To the pastor and congregation of . . ."

2. A "thus sayeth" statement that includes components of Jesus' identity that are important to you

3. Celebration of fruit: a commendation for things your congregation is doing right!

4. Confrontation of unfaithfulness: a rebuke for things your congregation is doing wrong

5. Promise of reward connected to your repentance: "If you repent/overcome . . ."

6. A closing "who has ears" statement

Save the document to reflect on in the future. Maybe share it with the entire congregation. It's a requirement to have fun with this!

Part Two

APPLICATION: THE FIVE CONGREGATIONAL PERSONALITY TYPES

THE ARRANGED MARRIAGE

Let us rejoice and be glad
and give him glory!
For the wedding of the Lamb has come,
and his bride has made herself ready.
—Revelation 19:7 (NIV)

Every relationship between a congregation and a clergy person is in a sense an "arranged marriage." Arranged marriages are a type of marital union in which the bride and groom are chosen by persons other than the couple themselves, in many cases by family members or sometimes a professional matchmaker. Arranged marriages have been the dominant model of marriage across history and remain common in many regions, notably South Asia and the Middle East.

In some cases, the husband and wife have never even met! This is literally a foreign concept for those of us in the West who talk about "soul mates" and "love at first sight" and who often go through an extensive dating process. Some would argue that dating apps could be considered a modern iteration of "arranged" couples today. For emerging generations, marriage itself is not necessarily a foregone conclusion.

Over half of the marriages in the world today are arranged marriages with a staggeringly low global divorce rate of 6.3 percent.[53]

---

53.   "Arranged / Forced Marriage Statistics," Statistic Brain, https://www.statis-

Obviously some forms of arranged marriages are exploitative of women. Forced marriages, particularly those involving children, have been rightfully condemned by the United Nations. In some cultures death by stoning is still the penalty for adultery or divorce. These patriarchal and oppressive arrangements should be challenged and eliminated.

And yet millions of couples across world history have learned to appreciate and even thrive in arranged marriage unions. People with completely different and in some cases seemingly noncompatible personalities are coupled together for a lifelong union. No dating, no questions, no personality assessments, but married. Over time people can learn to love each other, whether they were total strangers or high school sweethearts. In every marriage, arranged or otherwise, the real marriage begins when the honeymoon is over, and much of that work involves learning to navigate our partner's unique personality traits as they in turn learn to navigate ours.

Again, the relationship between a pastor or pastoral team and a congregation is an arranged marriage. Whether the clergy were evaluated and interviewed in a call system, grew up through the ranks of the congregation, or were sent to serve the congregation by an episcopacy, this union has been *arranged*. Even if you think you fell in love and had a honeymoon, a matchmaker was involved. Somehow, by the grace of God, the pastor(s) and congregation have been brought together in a divine union to serve the larger community on mission together.

Within each of the congregations I've served, I preached some version of an opening sermon called the *arranged marriage*. As an ordained clergy person in an itinerant system, I am sent by the episcopal leadership to serve a congregation as the appointed pastor. However, in my experience *pastor* is a title that is earned, not given. I am fond of saying in that opener, "I don't know you, you don't know me, but here we are standing on the altar together." I've stood on enough altars with enough groups of people in a wide range of contexts to come to realize, "Some of you are going to want a divorce one day." One day our honeymoon will be over.

---

ticbrain.com/arranged-marriage-statistics/

In that opening sermon I have an opportunity to set the tone and pace of the relationship. One of the important things I find to lead off with is the three L's I referenced earlier. I'm here to listen, to learn, and to love. It's also an opportunity to share a little about myself: where I come from, how God called me, and what my passions for ministry are. In one sense I'm doing two things simultaneously: I'm letting the congregation know I'm here to learn about their distinct personality, and I'm giving them a little spoiler alert around my own. The goal is not for the congregation to love me as their pastor but rather to more fully love one another and the larger community that cradles their lives.

I ground all of this in the biblical passage that most defines my part in God's story. My go-to Scripture is a minor prophet named Amos, who finds himself at odds with a bankrupt religious system. Amaziah, the head priest at the religious center of Bethel, says to Amos, "O seer, go, flee away to the land of Judah, earn your bread there, and prophesy there, but never again prophesy at Bethel, for it is the king's sanctuary, and it is a temple of the kingdom" (Amos 7:12–13). The little nobody prophet is stirring up trouble in the church, and Amaziah is not having it!

But Amos answers Amaziah, "I am no prophet nor a prophet's son, but I am a herdsman and a dresser of sycamore trees, and the LORD took me from following the flock, and the LORD said to me, 'Go, prophesy to my people Israel'" (Amos 7:14–15). Like Amos, I find the typical religious-leader clothes don't fit. Like Amos, I'm a nobody in the hierarchy of the religious system. I come from a line of drug addicts. I was abandoned, adopted, and then orphaned as a child. Much of my youth was spent incarcerated. I don't have the religious pedigree, don't come from a family of priests, and don't necessarily fit the typical pastoral profile. I have tattoos all over my hands and arms. After running an illegal enterprise, I started my first corporation as a teenager: a tree service, land clearing, and site preparation company. Like Amos, I was a tree trimmer and an everyday worker. Worse than Amos, I was a criminal. I've got no business preaching the Word, especially in a disruptive way to the religious powers!

And yet, like he called Amos, God called me and said, "Go preach to my people!" So here I am, underqualified, a nobody from nowhere, and an outlier to the clergy caste system.

The thing about Amos is he knew who he was. He knew the gifts God had given him. He knew the people God had called him to. This is utterly important for all people called to some form of ministry. Our unique personhood, both our good and bad traits, are a gift to the church. We need to stand in our identity, calling, and particular giftings, lest we become what Stanley Hauerwas once called "a quivering mass of availability."[54]

Learning the unique personality of our congregation and adapting our own leadership style is not about diminishing our identity or becoming an on-call spiritual butler to every whim and desire of the people. It's about asking what Eugene Peterson called the pastor's question: "Who are these particular people, and how can I be with them in such a way that they can become what God is making them?"[55] Many pastors stop at "Who are these particular people, and how can I be with them?" But the second half is where the real magic happens: "in such a way that they can become what God is making them?"

My own childhood abandonment—being recovered and nurtured by the church—shapes my posture toward her. My own experiences as a drug addict and criminal—living a life in a dark land far from the church—shape my orientation to go after those still living there. My own supernatural encounter with Jesus Christ in a jail cell and his calling me to pastoral ministry informs how I see the nature and work of the church. Mine is only a single story, a single perspective in the ongoing saga of God's graceful activity in the world, but I need to know and live that story, my story, not someone else's.

On the fivefold APEST (Apostle, Prophet, Evangelist, Shepherd, Teacher) gifting from Ephesians 4, I'm a high Apostle, with Teacher coming in close behind. I love to be involved in innovative, entrepre-

---

54. Stanley Hauerwas, as quoted in William H. Willimon, *Pastor: The Theology and Practice of Ordained Ministry* (Nashville: Abingdon Press, 2002), 60.

55. Eugene H. Peterson, *The Contemplative Pastor: Returning to the Art of Spiritual Direction* (Grand Rapids, MI: William B. Eerdmans, 1993), 4.

neurial ministry that connects people currently outside the church with Jesus. This is an essential aspect of my personality, openness, and extroversion. But also, I greatly enjoy thinking deeply about how these innovations intersect with theology, church history, and ecclesiology. Then I love to teach others from those practitioner-oriented learnings.

This doesn't mean some apostles won't score high in agreeableness or that some shepherds can't score high on openness. People are too complex to fit neatly into these categories. There are apostolic teachers, prophetic pastors, and evangelistic apostles. But generally speaking, we find a correlation between personality traits and the spiritual archetypes from Ephesians 4.

It also doesn't mean that there exist only five types of congregations in the generic sense. Every congregation has a unique personality in the same way a human does. Just like no person is exactly the same, so neither are any two congregations. Yet just as psychologists can simplify hundreds of unique personality traits into the Big Five categories, so too can congregations be understood through the five congregational types. There will be a multitude of unique variations, but the types give us a framework through which we can grow in maturity. It's by identifying the personality types involved in the love triangle of relationships, how they interact, and where the areas for growth are that we can "grow the center, experiment on the edge."

In my personality assessment you may have noticed that I didn't mention being a "shepherd" there. Admittedly, the conventional responsibilities associated with being a pastor don't exactly light my fire. Home visits, trips to the hospital, and regular office hours are not things that come naturally to me. But that doesn't let me off the hook from being a pastor! The sign in front of the church says "Pastor Michael Beck," after all. No one is exempt from serving people's needs, washing feet, and visiting folks in moments of pain and confusion. Yet I've found a way to be a pastor in traditional congregations while remaining faithful to who I am. By employing a team-based ministry approach, I equip people to join me in the work of ministry.

By listening, learning, and loving the unique personality of my congregation, I can see the places where I need to adapt and grow. In my willingness to do this, the congregation begins to grow in a sense of trust. Then together, we can have real conversations about our blind spots. We can identify people who have personality traits and spiritual gifts who can lead us into new areas of growth. Finally, we can equip and empower them to lead out on those edges.

My pastoral personality embraces outreach. The church of my youth was an outreach-centered congregation, so my personality was formed in that kind of a culture. As a juvenile delinquent and ninth-grade dropout addicted to drugs and alcohol, I was the "least of these" (Matt 25:40). I was on the receiving end of "outreach" in a dark time of my life. Perhaps that shapes my own passion for those kinds of ministries today.

Whether I chose the people I serve or not, we have been brought together into a relationship that has eternal implications. Just like with a healthy arranged marriage, we will need to navigate how our unique personalities synergize and where they collide. Listening, learning, and loving, over time, becomes leading. No relationship can be healthy long term when both parties are not willing to become students of each other.

When congregations seek to understand the unique personality of their pastor like in an arranged marriage, we can grow to a healthier place together, to more effectively serve the larger community. We can make sure love is flowing through each of the essential relationships in the love triangle we discussed earlier: a divine dance of love, flowing back and forth among pastor, congregation, and community, all equally derived from the life of God.

APPLYING THE FIVE CONGREGATIONAL PERSONALITY TYPES

1. Proclamation Centered

But speaking the truth in love, we must grow up in every way
into him who is the head, into Christ.
—Ephesians 4:15

This is a congregation of people who rally around the faithful preaching and teaching of God's Word. Worship services and Bible studies are the life stream of this congregation. Usually, they were founded or led for a significant period of time by a conscientious teacher who created a culture in which the study, proclamation, and transmission of scriptural truth (ἀλήθεια, *aletheia*) was a central value. Proclamation-centered congregations are the communal embodiment of conscientiousness. A central activity for this community of learners is thoughtful, attentive, and disciplined engagement with Scripture. People often feel compelled to act dutifully and excel as students as they integrate learnings in their daily life.

It's possible that when people talk about the "golden days" of this congregation's history, it involves a teaching pastor or preacher, who was exceptionally gifted in the proclamation of God's Word. It's easy to see how this is a congregation that can become all head and no heart. But healthy conscientious people are also thoughtful and attentive to the needs of others.

While many styles and approaches to preaching and teaching exist, I believe that some fundamental underlying principles can help a proclamation-centered congregation grow. It all traces back to a universal human desire for and recognition of truth. The truth we discover unveiled in Jesus of Nazareth as "way, truth, and life" (John 14:6) is a God of unconditional love. A God who "is love" (1 John 4:8). This truth stirs within us the desire that all people have to be loved and appreciated. From their most formative years, children seek the admiration and praise of their parents. When that element is missing, it can have lifelong implications.

When we are never affirmed by our parents with "I love you," "You are special," or "That was a really great thing you did" as children, we can become adults who constantly try to seek the approval and affirmation of others. Sometimes this can lead to unhealthy patterns and harmful behaviors.

In Ephesians Paul is highlighting the fact that "speaking the truth" and "in love" need to be held together. Furthermore, "speaking the truth in love" leads to the church "growing up" in Christ in every way (4:15). Speaking the truth in love is an essential part of a healthy body.

Good teaching and preaching builds up a congregation. Proclaiming the word of God in a transformative way requires those two essential ingredients: truth and love. Faith comes through hearing the truth of God's Word. Again, Jesus Christ himself is "the way and the truth and the life." The content of the gospel is a person, and that person is Jesus of Nazareth. Jesus is truth with skin on.

If we study the interactions of Jesus with most people, he is almost always affirming, always graceful, and always loving. The only places we see the tone and content of Jesus' message change are in his interactions with religious leaders who are living in hypocrisy.

This doesn't mean that all our preaching must be of the Barney variety: "I love you, you love me, we're a happy family." We can't evade truth in the name of love. Truth and love go together. They are lovers. When we speak the truth in love, we can say hard things that need to be said, but we can do this in a way that's not harmful or condemning.

Honestly, this is a place where I struggle in my own preaching. I harbor a miniature prophet inside my heart who likes to come out and say radical and challenging things. My first impulse is to communicate those things in a tone and language that can seem like I'm "speaking the truth in anger." I can tell I've gone astray when I start using "you" statements rather than "we" statements. As we say in recovery, "When you point the finger at someone else, you have three pointing back at you," or in other words, "You spot it, you got it." Should we confront racism, highlight corrupt behavior in political leaders, and call ourselves to examine unjust systems and policies that cause harm from the pulpit? Yes; it would be an act of cowardice not to no matter how we dress it up. But this can be done in the spirit of love and truth. I must constantly be on guard about that.

Perhaps Proverbs 13:17 can be our guide here: "A bad messenger brings trouble, but a faithful envoy, healing."

We can say the things we feel God calling us to say, but how we say them is important. For one, our connection with the congregation needs to be real and rooted in love. Think about the people in your own life who can say hard things to you. Why do you receive it from them? Because we know they love us and want God's best for us. That relational currency must be there.

If something in the Scriptures needs to be said that confronts some attitude or behavior in the church, we need to say it. But for me I try to keep that a very small part of the sermon. As Mary Poppins famously said, "A spoonful of sugar helps the medicine go down." If there's some medicine in the sermon that's not going to taste so good, I better make sure it's wrapped in the sugar of love.

Dwayne Butler, one of the lay preachers on our team at Wildwood, is incredible at creating sermons with this blend of truth and love. Wildwood was a fellowship-centered congregation for many years but has recently been growing in proclamation and outreach.

Dwayne has no formal seminary education, but he is passionate about proclaiming the Word of God. His gift has helped us grow into a more robust congregation.

Dwayne is one of the first black members to join Wildwood since its planting as a Methodist Episcopal Church, South congregation in 1882. Sadly, racism is an enduring legacy of Wildwood UMC and its surrounding community. Dwayne, through his charisma and commitment to form real relationships with fellow congregants, has forced people to come to terms with long-held unexamined racist ideas.

As a lay pastor he lacks the kind of institutional credentials often expected but brings others that are more important. Dwayne serves in a pastoral-leadership role. This shared-leadership approach allows the congregation to be anti-racist not just theoretically but also structurally. When Dwayne preaches, he can do so from his own experience as a black man while directly challenging racist assumptions with the anti-racist truths inherent in the biblical passages themselves. He is speaking the truth in love in a way that is transformative for us all.

A sermon can be filled with many simple, straightforward statements of affirmation, celebrating the good, beautiful, and true and lifting up the sacred worth of God's people. That should be the primary content of a sermon, whether it's wrapped in story, projected on slides, recited as a poem, or delivered as a first-person narrative. Speaking the truth in love is about edification, uplift, and encouragement.

When it comes to preaching, a sermon is not just a speech. A sermon is a missional phenomenon, so it should motivate the hearers to actually do something: to love others, to start a new ministry, to give generously, to repent of some sin, or to come down and receive communion. People are motivated to change or act more through encouragement and love than through judgment and condemnation. In the teachings of Jesus, what percentage would you guess is encouragement and what percentage judgment? Jesus is disproportionately more encouraging than he is condemning.

Good proclamation can build up the well-being of others. It can be an experience of affirmation that inspires motivation. Just like a spouse appreciates and is motivated by words of affirmation, so a congregation is moved to act by truth spoken in love.

Affirming words can motivate people to go deeper in their calling. It can encourage, or "inspire courage." This helps people overcome things that hinder them. Encouraged people can accomplish things they might not have believed they could do. The Bible gives us lots of content to work with here. It is a treasure trove of encouragement, so much so that some have called it one extensive "love letter from God." From the God who seeks us with the gentle call of "Where are you?" in the garden, to the God who says, "I'll be with you always" until the final garden, God's Word encourages us to press into the life of faith.

Good teaching and preaching require empathy and understanding for what the people in the congregation are going through. This requires the pastor(s) to spend more time listening than talking. We must create some mechanism to be with people and hear their stories, whether that's home visits, large fellowship gatherings, visit with people at work, or parking-lot conversations. The best preachers I know are expert listeners. In the context of a large church, we need teams of people who are tasked with connecting and listening to people's stories and struggles. Those realities need to inform the preaching.

An inspired word can be a catalyst that changes someone's life trajectory. A word of hope in a moment of despair. A word of challenge in a season of sin. A word of healing in a time of woundedness. A word of resurrection in the valley of death.

The tone with which we communicate becomes its own communication. You've heard the adage "It's not what you say but how you say it." This is true for proclaimers of God's love. If we are sharing the sweetest words of life ever preached in a tone that is sarcastic or demeaning, then, in the words of Canadian philosopher and technological prophet Marshall McLuhan (1911–1980), the "medium is the message."[56] People can't hear the words through the tone with which they are delivered.

---

56. Marshall McLuhan, *Understanding Media: The Extensions of Man*, critical edition, ed. W. Terrence Gordon (Corte Madera, CA: Gingko Press, 2003), 9.

Preaching and teaching can be a vehicle through which the Holy Spirit brings healing. On many occasions "truth in love" penetrate someone's heart, bring clarity from confusion, shift a negative attitude, unleash a cascade of forgiveness, and so on. The words of life bring healing to the soul.

If this kind of proclamation seems challenging, we need to do a heart examination. What is blocking us from speaking the truth in love? Where there exists a track record of contention or abuse between the pastor and the congregation, there needs to be a time of confession, repentance, and forgiveness.

If the congregation is resentful of the pastor, all the words of affirmation in the world will fall on deaf ears. If the pastor is carrying resentment against the congregation, preaching and teaching will be inauthentic or even harmful. Perhaps reading this book will be an opportunity to change the conversation? Working through these ideas with a team can provide a vehicle to clear the air. After all, as we say in the recovery community, "Resentment is liking drinking poison hoping the other party will die."

A conscientious teacher makes not demands, pounding their fists on the pulpit, but thoughtful suggestions and requests. Requests affirm the worth and giftings of the congregation. Speaking the truth in love is not about making demands. As we all know, only the Holy Spirit can do the real heavy lifting of conviction, transformation, or healing. When we find ways to turn our sermons and Bible studies into conversations, ones in which we can lay before people requests, we can see amazing results.

Jesus was primarily a dialogical preacher. He gave extensive sermons, like the Sermon on the Mount, for example (Matt 5–7). But more frequently he asked questions—as many as 307, to be exact![57] He told stories and parables that didn't so much give answers but rather invited people to ask deeper questions.

"You need to go out there and love and serve the lost!" is a demand. "How might each one of us find ways this week to love and serve the people in our community?" That is a request. The best teachers understand the difference between extrinsic and intrinsic

---

57. Martin B. Copenhaver, *Jesus Is the Question: The 307 Questions Jesus Asked and the 3 He Answered* (Nashville: Abingdon Press, 2014).

motivation. The church has used extrinsic motivation in harmful ways for two thousand years. For example, scaring people into a relationship with Jesus through fear of hell. "You should do this because the Bible says it!" That's a textbook example of extrinsic motivation.

Intrinsic motivation involves helping people hear the voice of the Holy Spirit in their own lives. A biblical truth that resonates with one's own unique personality and giftings can motivate us to change the trajectory of our future. This is the beauty of movements like Fresh Expressions, which plugs into intrinsic motivation by inviting people to gather a group of friends to do something together in a time, space, and rhythm that works for them. There we center around Jesus and think about how that can become church in and of itself. Intrinsic motivation is entirely more effective in my experience.

A proclamation church can go about learning and growing in a variety of ways. Perhaps the discussion questions at the end of this chapter will spark some ideas.

People need to feel appreciated. They need to know they are loved. The teaching and preaching ministries of the church can be a place of explosive potential toward that end.

The Dark Side of a Proclamation-Centered Congregation

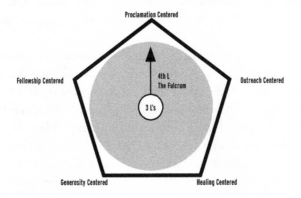

Remember that every congregation has a dark side or a blind spot. If Christ's "power is made perfect in weakness" (2 Cor 12:9), how do we yield that weakness to Christ in order to allow him to turn it into our superpower? How does a proclamation-centered congregation represent the fullness of the "love triangle" in which God's love flows in a continuous loop through pastor, congregation, and community?

The first movement is to communicate love well, thereby strengthening our center. In a proclamation-centered congregation, the leaders need to work hard to create vibrant preaching and teaching ministries that "speak the truth in love." Ministers need to work hard on delivering compelling and transformative sermons. Leadership teams need to work hard to create environments in which people can gather around the proclaimed Word and create a discipleship system that will help people bend their lives to the truth of Scripture. Faithful engagement with Scripture can lead people to an encounter with the One who is the "living Word," Jesus the Christ (John 1:1), much like we saw to be true in the little church in Asia Minor called Philadelphia.

From the strength of that center, we can begin to move out to the edges. As we have seen, the dark side of a proclamation-centered congregation can manifest in many ways. In larger churches it can become a shallow form of church, where people come to consume the preaching like a spiritual Happy Meal. In smaller congregations it can diminish authentic fellowship because the whole system centers around the sermon, or the deliverer, but leaves no space for quality conversations.

If a minister is particularly gifted in preaching, the minister and their gift can become an idol. People start worshiping the person and their abilities rather than the God they point to. If a preacher embraces that worship and idolization, it leads to a toxic culture that can result in harm. One way to avoid this dark side is to understand proclamation as a team-based and communal endeavor. If a preacher is particularly gifted in preaching and teaching the Bible, they should preach less, not more. This seems counterintuitive, but the best preachers I know equip teams in how to preach. They grow fruit on other people's trees. They do the behind-the-scenes work of training, encouraging, and unleashing others.

A proclamation-centered congregation should not become fixated upon one person but become a community of proclaimers in which every person is encouraged to play a role. Large congregations with lots of staff can accomplish this by having a rotation of employees who preach. But even small proclamation-centered congregations can accomplish this by empowering laity.

At the network of congregations Jill and I serve as part-time pastors, we have no staff. Our preaching team consists of two clergy and a diverse group of six lay preachers who cover the pulpits of two congregations. We have a dozen more folks who preach and lead sermonic conversations in our Fresh Expressions of Church. We go away together for preaching retreats, teaching seminary-level content about how to study, prepare, and deliver sermons. As a community of equals, we each bring sermon series ideas to the table. We talk these through and democratically decide which ones we will preach. We plan out the entire year's preaching calendar in advance.

Proclamation looks different in a post-Christendom setting. In our various fresh expressions of church, we have utilized a different approach by taking a page from the early church's playbook. Perhaps their strategy for a pre-Christian world can be applied to a post-Christian world?

Many scholars agree that the first apostles most likely carried an oral tradition about Jesus for a period of time before the gospels came into written form. This treasury of stories about Jesus' life and teaching came to be known as the *kerygma*, related to the Greek verb κηρύσσω (kērússō), literally meaning "to cry or proclaim as a herald." The apostles traveled the ancient world proclaiming these stories about Jesus and inviting hearers to respond. This ultimately became the core of the early church's teaching about Jesus.

We train our laity to do a simple version of this in home, work, and third places where these small contextual Christian communities gather. Many people who participate can't or don't want to attend more traditional forms of church, so we incarnate church with them where they are. The center of these gatherings are open and honest conversations about the joys and struggles in our lives.

In the context of these conversations we share "Jesus Stories," simple, short, retellings about something Jesus said or did in five minutes or less. We equip our laity with simple questions to frame the conversations: What would this story look like today? What if this Jesus story is true? If it is true, how would it make a difference in my life? What is this Jesus story saying to me? What is one small thing I can change in my daily life as a result of this Jesus story? Or what is one thing I might do differently? These questions give access for non-Christians to join into the conversation. They are intentionally designed to not be "right or wrong" answer questions, but to open curiosity and reflection.

People who are not quite comfortable getting "preached at" on Sunday mornings find space to ask questions and join this sermonic conversation. If a formal sermon is an orchestra, with a conductor on a stand guiding the community through predetermined sheet music, a sermonic conversation is a jazz band. We sit down together as a community of equals, and someone strikes a note. Then each person improvises their contribution in real time. It's entirely contextual and particular to the people in that circle. People respond with personal insights, questions, and challenges. The "proclaimer" must shift more into the role of "facilitator."

This interactive dialogue replaces the proclamation monologue with a didactic, inquiry-based approach. The engagement draws from the collective wisdom of the group. It is modeled after Jesus, the master teacher, who asked more questions than he gave answers. Jesus, who rarely read manuscripts, probably never wrote one, but told lots of stories and parables that invited deeper questions and reflection. These sermons are more dialogue than monologue, but they are a form of proclamation none the less.

There are some key advantages to proclamation in this form outside traditional church settings:

- Anyone can lead these Bible discussions. It's every member ministry (1 Pet. 2:9).

- Enquirers can easily join in, even if they are agnostic, atheist, or "spiritual but not religious" (Acts 8:26-40).

- Scripture does the evangelism and disciple making, as the Holy Spirit works on each person's heart at their own pace (Rom. 10:17).

- Christians share their faith almost without knowing, you don't have to be a long-term disciple, or seminary trained, to tell a story and ask some questions (Matt. 25:37-38).

- Seekers see how the Bible and the Christian community impact life (Jn. 8:30).

- Leadership is shared with newcomers, increasing their commitment to the group (Jn. 4:29).

- New Christians learn how to study the Bible, apply it to their lives, share it with their friends, and find helpful resources (Jn. 4:39-42).

- If the leader moves on, the group has the means to keep going—sustainability is built in (1 Thess. 2:17).

This helps a proclamation centered congregation own its strength but expand to become a constellation of little communities spread across an entire parish. These gatherings are distributed across a seven day work week, meeting at different times and places, making church more accessible to those not currently connected with any congregation.

The dark side is going to be different for every congregation. But we can use the concept of the "Fourth L" fulcrum to move the needle toward a weak area of our congregational life. As we do this, we need to keep the three primary relationships in mind: God's love flowing through (1) minister, (2) congregation, and (3) community. We may need to start with where we see the biggest "love blockage." Is the primary dysfunction a congregation feeling unknown and unloved by their pastor(s)? Or is it a community being unknown and unloved by a congregation? Or a pastor who is unknown and unloved or even resented by the congregation?

If we identify that *outreach* is our biggest weakness, we can use the preaching and teaching ministries of the church to empower the congregation for service to the community. If we identify *fellowship* as our most obvious dark side, we can plan fellowship gatherings alongside major proclamation events. If *healing* is a major blind spot, we can start with a series that highlights the importance of cultivating the shalom of God in our wider community, through both extraordinary and ordinary means of the Holy Spirit, and experiment with these impartations in worship or smaller, more intimate gatherings like a fresh expression. If *generosity* is our biggest challenge, we can do extensive teaching on giving from a biblical perspective.

We can create small groups focused on one of these areas in which people are invited to delve deeper into their discipleship journeys. The key to strengthening the center, while experimenting on the edge, is to use the gift of the congregation's particular strengths, to lead them into other expressions and growth of their weaknesses gently over time.

These are determinations your team must make for itself, but perhaps the guiding questions following each section can give you a starting point and help you move in the right direction.

Team Discussion

Gather your team. Make sure everyone has read the chapter. Open in prayer. Use these questions to guide your conversation.

1. Do you believe you are a proclamation-centered congregation? Why or why not? Give some practical examples that support your belief.

2. Is biblical truth a value for your congregation? How do you know?

3. Name some ways you spend time listening to understand one another.

4. How many on your team score high on Teacher in the FCPT typology? What does this say about your team or congregation?

5. What would you say is the "dark side" of your congregation's personality characteristics? Why do you think that? What are some practical ways you can begin to deal with it?

2. Fellowship Centered

They devoted themselves to the apostles' teaching and fellow-ship, to the breaking of bread and the prayers.

—*Acts 2:42*

Early in the life of the church, we see some consistent ingredi-ents that make up what it means to be the church. As we saw earlier, Acts 2 shows us that those first believers devoted themselves to the apostles' teaching (proclamation centered), breaking of bread (gener-osity centered), and the prayers and wonders (healing centered), and the Lord was adding outsiders to their numbers (outreach centered). If we're not careful, we might skip right over that little word *fellow-ship*. A healthy, growing church in Acts expressed all these character-istics at some level, and this is true of healthy, growing congregations today. But the word *fellowship* is somehow in the center of it all.

The Greek word that we translate as *fellowship* is κοινωνία (*koi-nonia*). The word occurs twenty times in four unique forms in the Greek text upon which many New Testament versions are based. It was an important concept to those first-century Christians, and it should be an important concept to us twenty-first-century Chris-tians!

Fellowship, κοινωνία, can mean partnership, social intercourse, financial benefaction, or communion. Within it is the concept of generosity, the share that one has in anything, participation in a gift jointly contributed, a collection or a contribution, as exhibiting an embodiment and proof of fellowship. But at the deepest level it also means mutual vulnerability, fellowship, and intimacy. This language that borders on spiritual eroticism envisions a group of people who share such a depth of union, it's as if they penetrate and are bound to one another at a soul level. In short, it describes a type of community that shares the deepest intimacy.

Agreeableness is the main personality trait of fellowship congregations. There is a quality of being friendly, considerate of others, and concerned about social harmony. Agreeable congregations value getting along with one another, making things work, and cherishing long-held relationships. When healthy, they have an optimistic view of human nature. They show genuine concern for community members and their happiness. Fellowship is the communal embodiment of healthy agreeableness. These are congregations where kind pastors thrive.

Fellowship-centered congregations love to be together. They enjoy a shared life. They are always creating ways to be in one another's presence. This is a congregation that has lots of get-togethers and social events, from potlucks to yard sales to church cleanups to sewing circles. Essentially, if there's a way they can meet somewhere, they'll find a way to do it!

I've served several fellowship congregations. Since my personality manifests best in outreach, I often found myself frustrated. More people would show up to the church potluck than to Sunday service. In one very rural congregation, the only people who came to the monthly church yard sale were other church members! The activities seemed to be ineffective, internal, a big waste of time. It seemed like all these folks wanted to do was make excuses to be together. Where was the missional thrust of that?

After years of failing forward as a pastor, I realized something deeper was going on at these gatherings. It wasn't about the activities themselves; it was all about making quality time together. It was about fellowship, κοινωνία, and that is quite a sacred endeavor in its own right. This was a kingdom value, embodied by those first Christians who gathered daily, devoting themselves to the apostles' teaching and fellowship, to the breaking of bread, and to prayers—a true Christian community.

I've realized now that quality time is one of the greatest gifts we can give to another person. Our slate of days is limited. Time is a resource we never get back. The world programs us for hurry, productivity, and results. Technology, while it can be an incredible tool for massive good, also monetizes our time and fragments our attention. We can't be fully attentive to the person in front of us if our attention is fixated on a screen with others elsewhere. In this sense fellowship-centered congregations are living out a subversive, countercultural witness within the world.

My dazzling sermons or edgy outreach ideas weren't the essence of church for them. Being together in a slow intentional way mattered most.

The key to quality time is not what we do together; it's about togetherness itself. Togetherness, true fellowship, is not just about being together either. It's about being together in a focused way. It's about attending to one another. It's about undivided attention. This doesn't mean we can't actively be doing something together, but rather as we are doing what we are doing, we are fully engaged with one another. We are offering one another the gift of presence.

Another aspect of what's happening during these "fellowship events" is the nature of the conversations happening.

Perhaps the bane of all fellowship-centered congregations is the opposite of that kind of conversation: gossip! In an unhealthy scenario the conversations are about other people or that pesky pastor! Unhealthy fellowship can result in speaking negatively or even maligning other people who are not present to defend themselves. Those kinds of conversations poison the well of a fellowship congregation. They spread like a virus throughout the whole body. I've witnessed my share of those conversations. I call them un-quality conversations. But for people who valued fellowship in a healthy way, these conversations were dripping with prayer and depth.

In a fellowship congregation the key tools of the pastor are giving time and listening. It's about sitting at the table, participating in the conversations, and being truly present with people. It's not just focusing on getting to whatever task the gathering has been called together for but attending to each person in a sacred way, really being there with them. I found that if I did my share of this, people really started to value my preaching and teaching. As I gave the gift of time in fellowship, I could even shape the kinds of gatherings and conversations that were taking place.

Being together, really listening, giving the gift of presence, can be the solution to so many problems in the church. We've been programmed for a McDonaldized, programmatized, and consumerized version of the faith. We show up to the church thing, do our part, sing a hymn, cook a meal, put a tip in the bucket, and then hurry back to the so-called important things of life, the laundry list of things we never seem to be able to accomplish.

In a larger congregation quality time is a challenge for the pastoral team. We have so many people. How could we ever give them all quality time? The other humbling thing I've had to realize is that it's not about the pastor. Just showing up was enough. Just spending time with the couple of people I was able to connect with was enough. This is why small groups are so important. They provide little churches within the larger church, a fellowship where people can really know and love one another. The sad part about many so-called megachurches is that they can be like a massive oak tree with a shallow root system. Because they have no depth, they blow over in a minor storm. A church can't fully be healthy without κοινωνία. It is an essential ingredient.

Think about the two primary types of listening: listening to respond and listening to understand. I'm really great at the former. I have to work at the latter. We are wired to listen to respond. While you're talking, I'm thinking about what I'm going to say. Before you're even finished, I've got the answer to your problem! Listening to understand is about empathy, withholding judgment, not trying to solve a problem, but just being present to another person.

The church is not a problem to be solved but more a mystery to be adored. It's not merely pews to be filled, food to be distributed, or sermons to be preached. The goal of the church for Jesus was not about growing a megachurch. It was about being relationally present with a handful of people, nurturing them, growing them, and then sending them. In the church-growth paradigm, when as pastors we are consumed with all the numbers being up and to the right, we are missing the essence of what the church is.

The church is not a series of goals or projects to be accomplished. The church is a web of relationships. Quality time is the fertilizer of good relationships. A relationship calls for listening to understand. It's about being present.

At their best these churches can become a place where healthy conversations and deep intimacy can help people grow and heal. This includes quality activities, potlucks, yard sales, hymn sings, sewing circles, chat over coffee, craft beer, yoga, or even a 5k. In the rapid pace of a world in a hurry, these moments of fellowship are a countercultural witness to the world. They embody a kind of community, a community that is Jesus' gift to the world, a community that devotes itself to the apostles' teaching and fellowship, to the breaking of bread and prayers.

It's not hard to see the dark side of a fellowship congregation. They can become self-absorbed, internally focused, and even hostile to outsiders. Every time a new person comes into the fellowship, it changes the social dynamics. Strangers can threaten the cohesiveness and the intimacy of the fellowship. This is exactly why the most important thing for a fellowship-centered congregation to do is move into outreach.

The Dark Side of a Fellowship-Centered Congregation

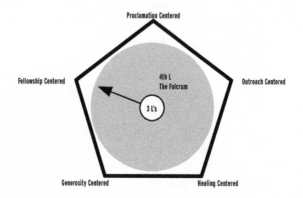

At some level every congregation is exclusive by nature. Any time we decide to gather in a particular place, at a particular time, and in a particular way, we will include some people, but we will inevitably by default exclude others. While this is true of every congregation, it is particularly so of a fellowship-centered congregation. Exclusion: this is the primary dark side of this kind of community.

In *Divided by Faith*, Michael Emerson and Christian Smith pull together research from psychologists and social scientists to explore the "natural" biases functioning in ingroup/outgroup dynamics. They highlight the "ethical paradox of group loyalty," which states that even when groups are made up of loving, unselfish individuals, the group can transmute individual unselfishness into group selfishness.[58]

The underlying research in group dynamics further reveals that whenever a new person enters a social system, it requires adaptation to the newcomer. This can leave tightly knit groups and families feeling vulnerable. A social system can find a certain equilibrium, a rhythm of community. Newcomers threaten that equilibrium. They send the system into chaos, at least momentarily. Unhealthy fellowship congregations exist as closed systems.

Professor and missiologist Kristine Stache describes the difference between open and closed systems. Closed systems exist in particular contexts, but the systems operations do not depend on those contexts. The environments are not taken into consideration when the system operates. Stache reflects on the Christendom ideal that "a church was a church, regardless of where it was. It looked like a church, acted like a church, and could be airlifted to any place around the globe and not change." In comparison, an open system not only takes its context into consideration but depends on its environment for input and resources. Therefore, an open system exists for the sake of that context.[59]

Fellowship-centered congregations, particularly those that exist in the same location for many years, can become closed systems. The

58. Michael O. Emerson and Christian Smith, *Divided by Faith: Evangelical Religion and the Problem of Race in America* (Oxford, UK: Oxford University Press, 2001), 207.

59. Kristine M. Stache, "Practice of Immersion in the Context," *Currents in Theology and Mission* 38, no. 5 (2011): 363–64.

context changes, but the church does not. The church continues to function under the assumptions of a previous societal form, while those assumptions have become largely invalid. These groups have thought and skill sets geared primarily toward a closed system. If a system stays closed for too long, its inhabitants perish. A system needs healthy input and output in order to thrive.

Sadly, creating homogeneous units has been a tactic of church-growth strategies at times. Like attracts like. People who have things in common can more easily connect and build meaningful relationships. But when that kind of intimate community becomes exclusive to outsiders—a closed system—it is a breeding ground for all kinds of evil: racism, sexism, and colonialism to name a few. This kind of thinking has led to racially segregated churches. Remember our friends in the congregation in Pergamum. Their internally focused nature led to all kinds of troubles with false teachers as well. Somehow, the truth of Jesus became less important than their being together.

Typically, a fellowship-centered congregation needs to move toward outreach. It requires moving out of its comfort zone, opening the system, and connecting with its community again. Yet the weakness of a fellowship congregation can also be its superpower. These are people who know the value of quality time. They know how to be present with people. Often finding ways for them to create fellowship gatherings in the community can be a useful adaptation.

George and Carole Vitale at St. Marks in Ocala, Florida, are dedicated lay leaders who have made this shift. They have the spiritual gift of creating fellowship-centered experiences around food. They believe that food is love. For decades they've prepared meals that seemed to be at the center of every church gathering. They value getting people together to break bread and share in conversations. Many times these gatherings were focused on existing members of the congregation.

One day George and Carole decided to transform the spiritual giftings that flow from their personalities into a way to turn strangers into friends. They turned fellowship meals into a form of outreach. Together with their team of volunteers, they started a Wednesday night community dinner called The Family Table. They host the gatherings in the fellowship hall between the 5:30 and 8:00 p.m. recovery groups that meet at the church. These meeting are typically attended by over a hundred people. Many are not prepared to "attend church," but they are more than willing to come enjoy the Vitales' food and join a dialogue around a Jesus story.

The Vitales and their team have pulled the "fourth L" fulcrum if you will, transforming the dark side of a fellowship-centered congregation into its strength. They have turned weakness into superpower. Now people who largely have no connection with a church are experiencing the love of Jesus through quality time being extended through gathering around the table together. George and Carole have used their church's strength to cultivate an outreaching fresh expression of church for those in the recovery community.

Fresh Expressions are open-system, contextual forms of church that come in many different colors, shapes, and sizes. While some, like The Family Table, can take place at the church compound in certain contexts, many form in "third places," meaning a location that is neither the primary location of home or workplace but spaces for relaxation, recreation, and connection. Stache defines the pastoral practice of "Immersion in Context" as "showing awareness of the context through listening to, dialogue with, and involvement in the local community." Adopters of this approach are to show competency in the ability to "interpret texts and contexts with insight."[60]

Fellowship congregations that employ the "immersion in context" approach can adapt and break the closed loop. The value of immersive learning has a wide history in multiple fields and is currently a significant focus in the business realm. It is a central practice in the development of contextual intelligence.[61] Being embedded in an unfamiliar setting precipitates a form of active learning about the new culture. This is a kind of transformative learning that does not typically occur by simply studying data about a culture but through learning a culture from the inside. One way to deal with the dark

---

60. Stache, "Practice of Immersion in the Context," 364.
61. Sweet and Beck , *Contextual Intelligence*.

side of a fellowship congregation is to empower teams to create little pockets of *koinonia* all over the community.

I was once pastor to a notoriously exclusive group: the United Methodist Women! These ladies had been meeting exclusively for decades. They were a thick community who loved to be together. They also were the ones who really ran the church! Part of their gatherings featured quilting, doing arts and crafts, and preparing wonderful meals for one another. These are all gifts our greater community needed desperately.

A small team of these women decided they would rent the local community center to start a Fresh Expression they called "Arts for Love." They passed out flyers in the neighborhood and the local schools. Young families with children who weren't quite comfortable coming to the church facility showed up at the community center. They gathered to have a meal together and spent time teaching how to make sea glass jewelry, paint, write poems, and so on. Then participants shared their creations with the group. Eventually, they also introduced a Jesus story, in which someone stood up and provided a brief story from Jesus' teaching or life. They were cultivating a new form of church by using their gift of fellowship.

This turned the congregation, which largely functioned as a closed system, into an open system. Over time people who connected at the gatherings in the community center made their way back to the church compound, and people who seemed to live at the church compound started to form new relationships with people in the community.

If you are a fellowship congregation, only you know your biggest blind spot and where to begin. Perhaps introducing sermonic conversations into the fellowship gatherings? Inviting people to explore healing practices or rituals like anointing with oil, yoga, or meditation? Or using some portion of a fellowship event to study a resource on generosity? The key is to leverage a strong center to move toward the edge. The team discussion questions are designed to help you explore contextually appropriate options.

Team Discussion

Gather your team. Make sure everyone has read the chapter. Open in prayer. Use these questions to guide your conversation.

1. Do you believe you are a fellowship-centered congregation? Why or why not? Give some practical examples that support your belief.

2. Name some ways you spend time being fully present with one another and engaging in quality conversations.

3. Do you feel your congregation is currently more of a closed system or an open system? Why do you feel that way?

4. What is the greatest dark side you see in light of what you've learned so far? Where is your edge, where you see needed growth?

5. What small experiments might you begin to "grow the center, experiment on the edge"? How might you get started?

3. Generosity Centered

*As for those who in the present age are rich, command them
not to be haughty or to set their hopes on the uncertainty of
riches but rather on God, who richly provides us with everything for our enjoyment. They are to do good, to be rich in
good works, generous, and ready to share, thus storing up for
themselves the treasure of a good foundation for the future, so
that they may take hold of the life that really is life.*
—*1 Timothy 6:17–19*

For generosity-centered congregations, you guessed it: *generosity*
is a central value! The NRSV translates the word ἀπλότης (*haplotēs*)
as generosity. Interestingly, the word also means singleness, simplicity, sincerity, liberality, bountifulness, and mental honesty. The word
denotes a virtue of one who is free from pretense and hypocrisy. As a
congregation this manifests as not being self-seeking but rather dis-
playing an openness of heart manifesting itself by generosity.

It is indeed interesting that the word that is translated as "generosity" in the New Testament also means singleness or fidelity. This
is exactly the primary work of prophets, to call the people to repentance when they have strayed into idolatry. Prophets are a voice for
the oppressed and marginalized.

I do wonder if the Old Testament prophets would score high on
neuroticism in the FFM assessment. Read through Jeremiah, Lam-
entations, Ezekiel, Hosea, and so on. Their ministry and writings are
marked with sadness and seem to lean toward emotional instability.
Sometimes as I'm reading through the prophets, I think to myself
they could have benefited from some therapy, or even a prescribed

mood stabilizer! Yet in the midst of their inner struggle, some of the most beautiful prophetic glimpses of the coming Jesus flow.

Many of the prophets seem high on being vulnerable, temperamental, worry-prone, self-pitying, and self-conscious—insert mental picture of Jonah sitting beneath the vine in misery over the repentant Ninevites! But the prophets have a consistent theme in their messages. Just consider how many times the Old Testament prophets condemn opulence and hoarding worldly possessions while neglecting the poor. Follow the thread of their concern for the oppressed, marginalized, and neglected, and their relentless cry for the protection of orphans and widows. Consider John the Baptist and his message of repentance in the wilderness preparing the way for Jesus. Or consider the prophetic song of Mary regarding her coming child:

> He has shown strength with his arm;
>> he has scattered the proud in the imagination of their
> hearts.
> He has brought down the powerful from their thrones
>> and lifted up the lowly;
> he has filled the hungry with good things
>> and sent the rich away empty.
>
> —*Luke 1:51–53*

Jesus is the ultimate vision of a healthy prophet. He was emotive—he wept, he sweat blood, he got upset and turned over tables. Yet he was also calm, emotionally stable, even-tempered, self-content, and seemingly free from persistent negative feelings. Jesus' own prophetic teachings were aligned with the prophets who preceded him in calling the people to repentance for religious hypocrisy, neglecting to care for the vulnerable and oppressed, and hoarding wealth. Think about how much he spoke about money. It was one of his favorite subjects. Eleven of Jesus' thirty-eight parables were directly about money and material belongings, or they used money as a way to convey spiritual truth. Approximately one out of every ten verses in the Gospels are devoted to the issue of money.[62]

Yet the heart of Jesus' teaching about worldly wealth was a consistent call for people to use it to care for the neglected, marginalized, and "least of these." He told the rich young ruler to sell his great possessions and give to the poor (Matt 19:16–23; Mark 10:17–22; and Luke 18:18–23). One of the most famous and revealing of Jesus' teachings on the matter is found here: "Do not store up for yourselves treasures on earth, where moth and rust consume and where thieves break in and steal, but store up for yourselves treasures in heaven, where neither moth nor rust consumes and where thieves do not break in and steal. For where your treasure is, there your heart will be also" (Matt 6:19–21). Storing up wealth and defining ourselves by it is a great perversion of the heart. It is idolatry.

The calling of prophets almost always involves a call to repentance amid unjust economic, political, and religious systems. Generally, in the current form of our society, we operate in a system of *capitalism* in which private ownership of the means of production and their operation for profit is the foundational assumption. Central characteristics of capitalism include capital accumulation, competitive markets, a price system, private property and the recognition of property rights, voluntary exchange, and wage labor. In this system we think about work in terms of punching a time clock, exchanging our time or skills for monetary compensation. If we earn lots of money, we can buy nice things and do what we like. This is a narrow way to understand ourselves and our vocation within the world.

Due to the dwindling number of resources in a capitalistic society, we have created a massive gap between the super wealthy and the desperately poor. Less than 1 percent of the world's population now holds over 50 percent of the world's wealth. When people have more than they need, when they hoard, it creates lack for those who are excluded from the center of wealth generation. We throw away more food from our tables in one day than others have to live on for

---

62. Consider this sampling: Matthew 6:24; Matthew 13:44–46; Matthew 22:15–22; Matthew 25:16; Luke 7:41–43; and Luke 15:8–10.

weeks. This inequality is unacceptable for people who follow a Savior who said we would find him in the "least of these."

Financial generosity can actually create systemic change in oppressive and unjust systems. In fact, in a sin-broken world governed by this particular economic system, which influences all other systems, including governmental, judicial, and justice, it is one of the only ways to create systemic change. Perhaps this is why Jesus referred to money as "mammon," which means treasure and riches personified and opposed to God. "No man can serve two masters: for either he will hate the one, and love the other; or else he will hold to the one, and despise the other. Ye cannot serve God and mammon" (Matt 6:24, KJV). This is why generosity-centered congregations are so important.

In the midst of these fallen realities, the early church came together and devoted themselves to breaking and sharing bread, and "all who believed were together and had all things in common; they would sell their possessions and goods and distribute the proceeds to all, as any had need" (Acts 2:44–45). Believers who mature in their faith begin to live a life that's ripe with the "fruit of the spirit," and one of those fruits is *generosity* (Gal 5:22–23). For churches that fully understand the true economy of God, their spiritual life is all about giving. From a worldly perspective this doesn't make sense. Particularly in individualistic cultures, we chase the dream of earning success and wealth. We see ourselves as the locus of this activity.

For followers of Jesus, we know that this is a false and dangerously deceptive narrative. We can love only because God first loved us. We can give only because God first gave. God is the source of all good things. There is nothing that we receive that is not a gift from God. The clothes we wear, the food we consume, the air we breathe, intimate moments of prayerful communion in the Spirit—all gifts from God.

In 1 Timothy we learn of a God who "richly provides us with everything for our enjoyment." Generous people understand this. I confess that in growing up in the context of poverty, generosity does not come easy for me. Sometimes as a child I stole things to eat or survive. What many considered basic necessities were not a given for me. I grew up in an atmosphere of scarcity. That environment bred in me an attitude of scarcity. Will there be enough? Will the well run dry? Will I be able to provide for my family? These were default questions for me.

It has taken years of healing work to embrace an attitude of abundance. I've come to the realization that God always provides, that in his kingdom there is always enough, and that the more generous I can be with others, the more God will help me meet those needs.

Literally everything we experience as reality is a gift from God. But then there's this little gem:

> For God so loved the world that *he gave* his one and only Son, that whoever believes in him shall not perish but have eternal life. (John 3:16, NIV, italics mine)

Arguably the best-known Bible verse in the world demonstrates the giving nature of God. Even atheists and not-yet-Christians know this verse, and it communicates something fundamental about God's nature and heart. Even before we did anything to deserve it, in the fullness of time, while we were yet far away, God gave us the gift of himself—Immanuel, "God with Us"—so that we might be restored into a right relationship with God and enjoy eternal life.

In a generosity-centered congregation, this is the prevailing attitude. The people have realized that God's nature is profound generosity. We can become a channel of blessing in the lives of others. The abundance of God is a faucet that never runs dry and never gets turned off. The more we give generously to others as God directs, the more there seems to be to give away.

On the other side of discovering that God "richly provides for our enjoyment" is the overflow of God's generosity "to do good, to be rich in good works, generous, and ready to share, thus storing up for themselves the treasure of a good foundation for the future, so that they may take hold of the life that really is life." Receiving richly from God, and giving richly to others, is the fuller life that Jesus promises we will have. That doesn't mean we will all be wealthy in the material sense; Jesus' promises that following him means carrying a cross. It means that whatever our financial situation may be, we will be rich. We will be blessed to bless others. That can be the widow's mite or checks with lots of zeros. The key idea is this: *God wants to give gifts through us!*

Paul, in his first letter to the Thessalonians, describes the heart of a generosity-centered congregation: "Just as a nursing mother cares for her children, so we cared for you. Because we loved you so much, we were delighted to share with you not only the gospel of God but our lives as well" (1 Thess 2:8, NIV).

As a mother desires to give good gifts to a child, so do those who understand generosity. We want to not just share the message "but our lives as well." Communities of people who share a spirit of generosity know God as a giving God, and they in turn learn how to give good things to others. Pastors of generosity-centered congregations learn to be proficient gift givers and witnesses to God's extravagant generosity. One thing that is utterly important here is that the pastor herself or himself exemplify the spirit of generosity. This does include being a generous financial contributor.

Many people, myself included, need an overhaul in the area of our attitude about money. Essentially, I had chalked up money to the "root of all evil." I missed the part about "for the love of . . ." (1 Tim 6:10). I served a Methodist megachurch, one of the fastest growing in the United States, for four years. It was four years longer than I needed to know I was not called to serve a megachurch! Since then I've realized that my particular calling is to serve smaller congregations in need of revitalization. If the church is on death's door, that's Jill's and my favorite space to work in.

This larger congregation existed in an affluent retirement community. It was in a very real sense a crosscultural appointment for a person who grew up in the ghetto. At first, I bristled against the affluent lifestyle of the congregation. It was as if following Jesus was about retiring to a comfortable life of recreation and lots of golf. The worship experiences seemed shallow, and the entire staff worked to ruffle as few feathers as possible—not a good scenario for an apostle-teacher with a mini prophet inside who longed to do outreach.

This was a textbook generosity-centered congregation. Over time I was able to see the massive good the congregation was able to accomplish through their resources. They could literally buy dilapidated properties and fix them up, fund all the food banks in the area, and donate the money to buy and build a substance abuse rehabilitation center. The congregation was able to have an impact on surrounding poverty-stricken communities like no church I had ever seen. Essentially, they were making tremendous kingdom impact with their checkbooks. It was there that I started to see that God can use money as a massive force for good in the world. Yes, the love of money is the root of all kinds of evil. But the generous giving of money is the root of all kinds of lasting good.

Generosity-centered congregations love to have financial campaigns and teach about stewardship. Typically, they have amassed many resources, including buildings, staff, and funds that can be given to the larger community. Their primary value is in giving generously to meet human need around them. Preaching and fellowship events need to be aimed at inspiring generosity. A generosity-centered congregation, led to serve in outreach and healing, can impact the world with massive good.

But a generosity-centered congregation is not all about writing checks. The most important resource they give is time. The congregation I served had a workforce of volunteers who engaged in a mentorship program at the local school, food pantries that fed thousands, and a ministry that renovated or rebuilt houses for those experiencing poverty. In crisis situations, they could show up and give the gift of presence. But they also possessed a wide range of skills, abilities, and knowledge that could be a huge gift to their neighbors.

In this case their gift was embodied in their presence and service. They would show up in force to get things done. This included neighborhood cleanups, disaster recovery, and volunteer work at the local soup kitchen. Generosity congregations tend to pull the fulcrum toward outreach. One of the dark sides can be in the preaching and teaching ministries of the church. The pastors have to work pretty hard at keeping everyone happy, so their sermons tend to be heavy on love with a little truth sprinkled in here and there. But a wise preacher can use the pulpit to motivate people to accomplish great good.

The Dark Side of a Generosity-Centered Congregation

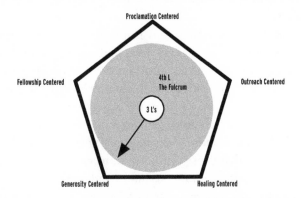

I know what you might be saying to yourself: "A congregation that probably has lots of resources and a large bank account? Now that's what I call a congregation with luxury problems. I'll take those any day!" I get that sentiment. As someone who serves congregations that live financially week to week, the generosity-centered congregation can seem like a dream come true. Yet these congregations all have their own sets of challenges and dysfunction. Remember our friends back in Sardis, the church where Jesus threatened to disconnect the cable and turn the lights out?

Generosity-centered congregations of the Sardis variety appear alive on the outside—big buildings, big crowds, and big budgets—but inside they are dead. The people live in relative ease, seemingly lacking for nothing, and that can lead to a state of apathy. It's easier to build new education wings and fellowship halls than to connect with real people with real needs in our community. We fulfill our religious duty, show up to service, put a tip in the bucket, but we miss a large part of living our Christian life in between church services.

I know several pastors who feel handcuffed in a generosity-centered congregation. They may see something deeply shallow and flawed about their church, but one wrong sermon in the pulpit or statement in the boardroom can spell disaster. People in generosity-centered congregations often don't like to be challenged. They have also learned how to control the church with their checkbooks. They can withhold funds when they are ready for a new preacher or designate funds to the most nonmissional of endeavors to frustrate an emerging vision.

Part of moving congregations like this from the center to the edge is about finding the broken places in the community. These are the tragic gaps where there is a disconnect between what currently is and the fullness of God's kingdom. It requires bringing to the awareness of the people the things about the larger community that break God's heart. In an unhealthy congregation that values "receiving gifts," the flow of generosity becomes a stagnant pond, all inflow and no outflow. That generosity needs to be redirected to become a stream, with a healthy continuous inflow and outflow.

Bringing mission moments and stories from the community into worship can help these congregations see the brokenness just outside their walls. Encouraging them to take prayer-walk days through the community, get involved in service projects, and volunteer at food pantries, soup kitchens, or school functions can make a huge difference. Challenging the shallowness and stagnation from the pulpit can be a risk. You may experience fallout, but unless we want Jesus showing up at our door like he did at Sardis, it's a worthy risk.

One often unforeseen opportunity with generosity-centered congregations is to help them re-vision themselves as a church-planting organism. I don't mean building more structures that the church owns to worship in but using their resources and connections to cultivate new forms of church throughout the community.

Do we have someone among us who owns a local shop or restaurant? Do we have a person of peace who has access to a community center in a remote part of town? Can we send congregants for training around missional forms of ministry? Can we adopt a blended ecology approach to church in which we seek to create meaningful, attractional forms of worship *and* experiment with more emerging forms? These are the kinds of questions that can help generosity-centered congregations awaken to their first love.

The discipleship system in a generosity-centered congregation needs to move people deeper, inward, on a spiritual journey toward the Jesus we discover waiting there. But it also needs to move people outward, out of themselves, out of the security bubbles and into the nitty-gritty facets of life in this place we call home. Perhaps introducing more disruptive, healing-touch elements to worship gatherings can break us free from the monotony of worship as a well-oiled machine. It provides opportunities for people to engage worship with their hearts, not just their heads. Providing outreach opportunities where people can connect names and faces to the checks that they write can be powerfully transformative as well.

Randy Cline is a dedicated lay leader who has done this well. His congregation in Wildwood lives on the edge of a massive and affluent retirement community called The Villages. While not an affluent congregation by any means, they are "property rich." Over its 140-year history, they have accumulated multiple homes, buildings, and even a city block with a duplex. When a local inpatient rehabilitation center for men called House of Hope ironically became homeless, Randy sprang into action. As the trustee chair, responsible for stewarding the many real-estate resources, he called the committee to turn one of the parcels with a home and adjacent apartment building into the new site for House of Hope.

The building was renovated and converted into an inpatient facility that could house up to twenty men and a live-in house father. Randy took a role as board chairman for the program, helping shape its internal processes as well as being a liaison between the church and the center. The congregation offers the space at no charge, using their generosity to literally fund the healing of the recovering men's lives. Randy often recruits volunteers from among the congregation to serve in the program, leading Bible studies, overseeing volunteer work, chairing meetings, and so on. This helps congregants connect faces and stories to the recipients of their generosity.

The proclamation ministries of the church can be a powerful tool here as well, grounding people not only in the practice of giving but also in the biblical foundation of the *why*. A generosity congregation that discovers they are drawing from a faucet that will never run dry can flood the community with healing. Knowing that God wants to redistribute his abundance through us, making us a channel of blessing to others, is one of the greatest joys a Christian can know.

A congregation that has lots of resources but doesn't value apeaking truth in love, spending time together, or loving and serving the needs of a community is in danger of embodying the very kind of hypocrisy that will cause Jesus to cut the lights out. But when we work to maximize our strengths and grow our weaknesses, a generosity-centered congregation can be a powerhouse for the kingdom.

Team Discussion

Gather your team. Make sure everyone has read the chapter. Open in prayer. Use these questions to guide your conversation.

1. Do you believe you are a generosity-centered congregation? Why or why not? Give some practical examples that support your belief.

2. Name some ways you spend time being generous in transformative ways for your community.

3. Can you identify ways you are rich in people and resources? How might you use those resources to create systemic change?

4. Considering everything you have read thus far, where do you see a dark side to your congregation? How might you begin to grow in your area of weakness?

5. What are some simple experiments you could begin to make flourish as the embodiment of God's generosity in your community? How can you get started?

4. Outreach Centered

*Then the king will say to those at his right hand, "Come, you
who are blessed by my Father, inherit the kingdom prepared
for you from the foundation of the world, for I was hungry
and you gave me food, I was thirsty and you gave me something to drink, I was a stranger and you welcomed me, I was
naked and you gave me clothing, I was sick and you took care
of me, I was in prison and you visited me."*
—Matthew 25:34–36

The outreach-centered congregation lives to serve its community. Their central value is *service* (διακονέω), meaning embodying
the good news in word and deed. A major personality trait of this
congregation is extroversion. Their heart beats to connect with new
people and build relationships. Loving and serving neighbors is a
primary way this flows from heart to hands.

These people truly understand Jesus' maxim to be a "servant of
all" (Mark 9:35). When the disciples are fighting over who will be
the greatest, Jesus shared the "not so with you" mandate: "You know
that the rulers of the gentiles lord it over them, and their great ones
are tyrants over them. It will not be so among you, but whoever
wishes to be great among you must be your servant, and whoever
wishes to be first among you must be your slave, just as the Son of
Man came not to be served but to serve and to give his life a ransom
for many" (Matt 20:25–28).

The idea of serving others is the raison d'être of these congregations. But service is not only about deeds of servanthood. It includes
evangelism, social justice, and overall engagement with the larger
community. Outreach is a way to embody the good news of Jesus

Christ. It emphasizes not only the words we speak but also the actions that accompany those words. Outreach congregations know in their bones that "talk is cheap" and that we must "be doers of the word and not merely hearers who deceive themselves" (Ja 1:22).

It's a holistic way to think about the nature and mission of the church, understanding that people can't hear the truth of Jesus if their stomachs are growling. They can't see a peaceable kingdom when all they see around them is a neighborhood experiencing racial inequality and systemic oppression. Outreach-centered congregations "practice what they preach" and "walk the talk," so to speak. Outreach congregations can emphasize that "religion that is pure and undefiled before God the Father is this: to care for orphans and widows in their distress and to keep oneself unstained by the world" (Ja 1:27).

At both of the congregations I currently serve, we weave an excerpt from Matthew 25 into the prayer time of every service: "For I was hungry and you gave me food, I was thirsty and you gave me something to drink, I was a stranger and you welcomed me, I was naked and you gave me clothing, I was sick and you took care of me, I was in prison and you visited me." We remind ourselves that our congregation exists to feed the hungry, give drink to the thirsty, welcome the stranger, clothe the naked, care for the sick, and visit the inmates. We celebrate how our congregations literally do these things every week. We also acknowledge that we see the face of Jesus in the faces of those experiencing poverty, pain, isolation, and incarceration.

We have a food pantry, a free community dinner, a clothing closet, recovery meetings around the clock, a care shepherd team, and a jail/prison ministry. On our property we house an inpatient rehabilitation program, two buildings dedicated as an AA and NA clubhouse, a shelter for those experiencing homelessness, and a sober house. These activities are the lifeblood of our congregation. It's how we measure if we are being faithful to Jesus or not. For us, all the spiritual growth, all the preaching, all the prayers, and all the worship must become embodied. What we carry in our hearts and heads must be expressed through our hands.

People who join our congregation say they love this church because: it "exists for the community," "believes in social justice," and "loves everyone no matter what." These are the heart expressions of an outreach congregation. There is an expectation that the real stuff of being a Christian will include acts of service in some capacity. "No pew potatoes" is a common cliché we throw around. Everything, from the worship to the committees, vision, and values, is oriented toward preparing people to serve in outreach.

No one needs to be coerced into this activity. They do it because for them it is the center of their Christian life.

Lana Young is a lay person who loves serving in an outreach-centered congregation. On her church's property was a small home that once served as the parsonage, the home that the clergy family lived in. The pastoral family was relocated to a nearby neighborhood decades ago, and the home became the church office. A part-time secretary used the office for a couple of hours each week, but otherwise it sat unused.

One day Lana asked the troublesome question, "Why have this entire space dedicated to something that's used only a couple hours per week?" Lana had inherited a clothing ministry that collected gently used clothing from an affluent gated community nearby. The clothes and household items were cleaned, inventoried, and then given away at a weekly gathering for those in the community in need. Lana had a vision: "Let's turn the office into a clothing closet!" Thus, "Twice Blessed Clothing Cottage" was born. The home was renovated and dedicated as a place where people could come throughout the week to browse the inventory and pick out what they needed. Lana and her team offered coffee, conversation, devotionals, and prayer to the community in the space. The cottage has now become a small expression of church.

If you haven't noticed, outreach is my passion. Sitting on my desk as I write these words is a statue of Jesus down on his hands and knees, washing the feet of a disciple. It reminds me of my primary calling to be chief foot washer. I am an extrovert. Being with groups of people, and especially making connections with new people, is just the way God wired me to be. It is a true gift to serve a congregation that has the same passion as I do, but that can also bring its share of problems as well.

Obviously, the outreach congregation appeals to a certain kind of people. It is action oriented. Everything is purposeful, even relationships. It's easy to become a community of Marthas, working in the kitchen, while Mary is at the feet of Jesus in the next room. An outreach congregation tends to be a community of doers and sometimes struggles just to *be with* one another. It's important that the motivation for outreach activities flows from a right heart.

My wife, Jill, recalls when one of her most active servants at an outreach congregation revealed his motivation. He and his wife were solid supporters of all things outreach. One of our ministries was a pancake breakfast church for kids. We met in the MLK Jr. Center of west Wildwood, a poverty-stricken area with lots of gun violence and drug dealing. We met on Saturdays to eat with the kids, play games, do arts and crafts, and share a Jesus story. One day this man whom Jill loved and cherished said to her, "Pastor, thank you for letting me do this. It's so meaningful. You know these people can't really help themselves." She was taken aback by his racist comment, and she asked him to unpack that some more. It turns out that his grandfather was a grand dragon in the Ku Klux Klan. He was raised in a very racist environment, and while he had grown by leaps and bounds, he still did not regard the people we were serving as his equals.

People can do outreach for the wrong reasons. One recurrent theme is the phenomenon of burnout. People begin to serve not as an expression of love but out of resentment. They do their work from a sense of religious duty rather than with a joyful heart. Compassion fatigue is a real thing, and in an outreach congregation we must be ever mindful of it. People who love to serve often don't realize when the flame of compassion has been snuffed out in their hearts. A key responsibility of the pastor is guarding that flame to keep it burning. Often that requires periods of rest.

When we are serving out of a place of fear, guilt, or resentment, our spiritual life is burning on the wrong fuel. We can't create anything good using bad tools. If we blaze new trails using resentment, religiosity, and self-righteousness, those paths will be crooked for the generations who follow behind us.

In the Fresh Expressions movement, we see outreach, or "loving and serving," as a movement in the journey toward forming new Christian communities. We get out into our communities and connect with people at their points of need as we commit to acts of service and begin to build relationships with people through repeated patterns of "withness." Over time, we share our faith and then see if a contextual form of church might form right where people do life.

It's an easy move for congregations with lots of outreach to shift those ministries toward becoming the church. For example, if you have a food pantry, why not invite the regulars of that ministry to a weekly community dinner? Who doesn't enjoy the gift of not having to prepare a meal? As you swap life and stories around the tables, might a dinner church emerge? If you have a strong visitation ministry to a local senior center, why not form a worship experience right there in the facility? If you are involved in or host youth sports leagues, why not invite parents to enjoy free lemonade, cookies, and a time of conversation around what spiritual practices are important to them? Could a tailgate church arise?

If you are providing breakfast for children in the community center of a poverty-stricken neighborhood, don't simply pass out free meals. Sit down at the table together. Learn names and stories. Create things. Play sports in the yard. Connect with one another in a deeper way than the act of outreach itself. Let it be a moment of inreach in which you allow another person to reach in and touch your own soul. This is where the magic of relationships happens. When those relationships are deep enough to sustain conversations around faith, prayer, and worship, well now outreach is suddenly transforming into something more in that community center.

As you can see, outreach is a deep and important part of forming community. It can be more than just doing good things for our neighbors. It can be a pathway to a relationship with them. Outreach becomes a form of toxic charity when we think we are the ones coming with all the answers or resources.[63] We need to take a posture of

---

63. See Robert D. Lupton, *Toxic Charity: How Churches and Charities Hurt*

vulnerability and mutuality. We need one another. It's not a one-way street in which one primarily gives and the other receives. That kind of outreach is better not to be done at all.

One of the major challenges in the outreach-centered congregation is that the pastor needs to be freed from stereotypical roles. The social contract needs to be renegotiated. One of the worst places to put an outreach pastor is cooped up in an office. These pastors need to be out among the people, making connections, learning names, and listening to people's stories. Typically, their focus is not those already in the congregation but the ones who aren't there yet.

Outreach pastors are typically guilty of shepherding malpractice in the eyes of some churchgoers. Jesus gives us a parable about a good shepherd going after a single lost sheep, searching until he finds it and bringing it back to the fold (Luke 15). Directors of the Shepherds Union who were present that day didn't appreciate Jesus' story. "No good shepherd leaves 99 good sheep *in the wilderness* to go after a single wild stray. That's shepherd malpractice!" They were going to pull Jesus' shepherd credentials.

But outreach ministers can't help but think of the lost sheep. That sheep is constantly on their minds. Their dream of a church is a community of shepherds on a search party for the lost sheep in the neighborhoods and networks that surround them. This doesn't mean the pastor doesn't love the sheep who stay in the pen. They are just called and gifted to run after the lost ones.

Pastors have a responsibility to set clear and reasonable boundaries. They can facilitate an open conversation around their schedule and how they spend their time in certain ministry tasks. If a pastor has an area of weakness, he or she can build healthy teams to share the ministry in areas like administration, care, visitation, education, worship, preaching, and so on. Congregations that can shift their expectations around conventional pastoral responsibilities can have a thriving relationship together. These kinds of leaders are dream pastors for an outreach congregation. But an outreach pastor in an inwardly focused congregation can be a challenging mismatch.

Those They Help (and How to Reverse It) (New York: HarperOne, 2012).

The outreach pastor must learn to understand a congregation's personality and strengths and then pull the fulcrum toward those outside the gates.

The Dark Side of an Outreach-Centered Congregation

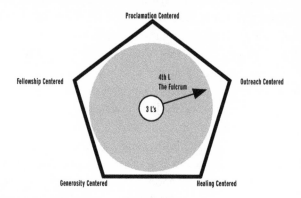

The outreach-centered congregation runs the risk of becoming a community of busybodies. Perhaps we run around doing lots of good things, but we get stuck in a routine in which our motivation goes astray. It becomes a hollow form of works-based religion with no real relationship with God or even one another. Congregations like this are in danger of burnout. First, we are running on fumes, and then we are out of gas. Like the church at Ephesus, we lose our first love, and unhealthy people hungry for power can cause a lot of damage.

In one congregation we served, a small handful of people were doing a massive amount of outreach. The output of service was incredible; I often joked that we were "the featherweight champions of mission in Methodism." Although we were small in number, we had a massive food pantry, an inpatient rehab, a thriving recovery ministry, and a dozen fresh expressions of church, and we were deeply involved in leading an anti-racism movement. However, we were fatigued.

In our state of exhaustion, a new couple showed up who were disgruntled with something that happened at the church just down the road from us. Red alert! It's only a matter of time before they will be disgruntled with us! But we were tired, and our warning radars were down. We needed some fresh faces to carry the work forward. Very quickly, this couple was integrated into the leadership of the church. Within a few months both were nominated into key committee level leadership positions, and one became the volunteer bookkeeper.

You already know how this story ends, right? Before long they were disgruntled with me as the pastoral leader. They began to spread their discontent among others in the congregation. Before long we had a full-blown mutiny on our hands, and a key leadership committee called a meeting to let me know they thought my time as pastor should be up.

Thankfully, the majority of the congregation did not agree, and they saw the kind of discord this couple was sowing. In all my ministry this has been the only time I had to ask a couple to find another church, but it came with a cost. They rallied as many people as possible to leave with them. They also vacated positions that we had become dependent on them to fulfill. This devastated the congregation, and we barely made it through that season without having to close our doors.

As a pastor who focuses on outreach, I know I have a significant blind spot here. Being focused on service to people in the community can lead to neglect. That neglect could be twofold: neglect of our own souls and of the community who are already here. When this happens in a church, it can foster resentment, both for the pastor and the congregation. When an outreach congregation and an outreach pastor are paired together, massive amounts of good can be done in the community. Yet this strength is also a weakness. It leads to compassion fatigue and a trail of fallen volunteers. We can become so consumed with helping others and taking the next hill that we run ourselves into the ground.

This kind of a culture is vulnerable for opportunists. Outreach congregations often function in a team-based way. The expectation is that everyone will chip in and do their part. Outreach opportunities are lifted from the pulpit and featured at fellowship gatherings. Everyone is expected to get up off their "blessed *ass*urance." People who are attracted to this kind of a culture are often action-oriented folks who love to engage in service to others. But when taken to extremes, this can lead to a lack of boundaries. The pastor who is "always on" is trying to model that behavior for the congregation, but people have limits.

When a group is stretched to capacity, we can hurriedly rush people into positions they are not ready for. This can lead to their own harm. Any individual with shining eyes who comes along is encouraged to jump in and get to work, partially because the rest of the group is worn out. But if we don't balance this with quality time, being together in a non-action-oriented way, we create superficial bonds overly focused on tasks. Doing tasks together is a shortcut to community building. Nothing can bond people together more quickly than sharing in some creative activity or common mission. Yet we need to work harder to make relationships more than that.

In that kind of culture, people can become disposable. We rally people to take the next hill, launch the next ministry, or start the next initiative, but what happens when they lose their energy for the work? Do they become disposable? Do we move to the next warm body with a pulse? Unfortunately, this can be the case in an outreach-centered congregation. But people are not disposable.

Through a long process of failing forward, I've learned a lesson. The mission is not the mission. Relationships are the mission. It's the community we build with one another that's more important than the task in front of us. And it's our relationship with God that is the absolute center of it all. We can get so busy working for God that we forget to walk with God.

It's very important for outreach congregations to remember that faithfulness precedes fruitfulness. Perhaps we are more oriented to action, but spending time with Jesus is even more important for this group. He is the vine; we are the branches (John 15:5). Our role to bear lasting fruit is not about effort and action but about "abiding" in Jesus and letting Jesus abide in us. This means our doing should flow from our being, not the other way around.

We need to build discipleship systems that encourage practices of stillness, meditation, prayer, and study of Scripture. We can then seek to find a balance between our works of piety, the internal things we do to abide in Christ and love God, and our works of justice and mercy, the things we do to love our neighbors.

Team Discussion

Gather your team. Make sure everyone has read the chapter. Open in prayer. Use these questions to guide your conversation.

1. Do you believe you are an outreach-centered congregation? Why or why not? Give some practical examples that support your belief.

2. Name some ways you spend time serving "the least of these" or building relationships with the marginalized and oppressed people in your community.

3. Do people in the congregation feel empowered to serve their neighbors? Do you balance this with practices that cultivate depth in relationship with God and one another? Why do you feel that way?

4. Based on what you've learned so far, do you see a blind spot where new focus and energy is needed? Describe it.

5. What are some small steps you could take toward growing in the area of outreach? Who should be on this team?

5. Healing Centered

And these signs will accompany those who believe: by using
my name they will cast out demons; they will speak in new
tongues; they will pick up snakes, and if they drink any deadly
thing, it will not hurt them; they will lay their hands on the
sick, and they will recover.
—*Mark 16:17–18 (non italics mine)*

Healing-centered congregations value wholeness (ἰάομαι, *iao-mai*) and the manifestation of Jesus' life in the world. They seek to be a community where people experience healing. Jesus' name literally means "he who saves." The Greek word used to describe how Jesus will "save his people from their sins" is σῴζω (sōzō) (Matt 1:21). The church in the West has often translated *salvation* to refer to a post-mortem destiny in which we will be rescued from hell and translated to heaven. Jesus "saves" by erasing penalties for sin from the divine scorecard.

Yet σῴζω (sōzō), *salvation*, more accurately denotes relief from suffering, healing from disease, making well and whole, and restoring to health. It has a present dimension that involves wholeness in this life, not just a condition in the next. Luke reports that Jesus began his ministry by going to Nazareth in the "power of the Spirit" and going into the synagogue, as was his custom. He then stood up to read the scroll of the prophet Isaiah and said,

The Spirit of the Lord is upon me, because he hath anointed me to preach the gospel to the poor; he hath sent me to *heal* the bro-kenhearted, to preach deliverance to the captives, and recovering

of sight to the blind, to set at liberty them that are bruised,
To preach the acceptable year of the Lord.
—*Luke 4:18–21, KJV (italics mine)*

Jesus rolled up the scroll, gave it back to the attendant, sat down, and with every eye in the room fixed on him, said, "Today this scripture has been fulfilled in your hearing" (v. 21). He is the fulfillment of Isaiah's prophecy—embodied. The word translated as "heal" (ἰάομαι) here means to cure or make whole. This is the meaning every time Jesus heals someone, not to give them a golden ticket to heaven but to heal the brokenness and fragmentation in their life.

The biblical vision of shalom (a world at peace) is much more expansive than saving souls for relocation to heaven when they die. It's about God's kingdom breaking into the world now. It's about the healing, renewal, and well-being of the entire cosmos. It's a holistic vision of God's reign on earth, of which the church is a foretaste. Salvation is a journey of restorative healing that begins in this life and is made complete in the next.

Healing-centered congregations see themselves as a manifestation and extension of Jesus' own healing life. Their key personality trait is one of openness, meaning the quality of being imaginative and open to experience. They are often highly creative and willing to experiment with reaching people in new ways. Expecting failure, they take risks, iterate, prototype, and adapt. They bear the mark of apostolic leaders who are intellectually curious, open to emotion, sensitive to beauty, and willing to experiment and expand to new edges. They are also open to the possibility of the Holy Spirit making people, communities, and systems whole.

Jesus of Nazareth healed the sick during his earthly ministry (Matt 9; 10:8; 25:34–36). This ministry has been continued by his followers ever since. For two thousand years, all across the globe, there have been an uncountable numbers of miracles. To this day stories of miraculous healings are reported mostly from the global South and East, often connected to apostolic forms of church.[64]

---

64. Henning Wrogemann, *Intercultural Hermeneutics*, trans. Karl E. Böhmer, vol. 1 of Intercultural Theology (Downers Grove, IL: InterVarsity Press, 2016).

But Christians have also learned to be healers in more practical ways as well. Christians who took Jesus' call to be healers seriously created the first medical systems, like St. Basil of Caesarea, who founded the first hospital to care for the poor and sick in 369. Christian hospitals spread across both the East and the West so rapidly that by the mid-1500s there were thirty-seven thousand Benedictine monasteries alone that cared for the sick.[65] Christians created educational systems, established shelters for those experiencing homelessness, and pioneered spiritually based mental health services.

Bill W. and Dr. Bob, the cofounders of Alcoholics Anonymous, were both Christians. They utilized the foundational tenets of the Oxford Group (1921), a Christian evangelical organization founded by Lutheran priest Frank Buchman, to create the twelve steps. Every day, in church basements and clubhouses all over the world, a million miracles gather together to celebrate healing from alcoholism.[66] Jesus is alive and well when it comes to healing, and much of it continues through the body of Christ that bears his name: the church.

All of these expressions of healing fall under the category of the kind of salvation that Jesus offers. It is exactly a diminished understanding of salvation that limits the good that churches can really do. It's much more expansive than saying the sinner's prayer. Obviously from this brief survey, we can see the diversity of what healing-centered congregations might look like.

Dr. Bessel van der Kolk, psychiatrist, researcher, educator, and author of *The New York Times* bestseller *The Body Keeps the Score*, writes, "Traumatized human beings recover in the context of relationships."[67] While spiritual formation is often thought of in an individualistic way in the West, this is a journey in which it's best to have company. Or, as the often-quoted African proverb states, "If you want to go quickly, go alone. If you want to go far, go together."

65. Albert R. Jonsen, *A Short History of Medical Ethics* (New York: Oxford University Press, 2000).

66. Michael Adam Beck, *Painting with Ashes: When Your Weakness Becomes Your Superpower* (Plano, TX: Invite Resources, 2022).

67. Bessel A. van der Kolk, *The Body Keeps the Score: Brain, Mind, and Body in the Healing of Trauma* (New York: Viking, 2014), 251.

One of the key ideas I set forth in *Painting with Ashes* is the African anthropological framework of *ubuntu*: a person is a person through other persons. Ubuntu highlights the interdependency of humanity. All individuals are woven together in a single interconnected organism. We are harmed in community, a bundle of relationships, and we can be truly healed only in community.

As Fred Rogers was fond of saying, there are a lot of people who "loved us into being."[68] We often think of healing as an individual enterprise. We go to the specialist, therapist, or spiritual director, who helps us form a healthy sense of self. But we cannot fully have a *healthy* sense of self that is not integrated in community. That kind of healing is illusory at worst, fleeting at best.

Regarding healing in the context of relationships, families, loved ones, AA meetings, veterans organizations, religious communities, or professional therapists, Dr. van der Kolk shows "the role of those relationships is to provide physical and emotional safety, including safety from feeling shamed, admonished, or judged, and to bolster the courage to tolerate, face, and process the reality of what has happened."[69]

People share healing when they invite others to touch their wounds. As an abandoned street kid, in and out of juvenile detention facilities, experiencing a healing church community that was accessible, safe, and real changed the trajectory of my life. Let me unpack what I mean by those words:

Accessible: close, contextual, speaking a shared common language.
Safe: an environment of grace and inclusion, a place of healing, not harm.
Real: authentic, transparent, where people are honest about their real wounds, and real healing is taking place.

---

68. Fred Rogers, *The World According to Mister Rogers: Important Things to Remember* (New York: Hachette, 2003).
69. van der Kolk, *Body Keeps the Score*, 251.

People find healing in a communal atmosphere of grace where they are free to be vulnerable. Communities that are accessible, safe, and real can allow people to process their trauma in an unfiltered way. Cultivating these healing communities can help heal the world. This is why healing-centered congregations are so vital.

There is a powerful connection between physical touch and healing. This is true for emotional, psychological, and physical healing. Physical touch is a necessary component of becoming a healthy, whole person. The same goes for a church.

One of the unique aspects of Christianity is its commitment to the body. The entire Bible bears witness to the fact that our bodies are who we are. While our being consists of multiple dimensions—soul, mind, heart, and body—those spheres are integrated into a single person, made in the image of God (Gen 1:27). While other religious traditions speak of an afterlife in which one becomes a disembodied soul, no longer bound to a physical body, or a state of nirvana, in which one escapes the great wheel of physical rebirth, Christianity's central claim is based on Jesus' resurrection from the dead.

Just as Jesus was raised from the dead, as the "first fruits of the resurrection," so every Christian will be raised in their glorified physical bodies. Whether we are cremated, buried, or preserved in a cryo-chamber, God is going to restore the physical molecules that make us who we are and imbue them with resurrection life. Christians believe in a heaven, which is described as a "new creation" (Rev 21–22) in which we live a glorified, physical existence in the presence of God for all eternity.

In some sense our bodies are us, and we are our bodies. And the church is intended to be a community where bodies gather together to be made whole. We are re-membered together from our fragmented and brokenhearted state.

On the other hand, nothing communicates non-love like inappropriate acts of physical touch. The worst kinds of abuse are perpetrated by those who use touch in a violent and exploitative way. No level of inappropriate touch is acceptable within a congregation.

The final chapter of Mark's Gospel is a complicated passage, so much so that the NRSV and NIV versions specifically say "another ending" or a "later ending." It is consistent among biblical scholars from across theological traditions that Mark 16 was a later addition to the original manuscript. It seems to be another version of a kind of great commission. We can notice some strange aspects of this co-mission, like drinking poison and snake handling, for example. Figuratively, every pastor knows ministry involves snake handling and even an occasional bite from toxic church members. However, churches who literally hold to these practices can be toxic and harmful and need some serious reevaluation. For most of us, this is absolutely a "do not try this at home!" situation.

Weaved into the passage is something fundamental to the Christian faith, and it has been for two thousand years. It's the connection between touch and healing. It reads, "They will lay their hands on the sick, and they will recover" (Mark 16:18). This is a summary of what had become common practice at the time of writing this alternative ending of Mark's Gospel. For Christians the connection between touch and healing goes back to the nail-scarred hands of Jesus himself.

In most of Jesus' healing miracles, an intimate form of touch was involved, and this continued in the early church. Just consider this selection of examples: Luke 13:13; Matthew 9:18; Matthew 19:13; Mark 6:5; Luke 4:40; Acts 8:17; Acts 9:12; Acts 19:6; Acts 28:8; James 5:13–16.

The laying on of hands, anointing with oil, and high-touch worship in general had largely fallen out of favor in many Western congregations for a time but is now becoming recovered. Globally speaking, most congregations in the world are healing centered.

I was able to experience these types of congregations firsthand in Guatemala. On Sunday church was planned out as an all-day event. When we gathered in the sanctuary, we enjoyed an extensive time of socializing. Each person traveled around the room greeting one another with hugs, kisses, and handshakes. When the music began, it was a fully embodied experience. Standing, singing, clapping, raising hands, and dancing were normative and even expected.

The sermon time was powerfully emotional. People shouted, spoke in tongues, and consoled one another with hugs, placing their arms around each other's shoulders and holding hands to pray. The service was concluded with a time of anointing with oil. The ministry team came up with big jars of oil, and people formed in lines to come down for prayer. It seemed that every person present came down for a time of prayer. They were anointed on their foreheads with oil in the sign of the cross, and their faces, shoulders, and even other places on their bodies were held and specifically prayed for. This went on for many hours, well into the afternoon.

The worship was physically intimate and high-touch, admittedly uncomfortably so for me. But I can only describe the experience as therapeutic. For many in attendance, just surviving another week was a celebratory occasion. They did not have access to therapists or psychiatrists, or even adequate medical care. The worship at church was their therapy.

For those of us formed in the Western church, we might think this kind of congregation is inappropriate. Let me describe to you two examples of healing-centered congregations, one made of predominantly white folks and another of black folks.

In the almost entirely white congregation, many showed up early to see their friends. The pastor was stationed at the door, shaking each hand or placing a hand on the shoulder of each person who entered. Occasionally, even a side-hug was exchanged. The people in the pews did likewise, greeting each other and exchanging some form of touch.

In the white congregation, shortly after the service began, there was a time to "greet your neighbor." People were up and about the pews, shaking hands, giving hugs, and kissing cheeks. When they stood to sing hymns, they shared hymnals and draped their arms across one another's shoulders. At several points in the service, they clasped hands in prayer. When they came up for communion, the pastor served each person at the altar, touching them in some way and saying, "The body of Christ broken for you." The Lord's Supper for them was a healing meal, as it has been for Christians across the ages. For instance, St. Ignatius of Antioch called communion the "medicine of immortality" back in the second century.[70]

---

70.   Ignatius, "Letter to the Ephesians 20.2," in Joseph Barber Lightfoot, *The*

The conclusion of the service consisted of everyone in the sanctuary standing and locking hands together as they sang a final stanza of "Blessed Be the Tie That Binds." They sang this together and then engaged in another final round of hugs, handshakes, and goodbyes. The pastor was back stationed at the door, physically touching each person as they departed back into the world. Later in the week they gathered in the sanctuary for a time of "healing prayer" in which members read Scripture, prayed for one another, and anointed one another with oil.

At God's Glory, a black Pentecostal congregation that meets in our fellowship hall, the worship has many of these same elements. People spend a great deal of time greeting and offering physical touch in the form of handshakes, hugs, and cheek kisses. This is part of the service, not a pre-session! The opening prayer does not begin until this time of exchanging physical intimacy is over. There is no expectation that the service will conclude at a certain time. They will worship as long as they feel the Spirit leading.

Almost every part of the service is embodied, meaning there is some kind of physical response: standing for the reading of the Word, lifting hands when the music is playing. Dancing and running in the aisles are normal. Coming down to kneel and pray at the altar together as the music plays is also part of the expectation.

When the sermon begins, the pastor leads the people to embody their response in physical ways. "Clap if you believe God is good!" "Slap your neighbor a high five and say amen!" "Tap your neighbor on the shoulder and say neighbor!" The sermon is not a monologue. It is a call and response dialogue between God, the preacher, and the people. It involves tactile exchanges of touch that create a deeper sense of solidarity.

People spontaneously gather to clasp hands and pray for one another as they are led. They embrace. They hold a person who is hurting. The service concludes with the pastor anointing each person with oil for healing. One by one they come forward to receive the imposition of the oil and the laying on of hands for prayer. Some people experience an overwhelming wave of God's presence; they

Apostolic Fathers, 2nd ed. (Grand Rapids, MI: Baker Books, 1989).

"catch the Holy Ghost" and become "slain in the Spirit." The ministry team catches these persons in an embrace, laying them gently on the floor, and then covers them with blankets.

The extended service concludes with a final round of physical tokens of affections, hugs, high fives, and special handshakes. Again, the worship experience feels therapeutic, like an extended healing session for the mind, body, and soul.

Part of this lies in the Afrocentric notion of self, which emphasizes personhood as a manifestation of community—a socially constructed self.[71] Again, a person's state of wellness is bound to a web of relationships. Connectedness, belonging, and social acceptance are emphasized rather than individuation. We are all bound together in a bundle of life, a social organism. In collectivistic cultures, community is the goal of life, not individuation.

The physical-touch congregation is centered in the life of worship, but it doesn't start there. Opportunities for study, healing prayer, and meals are also spread throughout the week. Obviously, in a generation in which the #MeToo movement and case after case of clergy sexual abuse have become the unfortunate reality, healing congregations have a big hill to climb. Women and children are disproportionately the recipients of unwanted physical touch. These congregations need to be hypervigilant and aggressive with rooting out those kinds of behaviors.

Personally, I have experienced the healing touch of these congregations. Human beings are created for intimacy. We are physical, embodied beings, and those bodies are meant to be touched in healing ways. We are created to worship with our entire bodies. This is the Old Testament concept of worship. The word הָוָחָשׁ (*shâchâh*) denotes fully embodied, fully physical worship, which includes raising our hands, lying prostrate, and joining hands.

Christianity is an embodied religion. We celebrate the sacredness of the body, the sanctification of the body, and ultimately the

71.   Makungu M. Akinyela, "Testimony of Hope: African Centered Praxis for Therapeutic Ends," *Journal of Systemic Therapies* 24, no.1 (2005): 5–18, https://www.academia.edu/2324704/Testimony_of_hope_African_centered_praxis_for_therapeutic_ends.

resurrection of our physical bodies in a renewed and embodied new creation. The healing-centered congregation must honestly deal with the challenges of the sinful and perverse misuse of physical touch. But perhaps this is something that needs to be recovered.

The COVID pandemic was hardest on congregations who value healing, and this continues to be a struggle. They have particularly struggled with online worship. How can I love my neighbor when I can only see them through a screen? When we as avatars lay our hands on those in need of healing prayer in virtual church, is it really touch? Can the healing power of Jesus manifest through the space of flows in the online built environment? Is Jesus Lord of the meta-verse and fediverse too? Some congregations have navigated this with creating smaller gatherings, often outdoors, where people can find a connection through some form of touch.

The Dark Side of a Healing-Centered Congregation

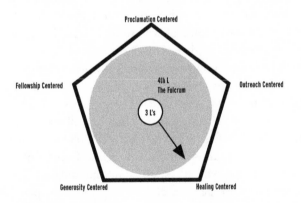

From the outside looking in, healing-centered congregations are weird. Let's just be honest here. This kind of congregation can seem fairly sketchy to an outsider. They employ secret handshakes and magical passwords that visitors don't seem to know. They may seem to have a lack of boundaries. People just get right up in our bubble and go straight for physical touch! Supernatural manifestations of the Spirit can be intimidating or even fanatical to a newbie. Overly touchy folks even with good intentions can make anybody uncomfortable. If a fellowship congregation can be exclusionary, a healing-centered congregation can be even more so.

Furthermore, from the book of Acts until now, people have been trying to counterfeit and purchase the power of the Holy Spirit. Remember Simon the magician, who had amassed quite a following with his sorcery? "Now when Simon saw that the Spirit was given through the laying on of the apostles' hands, he offered them money, saying, 'Give me also this power so that anyone on whom I lay my hands may receive the Holy Spirit'" (Acts 8:18–19). That's not exactly how the Spirit works. You can't buy and own it, but it doesn't stop people from trying. The false prophetess in Thyatira who was making all kinds of trouble is perhaps another case in point (Rev 2:20–24).

We don't have to look far to see the dark side of a healing congregation. US American Christianity can seem like an unending story of one televangelist and charlatan after another getting caught up in some scandal. High-profile leaders seem to fall from grace like a row of dominoes. The toxic church cultures they create leave a stream of victims in their wake, some of whom never actually heal from the abuse they suffered at the hands of Christian leaders.

Healing-focused ministry has ironically also led to scandals of sexual abuse, infidelity, and cover-ups. These blemishes on the face of the mother church have caused many to not even give her a second glance. I mean, for those outside the church, if all we knew were the headlines about Christianity, could we really blame them for closing themselves off to those kinds of churches? Can we not expect a movement of people who are "spiritual but not religious"?

We are embodied persons, and nothing seems to open the pathway to both healing and harm like physical touch. So then, is a healing-centered congregation even worth the risk? Having experienced some healthy healing-centered congregations, I believe so. A congregation where healthy forms of touch become a key value can help heal a wounded world.

In 2021 various people-helping professionals began to use the language of "the epidemic of loneliness."[72] Contrary to popular be-

---

72. Joseph E. Davis, "The Epidemic of Loneliness," *Psychology Today*,

lief, COVID did not create this phenomenon, but rather it accelerated a storm that had been brewing for at least decades. Gloo is an organization that serves the church by "supporting it with powerful technology." In a recent presentation I attended, a Gloo representative shared that the most popular search topics in 2022 were "sadness, relationships, and loneliness." In the last thirty days at the time of this writing, the three major internet searches were "loss, anxiety, and prayers."[73]

We need healing-centered congregations, where people can find community and wholeness, now just as always before.

One way to move the fulcrum here is to balance this congregation toward the other aspects of church. We need clear biblical teaching about spiritual gifts—what they are and what they are not. We need a discipleship system that builds in checks and balances to keep everyone in the community safe.

Perhaps we can see the main high-touch worship gathering with laying on of hands, speaking in tongues, and other impartations is a space that really is for mature believers who have been through an extensive catechesis process like that described in the *Didache*. Written in the first century, the *Didache* (Greek word for "teaching") is the first known Christian catechesis and the earliest known Christian writing outside of the Bible.[74] Church historians across the ages have well documented that the first-century church gatherings were not "open to all" in the sense as we think of them today. As Alan Kreider documented in his book *The Patient Ferment of the Early Church*, new Christian converts went through a series of mysteries before they joined the central gathering in which the Eucharist was shared.[75]

November 9, 2021, https://www.psychologytoday.com/us/blog/our-new-discontents/202111/the-epidemic-loneliness.

73. See various church polls at https://www.gloo.us/.

74. R. Joseph Owles, *The Didache: The Teaching of the Twelve Apostles* (CreateSpace, 2014).

75. Alan Kreider, *The Patient Ferment of the Early Church: The Improbable Rise of Christianity in the Roman Empire* (Grand Rapids, MI: Baker Academic, 2016), 41.

In a blended ecology of church, we need both centered-set and bounded-set communities. Centered-set communities primarily follow a "belonging before believing" journey, an inclusive community in which core convictions shape behavior, but one is free to explore moving toward the center, regardless of where in proximity they may be to those beliefs and behaviors. Bounded sets primarily have clear boundaries, established around beliefs and behaviors that are patrolled and enforced and in which one is included or excluded based on adherence.[76]

I'm suggesting that healing-centered congregations should function as bounded sets in most post-Christendom contexts. But these congregations should also move toward creating simpler, more inclusive forms of church that gather in the normal rhythms of life, that function in a symbiotic relationship with the central gathering. Many of my friends who are not Christians are much more comfortable coming to a church gathering in a dog park, yoga studio, running track, or tattoo parlor than a full-on worship experience where supernatural manifestations are expected. Smaller groups seem to create a deeper level of transparency and accountability.

Healthy healing congregations move toward outreach. They are openly apostolic and evangelistic. Evangelism is about healing. It's about being connected to the greater restoration of individuals, societies, and creation itself. These congregations give us a way to break free of the small-minded individualism so prevalent in the Western church. Evangelism is not about extracting people from the world back to the church compound where they can be rightly Christianized. It's done by the Spirit, in community with others, and it can happen anywhere human beings are connected together.

This is why Fresh Expressions of Church are so important. Outreach is built into the fresh expressions pathway of listening, loving and serving, building relationships, fostering discipleship, church taking shape, repeat.[77] As Dr. van der Kolk shows, the "body keeps

---

76. Stuart Murray, *The Church After Christendom* (Milton Keynes, UK: Paternoster Press, 2004), 28–31, 71.

77. Michael Adam Beck and Rosario Picardo, *Fresh Expressions in a Digital Age: How the Church Can Prepare for a Post-Pandemic World* (Nashville: Abingdon

the score"; the pathway to healing the mind must come through the body.[78] Fresh Expressions enable people to do this by connecting our bodies together around practices like doing yoga, tattooing, running 5ks, eating burritos, painting, and so on. As community builds around these practices, in an ecosystem of mutuality and vulnerability, people find healing in a community that is safe, accessible, and real.

Healing-centered congregations continue the apostolic aspect of the body. Always pushing out to the edge. Always creating new little pockets of healing in our larger community. The blended ecology allows many different forms of church to live together out of a single congregation. We can cultivate trauma-informed expressions of church that are sensitive to where people are in different stages of the journey of grace as *we grow the center, experiment on the edge*. Accompanying the more extraordinary elements of a healing-centered congregation, we should also consider balancing those with more socially acceptable forms of healing, for instance, having a therapist on staff or connected to the church or making space for recovery fellowships and grief share groups. It's important to balance gatherings where openness to the Holy Spirit's work is expected with a deep study of Scripture and knowledge from other people-helping fields. Create spaces where traumatized people can clasp hands and find a touch of healing in a subtler but very real way.

Fellowship events where people can sit around tables and hear one another's stories are important to a healing-centered congregation. Learning to be present with one another without being in full worship mode gives us space to know one another more intimately. All of this creates a more robust relational matrix in which congregations can thrive.

Press, 2021).
78.   van der Kolk, *Body Keeps the Score*, 114.

Team Discussion

Gather your team. Make sure everyone has read the chapter. Open in prayer. Use these questions to guide your conversation.

1. Do you believe you are a healing-centered congregation? Why or why not? Give some practical examples that support your belief.

2. Name some ways you use touch in a healing way. Name some ways it could be used in a harmful way.

3. Do you feel like your community sees your congregation as a safe place of healing? Why do you feel that way?

4. As a team do you feel open to the supernatural work of the Holy Spirit? Why or why not?

5. What are some practical ways your congregation can become an extension of Jesus' healing in the world? What might some first steps be?

WHEN THE HONEYMOON IS OVER

But I say to you: Love your enemies and pray for those who
persecute you, so that you may be children of your Father in
heaven, for he makes his sun rise on the evil and on the good
and sends rain on the righteous and on the unrighteous. For if
you love those who love you, what reward do you have? Do not
even the tax collectors do the same? And if you greet only your
brothers and sisters, what more are you doing than others? Do
not even the gentiles do the same?

—Matthew 5:44–47

I appreciate those couples who celebrate long-term anniversaries
with the statement, "We're on the fortieth year of our honeymoon!" It is a beautiful sentiment that two people can love each
other for decades and keep the flame of passion and intimacy burning. In some way preserving that flame is integral to a long-term
relationship.

But for many of us, there is a period when that first "honeymoon
phase" ends. The initial rush of endorphins and euphoria we felt
when we first met our spouse seems to fade. The intensity of longing
and the desire to be together seems to diminish. We start to really
know the person we are married to in a deeper way. In some cases
the personality traits and behaviors that first fascinated us can start
to become annoying.

Over time a relationship can lose its original brightness and shininess. The puppy love, the infatuation, starts to wear off. In an arranged marriage perhaps we never had any of those feelings in the first place. Our spouse is a stranger whom we are trying to understand and love. Their behaviors are peculiar, and their personality might be very different from our own. When our love reservoir is running low, we can feel unappreciated, unknown, and unseen by our spouse.

When the honeymoon is over, we reach a critical stage in the relationship. This is when we need to make the choice to *actually love*!

As we say in the recovery fellowships, "Expectations are premeditated resentments." At some point one of the parties in the relationship will fail to meet the other's expectations. Perhaps the congregation's and the pastor's personality types are a mismatch. We are a proclamation-centered congregation with an outreach-centered pastor, or an outreach-centered pastor serving a fellowship-centered congregation, and so on.

What are we to do? Perhaps it's time for a reset? Who will take the lead?

The answer to the question is *you*. Whether you are a congregant, group of leaders, or the pastor, the answer is still the same. You can't make the other party understand your personality and love you, but you can choose to learn their personality and love them. It could start with a simple commitment like, "I've decided I would like to be a better pastor to you. Can you show me how to do that?" Likewise, as a congregation, you could say, "We would like to be a better congregation, to more fully know and love you and our community, so can you show us how?"

Perhaps you are saying to yourself, "My heart has grown callous. I no longer love these people." Or as a congregation, perhaps you are saying, "We no longer love our pastor. In fact, sometimes we hate him/her." To now say "I love you" when it's not true would be an act of hypocrisy. That's okay, Here's the good news: you don't have to actually love one another to get started!

In the recovery community we say, "Fake it till you make it." This is not about being a phony or acting insincerely, but rather we try to change our actions to fit a new way of life. Another saying is "You can't think your way into sober living, but you can live your way into sober thinking." We know we need to have an entire psychic change to recover, but that change can't be manufactured by us through our own thinking. We need to start behaving in a new way. It starts simple: making coffee, setting up for the meetings or cleaning up afterward, helping newcomers, making phone calls, facilitating the groups. As we employ these new behaviors, over time our thinking starts to catch up with our living.

Perhaps you feel like the relationship between pastor and congregation is untenable. The honeymoon is over. You need a miracle. A congregation that is unhealthy or a pastor who is unhealthy can't possibly offer love to the larger community in a healthy way. But wait—what have you got to lose? You could start with some simple questions like these:

1. I've been thinking about our relationship, and I've decided I want to do a better job listening, learning, and loving. Can you give me some suggestions on how I might improve?

2. Based on all the discussions we have had around this book, what is the personality type of our congregation? What is our main dark side? What area can we begin to grow in right now together?

3. Based on knowing the FCPT type, how can the congregation come around and support the pastor(s)? Where do we need teams to strengthen the areas where we are weak?

4. In terms of "growing the center, experimenting on the edge," what small experiment can we begin right now? Who will lead it? Who will be on the team?

Another possibility for pastors is to ask the questions in reverse: What really drains you, or even harms you? Do you look at your calendar and say, *Oh no, got to start prepping for the sermon or Bible study . . . bummer!* Do you cringe when you see yet another potluck planned for this weekend? Are you tired just looking at another boxed set for a new stewardship campaign? Does the thought of showing up at yet another food pantry gathering make you want to bury your head beneath the pillow? Or, finally, are you dreading another extended prayer service this evening? These also are indicators of your primary identity, the most powerful and dominant part of your personality.

Another helpful tool is to look at your calendar. What typically do you spend the most time doing? Do you block out lots of time for teaching and preaching prep? Schedule lots of meetings to plan fellowship gatherings? Or do you pour through book after book on channeling generosity and cultivating a healthy culture of stewardship? Are you visiting other outreaches in the area to learn from what they're doing, or do you even volunteer because there's not enough going on in your congregation? Do you keep prioritizing prayer gatherings and healing services and restocking the anointing oil? Your calendar can tell you what your primary love language is.

What things do you enjoy doing for the congregation? What things would you do even if you weren't paid to do them?

Questions like these can help clear the blockages in the love triangle. Even if the honeymoon feels over, this is an opportunity for a new beginning. All you need is love.

Team Discussion

Gather your team. Make sure everyone has read the chapter. Open in prayer.

We have explored the FCPT types throughout the book. Here's a review of the five leadership types for the FCPT, according to the APEST framework discussed earlier.

1. **Apostle**: the "sent one" and "healer." Innovating, moving to the edge, connecting outsiders, and expecting the supernatural are primary giftings. Openness is a primary personality trait of the apostle.

2. **Prophet**: the "activist" and "truth teller." A heart for justice and allegiance to God are primary giftings. The personality of a prophet is understood as a spectrum of neuroticism. Think about Jesus as a healthy prophet: emotive, sensitive, but calm and grounded.

3. **Evangelist**: the "recruiter" and "promoter." Proclamation, networking, and being a connecter of people are primary giftings. The primary personality trait of the evangelist is extroversion.

4. **Pastor**: the "nurturer" and shepherd." Creating fellowship, care giving, and cultivating others are primary giftings. The primary personality trait of the pastor is agreeableness.

5. **Teacher:** "the preacher" and "educator." Proclamation and teaching are primary giftings. The primary personality trait of the teacher is conscientiousness.[79]

Use these questions to guide your conversation.

---

79. The APEST typology comes from Alan Hirsch, *5Q: Reactivating the Original Intelligence and Capacity of the Body of Christ* (100 Movements Publishing, 2017).

1. As we have seen, sometimes a minister and congregation can be a mismatch. Do you feel the pastoral and congregational personalities are aligned?

2. What is the weakness of a perfect match between congregation and pastor? What are the challenges with a mismatch?

3. Which of the five APEST types are missing most in your congregation? How might you connect with new people in the larger community?

4. How does the existence of these personality types create the possibility of conflict? How might you go about doing healthy conflict that speaks the truth in love and builds up the body?

5. What is one small experiment you can start together in an area of weakness? Who will start it? When? How will you measure its development?

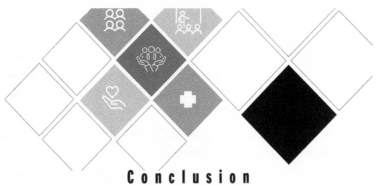

LOVE–THE FINAL WORD

The Love Triangle

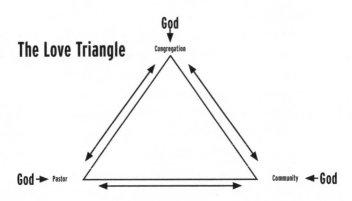

H ow are we growing in our love for God together? Loving God with all our heart, mind, strength, and soul? What practices help us grow in love with God, like prayer, fasting, study, generosity, and worship? As God's love flows through and among you as a healthy congregation and pastor, begin to think about how it can be shared in the community. How can we grow in our love for neighbor? What practices help us do that, like feeding the hungry, clothing the naked, welcoming strangers, and visiting the sick or incarcerated?

Every congregation is a unique gift to the world. Every person within the congregation brings a unique personality, gifting, and passion. The very nature of Jesus' design for the church, different personalities living together in deep community, is both an asset and a liability.

Different personalities have different perspectives, values, and hopes. People who are high on openness will always be chasing new ideas and focusing on the next horizon. People who are naturally agreeable will want to spend time together and nurture one another. People who are extroverted will always be thinking about who is not in the room and how we can connect with them. People who are conscientious will always value truth, strategy, and doing things in an orderly way. People who are neurotic will feel deeply and be concerned with calling us back to the heart of God.

Those differences will be a source of conflict at times. As we speak the truth in love to one another, we must understand the lens that we bring to each situation but also work hard to understand the lenses of others. We are seeing the same thing but from different angles. We are focused on loving and serving the same Lord, but we are literally wired to see and do that in different ways. While these differences make communal life in Jesus hard, they also make us better. In fact, we need each of these unique perspectives and values "until all of us come to the unity of the faith and of the knowledge of the Son of God, to maturity, to the measure of the full stature of Christ" (Eph 4:13). No one of us has the full perspective, the only right answer, and the singular way. But we do have that—together.

It's unrealistic to think that we will begin to love one another perfectly within the church before we start loving the people outside of it. If you wait for that, it will never happen. This is why the triangle can be so helpful. How is God's love flowing through each of the key relationships: congregation, pastor, community? This is a question to continually guide you along the journey as you "grow the center, experiment on the edge."

As you navigate the complexity of deep relationships with the unique personalities involved, it's time to "pull the fulcrum" and help that love spread out into the wider context.

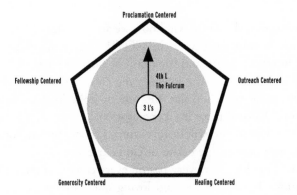

Again, the key to (re)missioning is found in this simple principle: "grow the center, experiment on the edge." Or in short, helping congregations live into a blended ecology of church in which diverse forms of church live together in a symbiotic relationship. This requires us to work hard to ensure the community does not take on the life of any one leader with a big personality. We need teams of people operating in their uniqueness, working in areas where they have gifts and passion. The only personality the community should seek to embody is Jesus himself.

The Key Word Is *Love*

Nothing I have written here will be particularly helpful if you don't actually care for one another. Love is the secret ingredient to everything we have explored.

Jesus said to his disciples in his farewell address, "A new command I give you: Love one another. As I have loved you, so you must love one another. By this everyone will know that you are my disciples, if you love one another" (John 13:34–35, NIV).

The secret ingredient of any revitalization is *love*. Love created us, love redeems us, love sanctifies and sustains us. The love of God awakens congregations from the brink of death. The love of the leader for his/her people can lead them through a journey of transformation. The love of a congregation for a community can transform a city.

Love is how the world will know we are disciples of Jesus.

After years of navigating the COVID pandemic, political upheaval, internal schism, and the death of the church as we know it, some leaders have lost the love for the church that drew them to ministry. Some churches, like the one in Ephesus, have lost their "first love." What if these five congregational personality types are a deeply theological and wildly adventurous model for our local congregations to unleash the power of God's love afresh?

This is my hope for every pastor, every congregation, and every community. Fully knowing and loving one another is the way of Jesus and his disciples. Loving one another through differences is the church's most profound witness to the world. Love is the ancient pathway for congregational renewal in the twenty-first century. Love well, my friends, as Jesus has loved you.

REFERENCES

Akinyela, Makungu M. "Testimony of Hope: African Centered Praxis for Therapeutic Ends." *Journal of Systemic Therapies* 24, no. 1 (2005): 5–18.

"Arranged / Forced Marriage Statistics." Statistic Brain Research Institute. February 7, 2018. https://www.statisticbrain.com/arranged-marriage-statistics/.

Beck, Michael Adam. *Deep and Wild: Remissioning Your Church from the Outside In.* Franklin, TN: Seedbed Publishing, 2021.

Beck, Michael Adam. *Painting with Ashes: When Your Weakness Becomes Your Superpower.* Plano, TX: Invite Press, 2022.

Beck, Michael Adam, with Jorge Acevedo. *A Field Guide to Methodist Fresh Expressions.* Nashville: Abingdon Press, 2020.

Beck, Michael Adam, and Tyler Kleeberger. *Fresh Expressions of the Rural Church.* Nashville: Abingdon Press, 2022.

Bosch, David J. *Transforming Mission: Paradigm Shifts in Theology of Mission.* American Society of Missiology Series, No. 16. Maryknoll, NY: Orbis Books, 1991.

Chapman, Gary D. *The Five Love Languages: How to Express Heartfelt Commitment to Your Mate.* Chicago: Northfield Publishing, 1995.

deSilva, David A. *Seeing Things John's Way: The Rhetoric of the Book of Revelation*. 1st Edition. Louisville: Westminster John Knox Press, 2009.

Emerson, Michael O., and Christian Smith. *Divided by Faith: Evangelical Religion and the Problem of Race in America*. Oxford, UK: Oxford University Press, 2001.

Friedman, Edwin H. *A Failure of Nerve: Leadership in the Age of the Quick Fix*. 10th Anniversary Revised Edition. Edited by Margaret M. Treadwell and Edward W. Beal. New York: Church Publishing, 2017.

———. *Generation to Generation: Family Process in Church and Synagogue*. New York: Guilford Press, 2011.

Gottdiener, M., Boklund-Lagopoulou, K., & Lagopoulos, A. P. (Eds.) (2003). *Semiotics*. SAGE Publications Ltd, https://dx.doi.org/10.4135/9781446263419

Hemer, Colin J. *The Letters to the Seven Churches of Asia in Their Local Setting*. Grand Rapids, MI: William B. Eerdmans, 2001.

Hirsch, Alan. *5Q: Reactivating the Original Intelligence and Capacity of the Body of Christ*. 100 Movements Publishing, 2017.

Hiser, Bethany Dearborn. *From Burned Out to Beloved: Soul Care for Wounded Healers*. Downers Grove, IL: InterVarsity Press, 2020.

Jones, E. Stanley. *The Word Became Flesh*. Nashville: Abingdon Press, 2006.

Kreider, Alan. *The Patient Ferment of the Early Church: The Improbable Rise of Christianity in the Roman Empire*. Grand Rapids, MI: Baker Academic, 2016.

Lightfoot, Joseph Barber. *The Apostolic Fathers*. 2nd Edition. Grant Rapids, MI: Baker Books, 1989.

Murray, Stuart. *The Church After Christendom*. Milton Keynes, UK: Paternoster Press, 2004.

Owles, R. Joseph. *The Didache: The Teaching of the Twelve Apostles*. CreateSpace, 2014.

Peterson, Eugene H. *The Contemplative Pastor: Returning to the Art of Spiritual Direction*. Grand Rapids, MI: William B. Eerdmans, 1993.

Stache, Kristine M. "Practice of Immersion in the Context." *Currents in Theology and Mission* 38, no. 5 (2011): 363–64.

Sweet, Leonard, and Michael Adam Beck. *Contextual Intelligence: Unlocking the Ancient Secrets to Mission on the Front Lines*. Oviedo, FL: HigherLife Publishing, 2021.

Willimon, William H. *Pastor: The Theology and Practice of Ordained Ministry*. Nashville: Abingdon Press, 2002.

Witherington, Ben, III. *Revelation*. The New Cambridge Bible Commentary. Cambridge, UK: Cambridge University Press, 2003.

Vatican Council II. *Ad Gentes (Decree on the Missionary Activity of the Church)*. Vatican Archives. Accessed November 5, 2022. https://www.vatican.va/archive/hist_councils/ii_vatican_council/documents/vat-ii_decree_19651207_ad-gentes_en.html.

SCAN HERE to learn more about Invite Press, a premier publishing imprint created to invite people to a deeper faith and living relationship with Jesus Christ.

STAR COCKTAILS

STAR COCKTAILS
Classic Drinks from Classic Movies

Oliver Hamilton

Published in 2009 by Max Press,
an imprint of Little Books Ltd,
Notting Hill, London W11 3QW

10 9 8 7 6 5 4 3 2 1

Text copyright © 2009 by Oliver Hamilton
Illustrations © The British Film Institute

Design and layout copyright © by Max Press

A CIP catalogue record for this book is available from the British Library.

ISBN 978 1 906251 25 3

Every attempt has been made to trace any copyright holders.
The author and publisher will be grateful for any information
that will assist them in keeping future editions up to date.
Although all reasonable care has been taken in the
preparation of this book, neither the publisher, editors
nor the author can accept any liability for any consequences
arising from the use thereof, or the information contained therein.

Printed and bound by SNP Leefung, China

CONTENTS

Introduction 7

A to Z of Cocktail Recipes 12

Index of Cocktails and Ingredients 205

Index of Films 221

INTRODUCTION

Drinking has never been as elegant as where cocktails are concerned, and nowhere has it been more glamorously portrayed than Hollywood. This collection contains the best of the classics so you can make your own star cocktails. The recipes chosen are simple to make and require the minimum equipment. Many of those included have endured over the decades. Some are derived and adapted from Harry Craddock's classic *Savoy Cocktail Book* published in 1930 and David Embury's *Fine Art of Mixing Drinks* which appeared two decades later. Others are taken from the original historical recipes. All are guaranteed to make an entrance at any social occasion.

The Art of Mixing

Although various technical terms are used in the preparation of a cocktail, there are essentially four ways of mixing a drink: shaken, blended, stirred or layered. Of all these methods, shaking is by the far the most common, intended to chill and dilute the ingredients as well as mixing them thoroughly together. A good shaker is a solid investment. If possible, use a standard three-piece shaker with a capacity of at least a pint and preferably made of stainless steel.

For best results, firstly combine the ingredients in the base of the shaker, then fill it with roughly two thirds of ice. (This rule applies equally to blending, when a better result will be achieved if the liquid ingredients of the drink are placed in the blender first before the ice is added.) When shaking the cocktail always secure the top and cap. Then pick it up with one hand on top and the other gripping the bottom and shake vigorously for about twenty-five seconds. When shaking, always direct away from your guests. Afterwards, remove the cap and pour through the strainer into the glass which ideally will have been already chilled in the fridge or freezer.

Occasionally, one of the recipes requires muddling, a term used by bartenders which refers to pummeling fresh fruit or herbs. A muddler is similar to a pestle, but any blunt instrument will do the job just as well. When muddling take care not to press too hard and if possible use a twisting action to ensure the maximum release of flavour and aroma. Layering different ingredients in a glass can take practice and patience. Every liquid varies in its density and weight. Syrups containing high sugar levels are most commonly the heaviest and line the bottom of a drink, but creamy liqueurs can be the lightest and usually 'float' well on top. For the best and most professional effect, slowly pour each layer of liquid over a bar or soup spoon onto the inside side of the glass.

Staying Cool

When preparing any cocktail, always ensure you have a plentiful supply of ice to hand. If you are making your own ice cubes it's best to avoid tap water if possible and use mineral water and filtered water to avoid any chemical or chlorine aftertaste. If a recipe calls for an ice-filled glass, always fill it up to the top and don't just add a few cubes. Temperature is crucial to a truly refreshing drink. Luke-warm cocktails belong down the plug hole.

Balancing Your Act

Proportion and balance of flavour and texture is at the heart of any cocktail, so accurately measuring your ingredients is of paramount importance. Ideally a shot is 25ml or one US fluid ounce (29.6 ml). If you buy a measure, it is a good idea to choose one with the quarter and half measure shots indicated on the side.

The Basic Ingredients

Many would-be cocktail makers are put off by the baffling array of exotic ingredients in some recipes, yet it is a fact that most of the greatest cocktails require just a few basics. It is unnecessary to feel you have to fill your cupboard with strange liqueurs, then watch them sitting there mainly unused for years to come. Many drinks can be made with the following dozen core ingredients:

Vodka	Gin	Rum
Bourbon	Whisky	Cognac
Dry Vermouth	Sweet Vermouth	Tequila
Cointreau	Grand Marnier	Apricot Brandy.

Dressing Up for the Occasion

A tasteful garnish will make any drink look like a star. The most stylish cocktails are presented with edible garnishes. Avoid the use of garish plastic paraphernalia or paper parasols. Understatement is what you are aiming to achieve. If you are using a wedge of lime or lemon, always use the freshest fruit and make sure it is clean. Rinse olives previously stored in brine before piercing with a cocktail stick.

Making an Entrance
Finally, if you are mixing drinks in front of people, remember that the act of preparation itself is an essential part of the fun and enjoyment of cocktails. Don't worry if it all goes wrong. Just relax, sit back and have a drink.

A–Z
OF
COCKTAIL
RECIPES

ALAMAGOOZLUM

¾ Shot Yellow Chartreuse
¾ Shot White Rum
¼ Shot Grand Marnier
¾ Shot Sugar Syrup
½ Shot Jonge Jenever
¼ Shot Angostura Bitters
¼ Fresh Egg White

Shake all ingredients in an ice-filled shaker. Strain into a chilled Martini glass.

In *The Fine Art of Mixing Drinks* published in the 1930s David Embury stated this cocktail was 'a speciality of the elder Morgan of the House of Morgan, which goes to prove as a bartender he was an excellent banker'.

ALASKA

2 Shots Gin
1 Shot Chartreuse
1 Shot Dry Sherry
3 Dashes Orange Bitters

Shake all ingredients with ice and strain into a chilled Martini glass.

Bing Crosby, *High Society*

HIGH SOCIETY (1956)
Directed by Charles Walters

Starring Bing Crosby, Grace Kelly, Frank Sinatra, Celeste Holm, Louis Armstrong and John Lund

This MGM musical was the final acting role for Grace Kelly before she married Prince Rainier of Monaco and the film was released three months after her marriage. It is a remake of *The Philadephia Story*, which starred Kathryn Hepburn, Cary Grant and James Stewart and the music and lyric are by Cole Porter.

In *High Society* a jazz musician, C.K Dexter (Crosby) is the former husband of Tracy Lord (Kelly), but is still in love with her. She is set to re-marry. Her prospective husband is George Kittredge (Lund), a dull but respectable man. The third side of the triangle is reporter Mike Connor, (Sinatra) who is covering the wedding for a magazine and falls in love with Tracy. She must make a decision about which man she wants to be with.

The Philadelphia Story follows a similar line. Kathryn Hepburn is arranging her second marriage when things are disrupted by the entrance of a number of unwanted and unwelcome guests including her father, her first husband and two reporters from a tabloid rag. Cary Grant is the first husband, and James Stewart and Ruth Hussey are the reporters.

Cole Porter got an Oscar nomination for his song *True Love* and Johnny Green and Saul Chaplin were nominated for Best Musical Score.

AMERICAN BEAUTY

½ Shot Freshly Squeezed Orange Juice
½ Shot Grenadine
½ Shot Vermouth
½ Shot Brandy
Dash Crème de Menthe
Dash Port

Shake all ingredients in an ice-filled shaker, strain into a chilled glass and top with port.

ANGEL FACE

½ Shot Gin
½ Shot Apricot Brandy
½ Shot Calvados

Shake all ingredients in an ice-filled shaker and strain into a chilled glass.

ANGEL'S TIP

¾ Shot Crème de Cacao
¼ Shot Fresh Cream

Pour the liqueur into a port glass and float the cream on top.

APPETISER

½ Shot Gin
½ Shot Dubonnet
Freshly Squeezed Orange Juice

Shake all ingredients in an ice-filled shaker and strain into a chilled glass.

APPLE JACK

½ Shot Vermouth
½ Shot Calvados
1 Dash Angostura Bitters

Shake all ingredients in an ice-filled shaker and strain into a chilled glass.

APPLE MARTINI

2½ Shots Vodka
½ Shot Apple Schnapps
2 Shots Apple Juice

Shake ingredients with ice and strain into a chilled glass.

APPLE OF MY EYE

In the Southern states of America, after a heavy evening and a hard day's work, there is nothing more relaxing than to mix a drink of fresh apple juice laced with Bourbon. The ravages of the previous night, and the stresses of the day, are forgotten once the Bourbon has revived flagging spirits and the apple has restored vitamin levels and provided a few calories. Mint adds just the freshness that a jaded mouth needs.

6 Apples
Mint Leaves, to taste
1½ Shots Bourbon

Core and peel the apples. Place them in a blender or a juicer. Add ice to the juice and mix in the Bourbon.

APRICOT COCKTAIL

½ Shot Apricot Brandy
¼ Shot Freshly Squeezed Lemon Juice
¼ Shot Freshly Squeezed Orange Juice
Dash Gin

Shake all ingredients in an ice-filled shaker and strain into a Martini glass. Garnish with a slice of apricot.

ATTA BOY COCKTAIL

¼ Shot Dry Vermouth
½ Shot Gin
4 Dashes Grenadine

Shake all ingredients in an ice-filled shaker and strain into an ice-filled Martini glass.

AVIATION COCKTAIL

¼ Shot Freshly Squeezed Lemon Juice
½ Shot Gin
2 Dashes Marashino Liqueur

Shake all ingredients into an ice-filled shaker and strain into an ice-filled Martini Glass.

AVIATOR

1 Shot Gin
1 Shot Dry Vermouth
1 Shot Sweet Vermouth
1 Shot Dubonnet

Stir ingredients with ice and strain into a chilled glass.

THE APOTHECARY

Herbs have almost magical qualities, but it requires a skilled apothecary to recognize these. Luckily, many herbal-based spirits are available that overcome this problem. This recipe, frequently recommended by Salvatore Calabrese, formerly of The Lanesborough Hotel in London and now at 50 St James, could have been designed to restore the equilibrium of your stomach. After the herbal-rich Italian Punt e Mes and Fernet Branca combine with Crème de Menthe, you will be able to face the world.

1 Shot Fernet Branca
1 Shot Crème de Menthe
1 Shot Punt e Mes

Pour all ingredients into a mixing glass filled with ice. Stir. Strain into a cocktail glass.

THE ASSASSIN

¼ Shot White Crème de Menthe
¼ Shot Fernet Branca
½ Shot Port

Mix together all the ingredients and serve in an old-fashioned glass without ice.

AURA

60ml or 2 fl oz Milk
2 Tablespoons Honey

Stir to boiling point in a saucepan. Pour into a mug and drink as hot as you can. If you're strong enough to go to work, a tot of rum at about 9am, after you're at your desk, will give you the energy to face another day. The recipe provides much-needed fluid and sugar.

Freshly Squeezed Juice of 1 Orange
Freshly Squeezed Juice of Half a Lemon
30ml or 1 fl oz Light Rum

Stir to boiling in a saucepan.
Serve in a heat-proof glass.

The third stage of the Aura is a modified coffee break. By 11am, you're already feeling more chirpy, you may even be better company and able to smile at your colleagues.

¼ Shot Campari
1 Shot Vodka
3 Shots Tomato Juice
¼ Shot Freshly Squeezed Lemon Juice
3 Dashes Worcestershire sauce

Pour all ingredients into a shaker filled with ice and shake. Strain into a highball glass filled with ice.

John Gilbert, *The Merry Widow*

BACK TO WORK

This hangover cure is recommended by Francis Ane, head bartender at the Orly Hilton in Orly, France. It contains some spirits, some refreshing, vitamin-rich lemon, and tomato juice packed with lycopene, a strong antioxidant. The Tabasco will sharpen a jaded tongue and mouth. This potion should be followed by a long, cool glass of water.

1 Shot Bourbon or Rye Whiskey
1 Shot Tomato Juice
2 Shots Freshly Squeezed Orange Juice
Dash Tabasco sauce

Shake all ingredients together and serve in a highball glass with lots of ice.

BATIDA DE COCO

2½ Shots Sagatiba Cachaca
1½ Shots Cream of Coconut
1 Shot Coconut Milk

Blend ingredients with ice and pour into glass.

BELLINI

Fresh Peach Juice
Dry Champagne

Half fill a Champagne flute with peach juice. Top up with the Champagne and stir. Serve well chilled and garnish with a peach slice on the rim.

The original Bellini was created by Giuseppe Cipriani at Harry's Bar, on the edge of the Grand Canal in Venice, in 1945. Cipriani named the cocktail after the Renaissance painter Giovanni Bellini on account of the pink colour which was the same as the ubiquitious pink hues of the artist's works.

Harry's Bar famously went on to be patronised by the likes of Ernest Hemingway – arguably the world's greatest drinker, Orson Welles, Sinclair Lewis, F. Scott Fitzgerald and Dorothy Parker. Nowadays cocktail lovers from all over the world make pilgrimages to the tiny bar to test the original for itself. The white peaches used to make the drink are in season only between May and September so many bars only serve the Bellini during these months.

BACARDI COCKTAIL

1 Shot Bacardi Light Rum
1 Teaspoon Freshly Squeezed Lime Juice
1 Teaspoon Grenadine
1 Teaspoon Chilled Mineral Water

For a perfectly delicious pink drink carefully measure out equal amounts of the rum, lime juice and grenadine. Shake all the ingredients in an ice-filled shaker and strain into a chilled glass.

Bacardi rum was first made by Don Facundo Bacardi in Santiago de Cuba. So strict was the company he founded about the uniqueness of their rum that in 1936 a New York bar discovered to be making the Bacardi Cocktail without Bacardi was sued. The court held the spirit was unique and the judge ruled that only Bacardi could be used in the Bacardi Cocktail.

BALLET RUSSE

2 Shots Vodka
1 Shot Crème de Cassis
1 Shot Freshly Squeezed Lime Juice

Shake ingredients with ice and strain into a chilled glass.

Leslie Caron and Louis Jourdan, *Gigi*

GIGI (1958)
Directed by Vincente Minnelli

Starring Leslie Caron, Louis Jourdan, Maurice Chevalier and Hermione Gingold

The film is widely considered the last great MGM musical.

Set in 1900s Paris, the film begins with Honoré Lachaille (Chevalier) suggesting that marriage is not the only alternative for wealthy young men like his nephew Gaston Lachaille (Jourdan), who is suffering from a case of ennui. The thing he enjoys the most is spending time with Madame Alvarez (Gingold), whom he calls Mamita, and her granddaughter, the gifted, Gilberte, also known as Gigi (Caron).

Following the family custom, Madame Alvarez sends Gigi to her Aunt Alicia to be raised as a courtesan, a mistress for rich men, and learn etiquette and allure. The young girl starts off as a useless student who fails to understand the rationale behind her education. She enjoys spending time with Gaston, whom she regards as an elder brother.

Gaston falls in love with Gigi, who is now far removed from little girl he wants knew and he tells Mamita he wants to take Gigi as his mistress, promising to provide the girl with luxury and benevolence. But Gigi dismisses the idea, telling him she wants more for herself than to be a sexual object to be shared by men. Gaston is appalled at this depiction of the life he wishes to give her and leaves shocked. But Gigi has also fallen in love with him and later decides she would rather be miserable with him than without him. Finally love conquers all and Gaston asks Marmita for Gigi's hand in marriage.

BALTIMORE EGGNOG

¾ Shot Brandy
¾ Shot Madeira
½ Shot Rum
1 Tablespoon Sugar Syrup
1 Fresh Egg
½ Shot Double Cream
2 Shots Fresh Milk

Pour all ingredients into a shaker filled with ice. Shake well. Strain into a highball glass filled with ice. Grate fresh nutmeg over the top.

BANANA COW

¾ Shot White Rum
1 Banana
2 Shots Fresh Milk
Dash Angostura bitters
Dash Vanilla Essence
1 Teaspoon Sugar

Pour all the ingredients into a blender and blend for ten seconds. Add half a scoop of crushed ice and blend again until smooth. Serve in a goblet.

BATONNET

Some people find that one of the most tiresome consequences of drinking is that it can destroy sleep. If you ever feel tired the next morning, Colin Peter Field, the bartender at Bar Hemingway in the Ritz Hotel, Paris, has the answer. He recommends that customers who lack energy the morning after should try a great reviver like Cognac, combined with tonic and white wine.

⅔ Shot Cognac
2 Shots Dry White Wine
Two Cinnamon Sticks
Tonic

Pour the Cognac and white wine into a tumbler filled with ice. Break the cinnamon sticks and drop them into the glass. Top up with tonic.

BARBARY COAST

¼ Shot Gin
¼ Shot Whisky
¼ Shot Crème de Cacao
¼ Shot Double Cream

Shake in an ice-filled shaker and serve in a Collins glass.

BELMONT

½ Shot Gin
½ Shot Grenadine
1 Teaspoon Fresh Cream

Shake all ingredients in an ice-filled shaker and strain into a Martini glass.

BENTLEY

½ Shot Calvados
½ Shot Dubonnet

Shake ingredients in an ice-filled shaker and strain into a Martini glass.

BETWEEN THE SHEETS

1 Shot Light White Rum
1 Shot Cointreau or Triple Sec
1 Shot Cognac
¾ Shot Freshly Squeezed Lemon Juice
½ Shot Sugar Syrup
½ Shot Chilled Mineral Water

Strain ingredients into an ice-filled shaker and strain into a chilled glass.

BIG BOY

⅔ Shot Brandy
¼ Shot Cointreau
¼ Shot Sirop de Citron

Shake all ingredients in an ice-filled shaker and strain into a Martini glass.

BLACK VELVET

2½ Shots Guiness Stout
Top up with Champagne

Pour ingredients into a chilled glass.

There can be few serious drinkers who haven't lunched on a Sunday by having a couple of Black Velvets. Yet just in case you haven't discovered its restorative powers, here is the recipe.

Combining Champagne and Guinness was an idea that started at Brook's Club in 1861, and is said to have been created by the barman who felt that, because Prince Albert had just died, a black drink was in order.

BLOODHOUND

2 Shots Campari
1 Shot Vodka
3½ Shots Freshly Squeezed Grapefruit Juice

Shake all ingredients with ice and strain into an ice-filled glass.

BLOOD TRANSFUSION

The alcohol provides the hair of the dog for your stomach, the Fernet Branca wakes you up, and the calories restore some blood-sugar levels. It is a long drink, so helps with rehydration. The combination is said to be either a kill or cure.

1 Shot Vodka
1 Shot Sherry
1 Shot Fernet Branca
4 Shots Tomato Juice
1 Shot Freshly Squeezed Lime Juice
Pinch Celery Salt
2 dashes Worcestershire sauce

Fill a highball glass with ice-cubes. Pour the vodka and sherry over the ice first, then add the tomato and lime juice, then the celery salt and Worcestershire sauce. Stir. Float a layer of Fernet Branca on top.

BLOODY BULL

1 Shot Vodka
1 Shot Beef Bouillon
1 Shot Tomato Juice
½ Shot Fresh Lemon Juice
2 Dashes Worcestershire Sauce
Pinch Celery Salt

Pour all ingredients into a cocktail shaker filled with ice. Shake. Strain into a highball glass filled with ice.

BLOODY CAESAR

1 Shot Vodka
3 Shots Clamato (a mixture of tomato and clam juice)
½ Shot Freshly Squeezed Lemon Juice
Pinch Celery Salt
Dash Tabasco Sauce
2 dashes Worcestershire Sauce
Freshly ground Black Pepper

Pour the Clamato and lemon juice into a highball glass filled with ice. Add the vodka and other ingredients. Stir. Garnish with a wedge of lime on the rim. Serve with a stirrer.

BLOODY MARY

50ml Vodka
Tomato Juice

Spice Mix:
2 Large Dashes each of Tabasco
and Worcestershire Sauce
Pinch Celery Salt
Pinch Cracked Black Pepper
1 Dash of Fresh Lemon Juice
1 Teaspoon Horseradish Sauce
Slice of Lemon
Celery Stick

Blend ingredients for spice mix together in a mixing glass. Pour vodka into a Highball glass filled with ice, add tomato juice and spice mix and stir vigorously. Garnish with a lemon slice and a celery stick.

Fernan Petiot was working at Harry's New York Bar in Paris when he came up with the legendary Bloody Mary. He named the drink after the entertainer Roy Barton, one of his customers, in honour of the Bucket of Blood nightclub in Chicago where he had performed. It was not, as some believe, named after Queen Mary, whose nickname was 'Bloody Mary' on account of her persecution of protestants in the seventeenth century. It was only later when Petiot was working at the King Cole Bar in Manhattan's Hotel Saint Regis that he famously mixed in the seasoning and

Worcestershire sauce, after the hotel's manager Serge Obolansky complained it was too flat.

The owner, Vincent Astor, when hearing the name, renamed it the Red Snapper, although this was largely subsequently ignored by the rich and famous customers who preferred the original name. The celery stick was only added later in 1960 when a bartender at the Ambassador Hotel in Chicago found inspiration from a customer stirring her drink with one.

BLOODY MARIA

1 Shot Tequila
3 Shots Tomato Juice
Dash Freshly Squeezed Lemon Juice
Pinch Celery salt
Pinch Black pepper
4 Dashes Tabasco Sauce
4 Dashes Worcestershire Sauce

Pour all ingredients into a cocktail shaker filled with ice. Shake. Strain into a highball glass filled with ice. Garnish with a celery stick and a wedge of lime.

Lauren Bacall, *The Big Sleep*

THE BIG SLEEP (1946)
Directed by Howard Hawks

Starring Humphrey Bogart and Lauren Bacall

This is the first film version of Raymond Chandler's 1939 novel and is one of Chandler's best hard-boiled detective mysteries. It is a very complex, confusing, logic-defying whodunit with private detective Philip Marlowe, false leads, unforgettable dialogue and wisecracks, raw-edged characters, sexy women and tough action.

The main protagonists in this rather convoluted film appear as confused about the plot during clue-chasing as audiences. What makes things particularly puzzling is that some important characters involved in the plot never appear alive on screen, several other characters appear only briefly or are quickly killed off, and important information is deliberately missing.

Whereas most examples of film noir relied on a voice-over narrative to explain plot points, in *The Big Sleep*, the audience is allowed to follow the point-of-view experiences of the detective and conclude what they want about his search for solutions.

Some critics have said that what is much more important than the basic blackmail-murder plot is the stylish method and process of the private detective's quest, that the viewer identifies with and shares, as he makes his way through the murky world of nasty crime from one oppressive setting to the next, or from one wicked character, fallen woman, or femme fatale to another, until eventually discovering love with his female protagonist.

BLUE BIRD

2 Shots Gin
1 Shot Blue Curacao Liqueur
¾ Shot Freshly Squeezed Lemon Juice
¼ Shot Almond Syrup

Shake all ingredients with ice and strain into a Martini glass.

BLUE BLAZER

2 Spoons Runny Honey
¾ Shot Boiling Water
3 Shots Scotch
6 Twists Lemon Peel

Stir honey with boiling water and lemon peel. Add Scotch and stir. Flame the mixture and stir with a spoon until the flame dies.

The Blue Blazer was originally devised by 'Professor' Jerry Thomas in the nineteenth century. Legend has it he set the ingredients alight in a metal mug, then mixed them by pouring the flaming brew into another. Do not attempt this at home.

BLUES COCKTAIL

½ Shot Whisky
½ Shot Curacau
Tablespoon Syrup of Prunes

Shake all ingredients in an ice-filled shaker and pour into a chilled glass.

BOSTON FLIP

Eggnogs may have been popularized in the Thirties, but similar drinks were being made in the seventeenth century. They contained beaten eggs, alcohol, spices and sugar. The Boston Flip used to be stirred by pouring the cocktail backwards and forwards between two containers until it was of a smooth consistency, then heated by putting a hot poker in the mixture before serving it. It is no longer served as a long drink, and is served cold. Nutmeg is usually sprinkled over it. For those who don't like rum or Bourbon, other spirits may be substituted.

½ Shot Bourbon
½ Shot Madeira
1 Fresh Egg Yolk
Dash Sugar syrup

Pour all ingredients into a cocktail shaker filled with ice. Shake well. Strain into a goblet. Garnish with grated nutmeg.

BOURBON MILK PUNCH

2 Shots Whisky
½ Shot Galliano
1 Shot Fresh Double Cream
1 Shot Fresh Milk

Shake all ingredients in an ice-filled shaker and strain into a chilled Martini glass.

BOURBON HIGHBALL

1 Shot Bourbon
Ginger Ale
Twist of Lemon

Pour the bourbon into a Highball glass filled with ice, top up with ginger ale and garnish with a twist of lemon.

A Highball traditionally contains only two ingredients, normally a spirit and a soft drink. The simplicity of a Highball makes it a perfect, refreshing choice for serving at parties.

Jack Lemmon, *How to Murder Your Wife* (overleaf)

HOW TO MURDER YOUR WIFE (1965)
Directed by Richard Quine

Stanley Ford (Lemmon) is a cartoonist. Stanley lives a carefree life as a single man, attending wild parties and chasing attractive young women. However, whilst at a friend's bachelor party, he has too much to drink and accidentally proposes to a gorgeous blonde Italian babe. An equally drunken judge at the party overhears Stanley's marriage proposal and obligingly performs an impromptu wedding ceremony. Stanley wakes up the following morning with a hangover. Lying naked in bed next to him is the beautiful woman who stepped out of the cake at the party. At first he remembers nothing of the previous night's events. Then, the awful truth begins to dawn on him.

Stanley's new wife proceeds to turn Stanley's world upside down. Buying expensive new dresses and shoes with his money, filling the bathroom with beauty products and watching television all night.

Stanley has just about had enough, when, purely by accident one day, his wife catches sight of a cartoon on his desk, takes offence and suddenly leaves. The police arrive and quickly formulate their own conclusions, arresting him for murdering his wife and disposing the body in a building site next door. At the trial Stanley fires his incompetent lawyer and decides to defend himself, pleading guilty to the murder and pleading that they should let him off on the grounds of justifiable homicide. The all-male jury, equally frustrated at the way their own wives have destroyed their bachelor fun, decide to find him not guilty and he is released, to the stony glares of all the women present.

Eventually his wife reappears from nowhere and they are reconciled. Stanley realises he loves her after all and that, despite their differences, life is far better with her than without her.

BOURBON PICK-ME-UP

½ Shot Bourbon
½ Shot Branca Menta
½ Shot Freshly Squeezed Lemon Juice
8 fresh Mint Leaves

Pour all the ingredients into a cocktail shaker filled with ice. Shake. Strain into an old-fashioned glass filled with ice. Garnish with a sprig of fresh mint. The Bourbon Pick-Me-Up is especially recommended by those who have drunk too much Bourbon the night before. Ben Reed, former barman at the Met Bar in London, suggests making it with fresh mint, combined with Branca Menta and Bourbon.

BOURBON SMASH

4 Mint Leaves
10 Raspberries
3 Shots Cranberry Juice
1 Shot Freshly Squeezed Lime Juice
2½ Shots Bourbon Whisky
½ Shot Sugar Syrup
1 Dash Angostura Bitters

Muddle the raspberries in the base of the shaker and add the remaining ingredients. Shake in an ice-filled shaker and strain into a chilled glass.

BRANDY ALEXANDER

1 Shot Brandy
½ Shot White Crème de Cacao
½ Shot Dark Crème de Cacao
½ Shot Fresh Double cream
½ Shot Milk
Ground Nutmeg

Pour all the ingredients and a dash of fresh cream into a cocktail shaker filled with ice. Shake sharply; strain into a chilled glass. Garnish with a sprinkle of ground nutmeg.

Originally the Alexander was a combination of Crème de Cacao, cream and gin, although the gin was later replaced by brandy. Drunk after dinner, it is a rich and delectible alternative – or addition – to pudding.

BRANDY FIZZ

1½ Shots Cognac
¾ Shot Freshly Squeezed Lemon Juice
1 Shot Sugar Syrup
Top up with Soda

Shake the cognac, lemon juice and sugar syrup in an ice-filled shaker. Strain into a Collins glass and top up with soda.

BRANDY FLIP

1 Shot Brandy
¼ Shot Double Cream
1 Egg Yolk
1 Dash of Sugar Syrup

Stir all the ingredients thoroughly in a mixing glass filled with ice. Strain into a chilled glass and dust with freshly ground nutmeg.

A Flip is any liquor shaken with an egg and sweetened, normally with cream and sometimes served hot as a delicious nightcap. This simple flip is made from egg yolk combined with brandy. The sugar restores the blood-sugar level and the fat in the egg ensures that it doesn't fall again as soon as the drink is downed.

BRANDY MILK PUNCH

2 Shots Cognac
3 Shots Fresh Milk
1 Shot Fresh Double Cream
Dash Vanilla Extract

Shake all ingredients with ice and strain into a chilled Martini glass.

Barry Nelson, *Mary, Mary*

BRADFORD

2½ Shots Gin
½ Shot Dry Vermouth
2 Dashes Orange Bitters

Shake all ingredients in an ice-filled shaker and strain into a chilled Martini glass.

BRANDY SOUR

2 Shots Cognac
½ Shot Sugar Syrup
½ Fresh Egg White
1 Shot Freshly Squeezed Lemon Juice
2 Dashes Angostura Bitters

Shake all ingredients in an ice-filled shaker and strain into a chilled glass.

BRAZEN MARTINI

3 Shots Vodka
½ Shot Parfait Amour

Stir ingredients with ice and strain into a chilled glass.

BREAKFAST EGG NOG

Here's a slightly more complicated eggnog. As with all nogs, this one is rich in fat and protein, as well as sugar to correct the blood-sugar level and alcohol to provide the hair of the dog and a bit of a lift. The milk has an alkaline effect on the acid being secreted by an irritated stomach. All in all, this is a good mixture, easily taken by those who can't face bacon and eggs and fruit juice.

1 fresh Free-range Egg
1 Shot orange Curaçao
1 Shot brandy
5 Shots Milk
Grating of Fresh Nutmeg

Pour all ingredients, except the milk, into a cocktail shaker filled with ice. Shake. Strain into a highball glass and add the milk. Stir. Sprinkle freshly grated nutmeg over the top.

BROOKLYN

2 Shots Bourbon
1 Shot Dry Vermouth
½ Shot Amaretto

Stir all ingredients with ice and strain into a chilled glass.

BULLSHOT

Bangkok is famous for many delights, but few know that this is where the Bullshot originated. Created by Axel Gorlach at the Rama Hotel, this hangover cocktail rapidly became world-famous. Some people recommend it instead of lunch; others serve it instead of soup, and countless hangover sufferers have drunk it medicinally. It owes its name to the presence of beef bouillon – an essential, but not overpowering, part of the recipe. The Tabasco and Worcestershire sauces provide its punch.

3 Shots Beef Bouillon
Dash Freshly Squeezed Lemon Juice
Pinch Celery Salt
Dash Tabasco sauce
2 Dashes Worcestershire Sauce
½ Shot Vodka
Freshly Ground Black Pepper
Lime Wedge

Pour the bouillon, lemon juice, celery salt, Tabasco and Worcestershire sauces into a cocktail shaker filled with ice, then add the vodka. Shake. Strain into a highball glass. Add a quick grinding of black pepper. Garnish with a wedge of lime on the rim. Serve with a stirrer.

Joan Crawford, *Sudden Fear*

SUDDEN FEAR   (1952)
Directed by David Miller

Starring Joan Crawford and Jack Palance

Based upon the novel of the same name by Edna Sherry, *Sudden Fear* was produced by Joseph Kaufman and was nominated for several Academy Awards, including one for the noir-ish cinematography.

Myra Hudson (Crawford) is an affluent San Francisco heiress and successful playwright. She meets actor Lester Blaine (Palance) while she is casting her new play. They meet again later that day on the train ride back and despite his unsuccessful audition they fall in love. After a brief romance they marry.

Upon finding out that Myra is writing her will and intends to leave the majority of her estate to a foundation and only $10,000 a year to him, Lester decides to murder her before the will can take effect. He involves an old girlfriend Irene Neves (Gloria Grahame) in his dastardly plot. But their conversation is recorded on Myra's dictation machine, and after listening to it Myra goes to Irene's apartment and steals a gun. She then lures Lester there where she plans to kill him and frame Irene for the murder. She is, however, unable to go through with the deed and leaves the apartment with Lester in Pursuit.

The film climaxes with all three meeting unexpectedly during an exciting chase. Marlon Brando was originally offered the role of Lester Blaine.

BUNNY HUG

2 Shots Gin
2 Shots Whisky
2 Shots Absinthe

Shake all ingredients in an ice-filled shaker and strain into a chilled glass.

BUCK'S FIZZ

Dry Champagne
Freshly Squeezed Orange Juice

Pour ingredients into a chilled glass and stir gently.

Like the Bloody Mary, Black Velvet and Bullshot, the Buck's Fizz is to cocktail drinkers what mince pies are to Christmas. Bucks Fizz was conceived in 1921 by Mr McGarry, bartender at the Buck's Club in London. He was always insistent that the drink should be two-thirds champagne to one-third fresh orange juice, and was greatly aggrieved when drinkers tried their own versions. A timeless classic.

CAMEL

For those not fond of too much hair of dogs, F. Krikzonis at Club 17, in Athens, Greece, has devised a combination of ouzo and tomato juice. As with all pick-me-ups it should be taken early in the morning, preferably with a breakfast that includes starchy carbohydrates such as oatmeal, cereal or even toast and a large glass of orange juice.

½ Shot Ouzo
2 Shots Soda
Freshly Squeezed Lemon Juice
Dash of Angostura Bitters
Ice

If you're still shaky two hours after drinking this mixture, try mixing an Alexandrette, which consists of ice, one egg white, one jigger Cognac, one jigger cream and about half a cup of coffee.

CAMOMILE FIZZ

2 Shots Vodka
4 Shots Camomile Tea
Soda

Shake the vodka and tea with ice. Pour into an ice-filled glass and top up with soda.

Richard Burton, *Bitter Victory*

BITTER VICTORY (1958)
Directed by: Nicholas Ray

Starring: Curt Jurgens, Richard Burton, Raymond Pellegrin, Ruth Roman and Anthony Bushell

In North Africa during WWII, two British officers, Captain Leith (Burton) and Major Brand ((Jurgens), a South African, are to lead a daring raid to steal crucial documents from a Nazi stronghold in Libya.

They don't like each other much and when Brand's wife, Jane (Ruth Roman), arrives, there is a great deal of awkwardness. When Brand introduces her to Leith, it turns out the two already know each other intimately. They were romantically involved long ago, until Leith broke it off without warning.

Jane later met Brand. Leith and Jane attempt to keep their relationship a secret from Brand, but he becomes suspicious when he finds them dancing together. Later gets his wife slips up and refers to Leith as 'Jimmy'.

The two officers go in the raid which goes fairly smoothly, until Brand can't bring himself to kill a German sentry, and Leith feels compelled to step in and do it for him. Brand's resentment of Leith grows.

The team steal the documents and heads out across the desert to make their escape. They're attacked by a German patrol, and after the melee, Brand arouses suspicions when he orders Leith to stay with three badly wounded soldiers while the rest of the group leaves for the rendezvous point.

Jean Luc Godard commented after seeing the movie, 'Cinema is Nicholas Ray'.

CAMPARI NOBILE

½ Shot Vodka
½ Shot Campari
¼ Shot Limoncello
2 Shots Combined Fresh Orange and Raspberry Juices
Bitter Lemon
Raspberries, a Mint sprig, and a Twist of Orange

Pour all ingredients, except the bitter lemon, into a cocktail shaker filled with ice. Shake. Strain into a highball glass filled with ice. Top up with bitter lemon. Stir. Garnish with five raspberries and a sprig of mint, plus a twist of orange on the rim. Serve with a straw and a stirrer.

CECIL PICK-ME-UP

1 Fresh Egg Yolk
1 Shot Brandy
1 Teaspoon Sugar
Dry Champagne

Pour all the ingredients, except the Champagne, into a cocktail shaker filled with ice. Shake. Strain into a Champagne flute. Top up with Champagne.

CHAMPAGNE COCKTAIL

Dry Champagne
½ Shot Brandy
1 White Sugar Cube
Angostura Bitters

Douse the sugar cube in Angostura Bitters and place into a Champagne flute. Add the brandy, then gently top up with Champagne.

The Champagne Cocktail, like the films in which it was sipped, remains a classic to this day. It appeared in the nineteenth century in *How to Mix Drinks* by Jerry Thomas but achieved worldwide fame when a New York bartender called John Dougherty won a cocktail competition with an almost identiacal drink named the Business Brace.

Humphrey Bogart and Ingrid Bergman, *Casablanca*

CASABLANCA (1942)
Directed by Michael Curtiz

Starring Humphrey Bogart, Ingrid Bergman and Paul Henreid.

In wartime Casablanca, Rick Blaine the owner of Rick's Café Americain, is forced to abandon his cynical view of the world and help an old-love and her Resistance leader husband escape from the Vichy-controlled Morocco to continue his fight against the Nazis.

Rick Blaine (Bogart) is a bitter, American expatriate who professes to be completely neutral with regards to the war, but we learn that he ran guns to Ethiopia during the 1935 Italian invasion, and fought on the Republican side in the Spanish Civil War against Francisco Franco's Nationalists.

Rick's ex-lover Ilsa Lund (Bergman) arrives with her husband, Victor Laszlo (Paul Henreid), a fugitive Czech Resistance leader long sought by the Nazis. The couple need documents to allow them to leave Casablanca for America to continue Laszlo's work. Rick has these priceless documents and eventually gives them over.

Rick shoots a Nazi Major who tries to prevent the couple flying out prompting the police chief Louis Renault (Rains) to deliver the memorable order, 'Round up the usual suspects'.

The police chief, seeing little future for himself or Rick in Casablanca suggests they leave and join the Free French at Brazzaville. They walk away from the airport and Rick says one of the most famous lines in film history: 'Louis, I think this is the beginning of a beautiful friendship'.

CHAMPAGNE CUP

¾ Shot Cognac
½ Shot Grand Marnier
¼ Shot Maraschino Juice
Top up with Champagne

Stir the Cognac, Grand Marnier and Maraschino juice with ice and strain into a flute glass. Top up with Champagne.

CHAMPAGNE DAISY

1 Shot Yellow Chartreuse
1 Shot Freshly Squeezed Lemon Juice
Dash Grenadine
Champagne

Shake the Chartreuse, lemon juice and Grenadine in an ice shaker. Strain into a flute glass and top up with champagne.

CHARLIE CHAPLIN

1½ Shot Sloe Gin
1½ Shot Apricot Brandy
1 Shot Freshly Squeezed Lemon Juice

Shake all the ingredients in an ice-filled shaker and strain into an ice-filled tumbler.

CLIPPER COCKTAIL

2 Shots Light White Rum
2 Shots Dry Vermouth
½ Shot Grenadine

Shake all ingredients in an ice-filled shaker and strain into a glass filled with crushed ice.

COLD COMFORT

6 Spoons Runny Honey
2 Shots Rum
1 Shot Freshly Squeezed Lime Juice

Shake all the ingredients with ice and strain into an ice-filled glass.

COLLINS

2 Shots Jonge Jenever
1 Shot Freshly Squeezed Lemon Juice
½ Shot Sugar Syrup
Soda

Shake the Jonge Jenever, lemon juice and sugar syrup in an ice-filled shaker and top up with soda.

CORPSE REVIVER

1 Glass Pernod
Freshly Squeezed Lemon Juice
Champagne

Pour the lemon juice and Pernod into a Champagne coupe over a cube of ice. Fill with Champagne. Stir slowly. Serve.

Later, the Savoy had its own version, published in 1930. To many people, this is the Corpse Reviver par excellence.

1 Shot Brandy
1 Shot Sweet Vermouth
1 Shot Calvados

Pour all ingredients into a mixing glass filled with ice. Stir. Strain into a cocktail glass.

More recently, Johnny Johnson, a barman at the Savoy's American Bar in London, introduced another variation.

1 Shot Brandy
1 Shot White Crème de Menthe
1 Shot Fernet Branca

Pour all ingredients into a mixing glass filled with ice. Stir. Strain into a cocktail glass.

DEAD RECKONING (1947)
Directed by John Cromwell

Starring Humphrey Bogart, Lizabeth Scott and William Prince

After World War II, paratroopers Captain Rip Murdock (Bogart) and Sergeant Johnny Drake (Prince) are inexplicably told to go to Washington, DC. When Drake learns that he is to be awarded the Medal of Honour, while Murdock receives the Distinguished Service Cross, he vanishes before newspaper photographers can take his picture. Murdock follows the clues and tracks his friend to Gulf City, where he learns that Drake has been burned to death in a car accident.

Murdock investigates and discovers that Drake joined the Army under an false name to avoid a murder charge. Drake was accused of killing a rich old man named Chandler because he had fallen for his attractive young wife Coral (Scott).

Murdock joins up with Coral in order to solve the crime but soon events lead him to grow suspicious of her. He confronts her and she admits to killing her husband in self-defence. Murdock is in love with Carol himself and they conspire to leave town together. In the final reel the guilty are revealed and Murdock discovers that Coral has been lying all along. She shoots Murdock while they are driving at speed, but while he survives she is gravely injured. While in the hospital Murdock comforts her in her final moments.

Humphrey Bogart and Lizabeth Scott, *Dead Reckoning*

COSMOPOLITAN

½ Shot Vodka
½ Shot Cointreau or Triple Sec
4 Shots Cranberry Juice
½ Shot Freshly Squeezed Lime Juice

Shake all the ingredients in shaker and strain into a chilled glass.

Although the Cosmopolitan was believed to be a version of a Harpoon, made up of vodka and cranberry, it transpires that the cocktail was created by a lady named Cheryl Cook while she worked at The Strand at South Beach, Miami. Cheryl based her drink on the recently available Absolut Citron vodka and added a splash of cranberry to create the pink colour.

CRANBERRY COLLINS

1 Shot Vodka
2 Shots Cranberry Juice
2 Shots Freshly Squeezed Orange Juice
Soda

Shake the vodka, cranberry and orange juices with ice. Pour into an ice-filled glass and top up with soda.

CUBA LIBRE

1 Shot White Rum
Freshly Squeezed Lime Juice
Coca Cola

Pour the rum into a Collins glass filled with ice. Cut the lime into quarters and squeeze into the glass. Stir and serve with straws.

Cocktail legend has it that in the early 1890s a group of American soldiers were gathered in a bar in Havana, drinking rum and Coca Cola. The Captain raised a toast to freedom, and the battle cry was 'Cuba Libre'. Unfortunately, since Coca Cola was not available in Havana at that time, it is likely to be untrue. However, the drink's association with the military was to continue until its popularity soared during World War Two.

CUBAN SPECIAL

2 Shots Rum
2 Shots Pineapple Juice
¼ Shot Freshly Squeezed Lime Juice

Shake ingredients with ice and pour into an ice-filled Martini glass.

DAIQUIRI

1 Shot Light or Golden Rum
½ Shot Fresh Lime Juice
2 Teaspoons Sugar Syrup

Pour all of the ingredients into an ice-filled cocktail shaker. Shake sharply and strain into a chilled glass. Serve straight up on the rocks.

It is said that the first Daiquiri was made by Jennings Cox, an engineer who was working at a copper mine in Cuba in 1896 when he met up one evening with his friend Pagliuchi, also an engineer, and created a drink from the ingredients they had to hand. Cox's grand daughter tells a different story, whereby Cox was entertaining American friends and served lime and sugar with their rum to make the neat spirit more palatable. From Cuba it travelled to America with an Admiral named Lucious Johnson who brought the drink to the Army & Navy Club in Washington in 1898 after fighting in the war against Spain in that year.

One of the Daiquiri's most famous fans was not an actor, but a writer. Ernest Hemmingway lived in Cuba and indulged his passion for the drink, often drinking doubles, known as Papa Dobles in his honour. He once wrote of the cocktail that 'it reminded him of the sea. The frapped part of the drink was like the wake of a ship and the clear part was the way the water looked when the bow cut it when you were in shallow water over marl bottom. That was almost the exact colour.'

Alec Guinness, *Our Man in Havana*

OUR MAN IN HAVANA (1959)
Directed by Carol Reed

Starring Alec Guinness, Burl Ives, Ralph Richardson, Noel Coward, Maureen O'Hara and Ernie Kovacs

The film is adapted from the novel of the same name by Graham Greene but adds a slightly lighter tone.

James Wormold (Guinness) is a vacuum cleaner salesman in pre-Catro Cuba. He is signed up by the British Secret Service to spy for them in Havana. But rather than enlist his own agents, Wormold just pretends to and makes up their characters from men he knows from just seeing around. He drafts plans for a rocket-launching pad based on vacuum parts to make himself indispensable to MI6 and so that he can get more money for himself and help fund his extravagant daughter, Milly.

As he becomes more important to the service, he is sent a secretary, Beatrice and a radioman to work for him. This throws a spanner in the works and means it's increasingly difficult to continue his deception.

Eventually all his false information starts to come true. One of his fake agents is killed and Wormold is the target in an assassination attempt. He confesses all to his secretary and is recalled to London. He resists the temptation to come clean but his commanders manufacture a story about his fabricated machines being dismantled. He is awarded with honours and is offered a job teaching espionage.

DANDY COCKTAIL

1½ Shots Bourbon
1½ Shots Dubonnet
½ Shot Cointreau or Triple Sec
3 Dashes Angostura Bitters

Stir all the ingredients in an ice-filled shaker and strain into a chilled glass.

DARK 'N' STORMY

2 Shots Rum
1 Shot Freshly Squeezed Lime Juice
½ Shot Sugar Syrup
Ginger Beer

Shake the rum, lime juice and sugar syrup in a shaker with ice and strain into an ice-filled glass.

DEATH IN THE AFTERNOON

1 Shot Absinthe
Champagne

Shake the absinthe with ice, strain and top up with champagne. Created by Ernest Hemmingway.

DIPLOMAT

2 Shots Dry Vermouth
2 Shot Sweet Vermouth
Dash Marashino

Stir all the ingredients in an ice-filled shaker and strain into a tumbler filled with ice.

DIXIE

2 Shots Gin
2 Shots Dry Martini
Dash Absinthe

Shake all ingredients with ice and strain into a chilled Martini glass.

DUBONNET COCKTAIL

2 Shots Dubonnet
2 Shots Dry Gin

Shake the ingredients with ice and strain into a chilled Martini glass.

DOCTOR

1 Shot Golden Rum
1 Shot Swedish Punsch
½ Shot Freshly Squeezed Lemon Juice

Shake all ingredients in an ice-filled shaker and strain into a chilled Martini glass.

DOLCE-AMARO

1 Shot Campari
1 Shot Dry Vermouth
1/2 Shot Amaretto

Stir all ingredients with ice and strain into a chilled glass.

DOWNHILL RACER

2 Shots Golden Rum
1 Shot Amaretto
2 Shots Freshly Squeezed Pineapple Juice

Shake all ingredients in an ice-filled shaker and strain into a chilled glass.

DRY MARTINI

1 Shot Gin
Dry Vermouth
1 Green Olive or Lemon Zest

Add a drop or two of vermouth into a mixing glass filled with ice. Stir and strain out the excess liquid. Add more ice, the gin and stir again. Wait until the mixing glass has frosted, then strain into a chilled Martini glass. Garnish with either a strip of lemon zest or a green olive.

The origins of the Martini are hotly contested and shrouded in mystery. Some argue that the man who first conceived of the Martini was Martini di Arma di Taggia, bartender at New York's Knickerbocker Hotel in the late nineteenth century, though this is guaranteed to raise temperatures amongst cocktail aficionados. Others argue the name came from the Californian town Martinez where a gold miner drank the first Martinez Special as far back as 1849. A few argue it evolved from the Manhattan into the Martinez, a Manhattan made with gin rather than whiskey.

However and and whoever invented it, for several decades the name Martini applied to any drink containing varying quantities of gin and/or vodka and vermouth and purists still define it as such. By the 1950s the drink we now know began to appear in cocktail books, traditionally stirred rather than shaken.

David Niven, *My Man Godfrey*

MY MAN GODFREY (1936)
Directed by Gregory La Cava

Starring Carole Lombard and William Powell

This is regarded as one of the 1930's most delightful, classic screwball comedies, appealing to depression era audiences. It was nominated for six Oscars. The screenplay by Morrie Ryskind and Eric Hatch was based on Hatch's short novel *1011 Fifth Avenue*.

The film displays the wacky characters of a wildly prosperous, unconventional family who employ a tramp to be their butler after finding in a hobo colony. This new position allows him ample opportunity for carrying and sampling trays of Martinis. He teaches them the realities of life, and eventually renews their perplexed, bewildering lives, and reverses the nobility of rich and poor. Finally they make the discovery that he is richer than they are.

It was the first film to receive nominations in all four acting categories and it remains one of the few films with that distinction.

EARTHQUAKE

1 Shot Gin
1 Shot Whisky
1 Shot Absinthe

Shake all ingredients with ice and strain into a chilled glass. If there is an earthquake happening while you are drinking, you won't notice it.

EAST INDIA COCKTAIL

½ Shot Pineapple Juice
½ Shot Orange Curacao
3 Shots Brandy
Dash Angostura Bitters

Shake all ingredients with ice and strain into a chilled glass.

EMBASSY ROYAL

1¾ Shots Bourbon
1 Shot Drambuie
1 Shot Red Vermouth
1 Shot Freshly Squeezed Orange Juice

Shake all ingredients with ice and strain into a chilled glass.

EL DIABLO

2 Shots Tequila
¾ Shot Crème de Cassis
1 Shot Freshly Squeezed Lime Juice
Ginger Beer

Shake the tequila, creme de cassis and lime juice in an ice-filled shaker and strain into a Collins glass filled with ice. Top up with ginger beer.

EMPIRE

1 Shot Apricot Brandy
1 Shot Calvados
2 Shots Gin

Shake all ingredients with ice and strain into a chilled glass.

ENGLISH GARDEN

2 Shots Gin
3 Shots Cloudy Apple Juice
½ Shot Elderflower Cordial
½ Shot Freshly Squeezed Lime Juice

Shake all ingredients with ice and strain into a glass filled with ice.

EPISCOPAL

1½ Shots Green Chartreuse
1½ Shots Yellow Chartreuse

Stir ingredients with ice and strain into a chilled glass.

E.T.

½ Shot Melon Liqueur
½ Shot Baileys Irish Cream
½ Shot Vodka

Layer the ingredients in a chilled shot glass.

FALLEN ANGEL

1 Shot Gin
Dash White Crème de Menthe
Dash Angostura Bitters
Dash Freshly Squeezed Lemon Juice

Pour all the ingredients into a cocktail shaker filled with ice. Shake well. Strain into a cocktail glass.

FASCINATOR

1 Shot Sweet Vermouth
2 Shots Gin
Sprig of Fresh Mint
2 Dashes Absinthe

Shake all ingredients in an ice-filled shaker and strain into a Martini glass.

FERNET BRANCA COCKTAIL

This recipe relies heavily on the power of herbs, and is a favourite remedy prescribed by many leading barmen. Fernet Branca is made in Italy and contains extracts from over forty herbs. It was first sold in 1844 by the Branca family – hence its name.

Among others, the herbs include aloe vera, angelica, camomile, cinchona, (from which quinine is prepared), gentian, peppermint, saffron, rue and wormwood.

1 Shot Fernet Branca
1 Shot Sweet Vermouth
1 Shot Gin

Pour all ingredients into a cocktail shaker filled with ice. Shake. Strain into a cocktail glass.

Joan Bennett, *Scarlet Street*

THE THIN MAN   (1934)
Directed by W. S. Van Dyke

Starring William Powell and Myrna Loy

The film was nominated for an Oscar for Best Picture and the script written by Albert Hackett and Frances Goodrich was based on the novel *The Thin Man* by Dashiell Hammett. It was the first in a series of six films.

The film is on the United States National Film Registry after it was judged to have filled the criteria of being culturally, historically, or aesthetically significant.

The 'Thin Man' eluded to the lead suspect, but practically everyone thought it refered to Nick Charles.

Nick (Powell), a former detective who enjoys a drink and Nora Charles, a wealthy heiress (Loy) are a married couple who engage in badinage as they use their considerable deductive skills to solve crimes. They are accompanied on their adventures their dog, Asta (played by Skippy).

Nick and Nora are trying to enjoy their retirement when Nick is called back to his former job by an old friend, Clyde Wynant's disappearance and his possible connection with a murder. Wynant's ex girlfriend has been found dead and he is a chief suspect. His daughter, Dorothy, refuses to believe he is to blame. She persuades Nick to take up the case, a situation that Nora finds highly entertaining. With a habitual drink wryly amused expression Nick heads off to look for clues. Events are complicated as more alcohol is consumed and more people perish along the way. In between the witty repartee Nick and Nora begin to get to the bottom of the crime. The murderer is finally exposed during a dinner party surrounded by all the other suspects.

FLIP

2 Shots Spirit (Gin, Brandy, Whisky etc)
1 Shot Sugar Syrup
½ Shot Fresh Double Cream

Shake ingredients with ice and strain into a chilled glass.

FLYING SCOTSMAN

2 Shots Whisky
2 Shots Sweet Vermouth
2 Dashes Angostura Bitters

Stir ingredients with ice and strain into a tall glass filled with ice.

FOG CUTTER

1 Shot Rum
½ Shot Cognac
½ Shot Gin
½ Shot Freshly Squeezed Lime Juice
2 Shots Freshly Squeezed Orange Juice

Shake ingredients with ice and strain into a glass filled with ice.

FOG LIFTER

This recipe, designed to lift the fog of despair after a night of heavy gambling losses, was invented by Walt Hudson at the Fabulous Flamingo Hotel in Las Vegas

1 Shot Brandy
1 Shot Pernod
1 Shot Fresh Double Cream
1 Fresh Egg

Mix all the above ingredients in a glass, and serve. Everything should seem clearer after drinking.

FOG HORN

2 Shots Gin
½ Shot Rose's Lime Cordial
Ginger Ale

Pour ingredients into a glass filled with ice.

Charles Hawtrey, *You're Only Young Twice*

FIFTH AVENUE

1 Shot Crème de Cacao
1 Shot Apricot Brandy
1 Shot Fresh Double Cream

Carefully pour ingredients into a liqueur glass. Try to ensure the ingredients do not mix.

FINE AND DANDY

1 Shot Freshly Squeezed Lemon Juice
1 Shot Cointreau or Triple Sec
2 Shots Gin
Dash Angostura Bitters

Shake all ingredients in an ice-filled shaker and strain into a Martini glass.

FIZZ

2 Shots Spirit (Whisky, Vodka, Brandy or Gin)
2 Shots Freshly Squeezed Lemon Juice
½ Shot Sugar Syrup
Top up with Soda

Shake the spirit, lemon juice and sugar syrup in an ice-filled shaker. Strain into a chilled Collins glass and top up with soda.

FOX TROT

2 Shots Bacardi Rum
2 Shots Freshly Squeezed Lime Juice
2 Dashes Orange Curacao

Shake all ingredients in an ice-filled shaker and strain into a chilled Martini glass.

FROUPÉ

2 Shots Sweet Vermouth
2 Shots Brandy
1 Teaspoon Benedictine

Stir all ingredients in an ice-filled shaker and strain into a chilled Martini glass.

FUZZY NAVEL

2 Shots Peach Schnapps
4 Shots Freshly Squeezed Orange Juice

Shake ingredients with ice and strain into an ice-filled tall glass.

FRANKLIN MARTINI

⅔ Shot Gin
⅔ Shot Dry Vermouth
2 Green Olives

Stir Vermouth with the ice and strain to discard the excess, leaving the glass and ice coated with vermouth. Then pour the gin over the vermouth-coated ice and strain into a chilled Martini glass. Garnish with the olives.

The Franklin Martini, named after Franklin Roosevelt, is always served with two olives.

Greer Garson and Lew Ayres, *Remember?*

GIBSON

50ml Gin
Dry Vermouth
2 Chilled Pearl Cocktail Onions on Stick

Fill a mixing glass with ice and pour in a few drops of dry vermouth. Stir for 15 seconds, or until vermouth has coated the ice, then strain out the liquid. Top up mixing glass with ice, add gin and stir until glass is frosted and the mixture is well chilled. Pour into a chilled Martini glass, or over ice into a rocks glass. Garnish with the cocktail onions.

The Gibson is said to have come into being early in the twentieth century. During the 1890s and in the decades that followed the pen-and-ink drawings of Charles Dana Gibson appeared regularly in the glamour magazines of the day. They were as significant then as the supermodels of the twenty-first century. The Gibson was named after the artist and the well-endowed Gibson girls - hence the two onions. Gibson was a member of The Players' Club in New York and the bartender there named Charley Connolly is credited with adding the garnish.

Betty Davis and George Sanders, *All About Eve*

ALL ABOUT EVE (1950)
Directed by Joseph L. Mankiewicz

Starring Bette Davis, Anne Baxter, George Sanders, Celeste Holm, Gary Merrill and Marilyn Monroe.

This gritty, realistic portrayal of show business and life backstage on Broadway was nominated for fourteen awards - more than any other picture in Oscar history, until *Titanic* (1997) equalled it. It one six Academy Awards, including Best Picture.

I*All About Eve* is widely regarded as a cinematic master-piece and one of the all-time classic films where both the acting and directing is flawless.

It is a attack against cunning, wannabe, glib, wannbee female thespians who seek success regardless of the cost and without thought for feelings or other people. The much-admired film also observes the fear that aging and loss of fame holds for many in the profession.

Bette Davis' leading role as Margo Channing is con-sidered by many as her greatest performance. At a time when roles were drying up for Davis the part of an aging, 40-year old Broadway actress fitted the 42-year old Davis brilliantly. The film is distinguished by Davis' memorable line: 'fasten your seatbelts, its going to be a bump night.'

The film was adapted and transformed into a Broadway play called Applause in 1970, with Lauren Bacall as Margo Channing. The film is frequently cited as a 'three suicide movie,' because of the subsequent deaths of three of it's cast, George Sanders, Marilyn Monroe and Barbara Bates.

GIMLET

1 Shot Gin
½ Shot Rose's Lime Cordial
Lime Wedge

Stir all the ingredients with ice and strain into a chilled Martini glass.

A gimlet was a small device originally used to tap barrels of spirits onboard British naval ships in the nineteenth century, and it was a shipyard owner who was responsible for creating Rose's Lime Cordial. In 1867 Lauchlin Rose devised a cordial of fruit juice and sugar, bottled it and patented the recipe and sold it to sailors who drank it to help prevent scurvy on their voyages.

Lauchlin Rose found a captive market for his product, since the Navy was compelled under the 1867 Merchant Shipping Act to carry lime juice to ward off disease. Naval officers on board with access to the gin, combined spirit and cordial to make Gimlets.

BORN TO DANCE (1936)
Directed by Roy Del Ruth

Starring Curt Jurgens, Richard Burton, Raymond Pellegrin, Ruth Roman and Anthony Bushell

This film was a follow up to the dancer, Eleanor Powell triumphant debut in Broadway Melody. Cole Porter wrote the film's score, the first time he had ever written directly for the screen. The plot treads a similar path of numerous other movies of the era. This time a sailor on leave, Ted (Stewart) meets a girl called Nora (Powell), they fall in love and then put on an extravagant cabaret show.

Born to Dance boasts a rare musical number by Stewart and a flamboyant finale called 'Swingin' the Jinx Away'. The film is set against a pre-Second World War naval backdrop, and contains a Depression period 'feel good' number, which lasts for ten minutes. It makes topical jibes at the economy and towards politicians of the time. It ends in a flurry of tap dancing and cannon fire. This finale was copied in a later Powell film, *I Dood It*, which also starred Red Skelton. Despite being good enough to use again, Musical director Roger Edens was often quoted as being embarrassed by the segment.

Porter's 'You'd Be So Easy to Love' (performed by Stewart and Powell) and 'I've Got You Under My Skin', which went on to be nominated for the Academy Award for Best Song.

GIN AND IT

2 Shots Gin
1 Shot Sweet Vermouth

Stir the ingredients with ice and strain into an ice-filled Martini glass.

GIN DAISY

2½ Shots Gin
¼ Shot Grenadine
¼ Shot Freshly Squeezed Lemon Juice

Shake all ingredients in an ice-filled shaker and strain into a glass filled with crushed ice. Stir and serve with straws.

GIN SLING

1½ Shots Gin
1½ Shots Cherry Liqueur
1 Shot Freshly Squeezed Lemon Juice
Soda

Shake the gin, cherry liqueur and lemon juice in an ice filled shaker. Strain into an ice-filled glass and top up with soda.

GIN & TONIC

1 Shot Gin
Tonic Water

Pour ingredients into an ice-filled Collins glass and serve without straws.

Some might argue the gin and tonic is not strictly speaking a cocktail, but in fact it is ranked as a Highball. Certainly it is one of the most popular mixed drinks around and one of the simplest to make.

It is generally accepted that the gin and tonic combination arose out of nineteenth century colonialism and thought to have been first drunk in India by the British and members of the Raj to help prevent disease in the hot climate.

Tonic was drunk throughout the British colonies after Schweppes launched their Indian tonic water in 1870, and even before that the quinine that gives the tonic water its bitter taste had been used specifically for the prevention of malaria. Likewise, gin had already been drunk neat for medicinal purposes as far back as the seventeenth century.

George Clooney, *Out of Sight*

OUT OF SIGHT (1998)
Directed by Steven Soderbergh

Starring George Clooney, Jennifer Lopez, Ving Rhames, Don Cheadle, Steve Zahn Albert Brook, Dennis Farina, Luis Guzman, Isaiah Washington and Michael Keaton

This was the first of a number of collaborations between Soderbergh and George Clooney. Out of Sight was nominated for two Academy Awards (adapted screenplay and editing). It won the Edgar Allan Poe Award for best screenplay and the National Society of Film Critics awards for best film, screenplay, and director. It also led to a spin-off TV series, Karen Sisco.

The story concerns the relationship between a bank robber, Jack Foley (Clooney), and a U.S. Marshal, Karen Sisco (Lopez).

The pair are forced into sharing her car trunk during Foley's escape from a Florida prison. After he completes his getaway, Sisco chases Foley while he and his friends, his right-hand man, Buddy (Rhames) and Glenn (Zahn), work their way north to Bloomfield Hills, a wealthy northern suburb of Detroit.

It is here they plan to pay a visit to shady businessman Ripley (Brooks), who foolishly bragged to them years before about a diamond stash he hides at his mansion. But a vicious criminal (Cheadle), who also spent time in jail with Jack and Ripley, is planning on raiding Ripley's mansion with his crew (consisting of Keith Loneker and Isaiah Washington) as well.

The question of whether Sisco is really pursuing Foley to arrest him or because she has fallen for him adds to the fun Foley claims they are having throughout the film.

GLOOM CHASER

1 Shot Grenadine
1 Shot Grand Marnier
1 Shot Orange Curaçao
1 Shot Freshly Squeezed Lemon Juice

Shake all ingredients in an ice-filled shaker and strain into a Martini glass.

This is a comparatively late pick-me-up that enjoyed popularity among the hippy generation who haunted the Tokyo Club bar in Rome, in the Sixties. Olive oil supplements the fat in the egg yolk, but like other eggnogs the brandy provides the hair of the dog, and the paprika gives it an unusual kick and enhances the Worcestershire sauce.

GODFATHER

2 Shots Scotch
1 Shot Amaretto Liqueur

Stir ingredients with ice and strain into an ice-filled glass.

GRAND MIMOSA

1 Shot Grand Marnier
2 Shots Freshly Squeezed Orange Juice
Champagne

Shake the Grand Marnier and orange juice in an ice-filled shaker and strain into a chilled flute glass. Top up with champagne.

HAIR OF THE DOG

1 Shot Scotch Whisky
1 Shot Single Cream
3 Barspoons Honey

Pour all the ingredients into a cocktail shaker filled with cracked ice. Strain into a Martini glass.

P. G. Wodehouse devised a recipe that the ever-faithful and tactful Jeeves served Bertie Wooster whenever his morning was troubled by a severe hangover. Some suggest that the use of honey maintains higher blood sugar than other sugars, but actually the opposite is true. The long-term success of Jeeves's cocktail is due to the fact that the alcohol and the sugary honey are combined with cream. Cream contains fat and protein that prevent the rapid absorption of this comparatively sweet drink.

Sydney Greenstreet, *The Way With Women*

HANKY PANKY

1 Shot Sweet Vermouth
1 Shot Gin
2 Dashes Fernet Branca

Shake all ingredients in an ice-filled shaker and strain into a chilled Martini glass.

HARRY'S PICK-ME-UP

1 Shot Brandy
1 Teaspoon Grenadine
Freshly Squeezed Lemon Juice
Champagne

Shake all the ingredients, except the Champagne, in a cocktail shaker filled with ice. Strain into a Champagne flute.

This is a simple mixture that was served by Salvatore Calabrese during his tenure at London's Lanesborough Bar, but it could be made in any household – even by someone whose head is pounding and whose brain is stultified. The grenadine adds distinction to a standard pick-me-up.

HEART STARTER

½ Shot Fernet Branca
½ Shot Crème de Menthe
Pernod

Stir the first two ingredients over ice until well-chilled, then strain into a glass. Float a liberal dash of Pernod on top.

The rest of the world thinks of Australians as beer-drinkers. John Burgess of the Diamond Bar at the Menzies Hotel in Sydney, Australia, developed this recipe which, so they say, will dispatch the worst of a beer-induced hangover. A refinement of the treatment is to sniff the drink first so that the Pernod can be inhaled to clear the head and improve the feel and taste of the mouth.

HEAVEN'S ABOVE

2 Shots Golden Rum
¼ Shot Dark Creme de Cacao
½ Shot Coffee Liqueur
3 Shots Pineapple Juice

Shake all ingredients with ice and pour into a glass filled with ice.

HEMINGWAY

1 Shot Anis
Champagne

Pour the anis into a chilled flute glass and top up with
Champagne.

HOBSON'S CHOICE

2½ Shots Cloudy Apple Juice
2½ Shots Freshly Squeezed Orange Juice
1 Shot Freshly Squeezed Lime Juice
½ Shot Grenadine

Shake all ingredients in an ice-filled shaker and strain
into a glass filled with ice.

HONEY BEE

2 Shots Light White Rum
2 Spoons Runny Honey
½ Shot Freshly Squeezed Lemon Juice

Stir the vodka and honey in a shaker. Add ice and
lemon juice, shake and strain into a chilled glass.

HOP TOAD

3 Shots Apricot Brandy
1 Shot Freshly Squeezed Lemon Juice

Shake ingredients in an ice-filled shaker and strain into a glass filled with ice.

HOT SHOT

¾ Shot Galliano
¾ Shot Hot Espresso Coffee
½ Shot Double Cream

Layer the ingredients in a shot glass. Begin with the galliano, then the coffee and top off with the cream.

HURRICANE

1 Shot Whisky
1 Shot Gin
1 Shot Crème de Menthe
2 Shots Freshly Squeezed Lemon Juice

Shake all ingredients in an ice-filled shaker and strain into a glass filled with ice.

ICED TEA

½ Shot Cognac
½ Shot Rum
½ Shot Cointrea or Triple Sec
½ Shot Freshly Squeezed Orange Juice
½ Shot Freshly Squeezed Lemon Juice
2 Shots Cold Tea
Coca Cola

Shake all but the Coke in an ice-filled shaker. Pour into a tall glass filled with ice and top up with the coke.

IDEAL

1 Shot Sweet Vermouth
2 Shots Gin
1 Tablespoon Grapefruit Juice
3 Dashes Marashino Liqueur

Shake all ingredients in an ice-filled shaker and strain into a glass filled with ice.

IMPERIAL

1 Shot Dry Vermouth
1 Shot Gin
Dash Marashino Liqueur
Dash Angostura Bitters

Stir all ingredients on ice and strain into a chilled Martini glass. Garnish with a green olive.

INCOGNITO

1½ Shots Dry Vermouth
1½ Shots Cognac
1 Shot Apricot Brandy
3 Dashes Angostura Bitters

Shake all ingredients in an ice-filled shaker and strain into a chilled Martini glass.

INK STREET

1 Shot Whisky
1 Shot Freshly Squeezed Orange Juice
1 Shot Freshly Squeezed Lemon Juice

Shake all ingredients in an ice-filled shaker and strain into a chilled Martini glass.

IRISH COFFEE

1 Shot Irish Whisky
Hot Filter Coffee
Lightly Whipped Fresh Cream

Pour whisky in a tall glass, top up with the coffee and stir. Float the cream on top.

IRISH FLAG

1 Shot Bailey's Irish Cream
1 Shot Grand Marnier
1 Shot White Crème de Menthe

Layer ingredients in the above order into a chilled glass.

IRISH LATTE

1 Shot Baileys Irish Cream
1 Shot Hot Espresso Coffee
Hot Milk

Pour ingredients in the above order into a tall glass.

JACK COLLINS

2 Shots Applejack Brandy or Calvados
1 Shot Freshly Squeezed Lemon Juice
½ Shot Sugar Syrup
Soda

Shake the brandy, lemon juice and sugar syrup in a shaker.
Strain into a glass filled with ice and top up with the soda.

JACKSON

1 Shot Dubonnet
1 Shot Gin
2 Dashes Orange Bitters

Stir all the ingredients with ice and strain into a Martini Glass.

JAYNE MANSFIELD

4 Fresh Strawberries
1 Shot Light White Rum
1 Shot Crème de Fraise
¼ Shot Sugar Syrup
Champagne

Muddle the strawberries in a shaker before adding the
rum, liqueur and sugar syrup. Shake with ice and strain
into a flute glass. Top up with the champagne.

JOCKEY CLUB

2 Shots Gin
½ Shot Amaretto Liqueur
½ Shot Freshly Squeezed Lemon Juice
1 Dash Orange Bitters
1 Dash Angostura Bitters

Shake all ingredients in an ice-filled shaker. Strain into a chilled Martini glass.

JOHN COLLINS

2 Shots Gin
1 Shot Freshly Squeezed Lemon Juice
½ Shot Sugar Syrup
Soda

Shake the gin, lemon juice and sugar syrup in an ice-filled shaker. Strain into an ice-filled glass and top up with soda.

JOHNNIE MACK

2 Shots Sloe Gin
2 Shot Orange Curaçao
3 Dashes Absinthe

Shake all ingredients in an ice-filled shaker and strain into a chilled Martini glass.

JOURNALIST

1 Shot Sweet Vermouth
1 Shot Dry Vermouth
2 Shots Gin
2 Dashes Freshly Squeezed Lemon Juice
1 Dash Angostura Bitters

Shake all ingredients in an ice-filled shaker and strain into a chilled Martini glass.

JUMPING JACK FLASH

1½ Shots Whisky
1 Shot Galliano Liqueur
1 Shot Freshly Squeezed Orange Juice
1 Shot Pineapple Juice

Shake all ingredients in an ice-filled shaker and strain into a chilled glass.

JOAN BENNETT

2 Shots Rum
1 Shot Parfait Amour
1 Shot Pressed Pineapple Juice

Shake ingredients with ice and strain into an ice-filled glass.

JUPITER MARTINI

2 Shots Gin
1 Shot Dry Vermouth
1 Teaspoon Parfait Amour Liqueur
1 Teaspoon Shot Freshly Squeezed Orange Juice

Shake all ingredients in an ice-filled shaker and strain into a chilled glass.

KIR ROYALE

½ Shot Crème de Cassis
Brut Champagne

Pour the Crème de Cassis into a Champagne flute, then top up slowly with chilled dry Champagne.

Easy to make and easy to drink, the Kir arose in honour of a French Canon named Felix Kir where it was originally made with white wine. An unbeatable combination.

James Stewart and Katherine Hepburn, *The Philadelphia Story*

PHILADELPHIA STORY (1940)
Directed by George Cukor

Starring Cary Grant, Katharine Hepburn and James Stewart

A socialite's wedding plans are complicated by the simultaneous arrival of her ex-husband and an attractive journalist.

Hepburn had had a string of movie flops and became known as 'box office poison'. She bought the film rights to the play of the same name in order to control it as a vehicle for her movie comeback. The film was a great success and was nominated for six Oscars. It won two: Stewart for Best Actor and Donald Ogden Stewart for Best Adapted Screenplay. In 1956 it was remade as the musical High Society.

The plot concerns Tracy Samantha Lord Haven (Hepburn), a well-to-do Philadelphia socialite who has divorced C.K. Dexter Haven (Grant), because he failed measure up to her standard. She is set to marry another rich man, George Kittredge (John Howard).

Then journalists Macaulay 'Mike' Connor (Stewart) and photographer Liz Imbrie (Ruth Hussey) turn up to report on the wedding. Tracy gradually finds her head turned by Mike and as the wedding nears, she finds herself torn between her fiancé, her ex-husband, and the reporter. After a clutch of misunderstandings, the engagement is broken off, Mike proposes, but Dexter wins his ex-wife's hand.

The film was shot in eight weeks, apparently with no retakes, and came in five days under schedule. At one point, James Stewart hiccupped on camera. Grant turned to him, surprised, and said, 'Excuse me?' There was no retake and the scene remained in the final cut.

LEAP YEAR

2 Shots Gin
½ Shot Apricot Brandy or Grand Marnier
½ Shot Dry Vermouth
Dash Grenadine

Shake all ingredients in an ice-filled shaker and strain into a well chilled Martini glass.

LEAVE IT TO ME

1½ Shots Gin
¼ Shot Apricot Brandy or Grand Marnier
¼ Shot Dry Vermouth
Dash Freshly Squeezed Lemon Juice
Dash Grenadine

Shake all ingredients in an ice-filled shaker and strain into a chilled Martini glass.

LEMON PIE

1 Shot Whisky
Lemonade

Pour the whisky into an ice-filled glass. Top up with lemonade.

LIMA SOUR

2 Shots Pisco Brandy
1 Shot Freshly Squeezed Lime Juice
½ Shot Maraschino Liqueur
¾ Shot Sugar Syrup
¾ Shot Grapefruit Juice

Blend all ingredients with a handful of crushed ice and pour into a tall glass.

LITTLE DEVIL

2 Shots Bacardi Rum
2 Shots Gin
1 Shot Cointreau or Triple Sec
1 Shot Freshly Squeezed Lemon Juice

Shake all ingredients in an ice-filled shaker and strain into a chilled Martini glass.

LITTLE PRINCESS

1 Shot Bacardi Rum
1 Shot Dry Vermouth

Shake all ingredients in an ice-filled shaker and strain into a chilled Martini glass.

LONDON

1 Shot Gin
2 Dashes Orange Bitters
2 Dashes Sugar Syrup
2 Dashes Absinthe

Shake all ingredients in an ice-filled shaker and strain into a chilled Martini glass.

LOUD SPEAKER

1 Shot Gin
1 Shot Brandy
½ Shot Cointreau or Triple Sec
½ Shot Freshly Squeezed Lemon Juice

Shake ingredients in an ice-filled shaker and strain into a chilled Martini glass.

LOTUS

1 Shot Vodka
1 Shot Lychee Juice (from tin)
Champagne

Shake the vodka and juice with ice. Strain into a glass and top up with champagne.

MANHATTAN

1 Shot Rye Whiskey
1 Shot Sweet Vermouth
Orange Bitters
Orange Zest
2 Maraschino Cherries

Pour the whiskey, the vermouth and the bitters into an ice-filled mixing glass. Stir until the mixture is chilled and blended, then strain into a frosted Martini glass. Garnish with a Maraschino cherry and a strip of orange zest.

The Manhattan was originally made with rye whiskey, although now many barmen substitute bourbon, when it becomes a Rob Roy. It first began to appear in cocktail books from the 1880s. Some believe it was invented at the Manhattan Club in New York for Lady Randolph Churchill on 18th November 1874 opposite what is now the Empire State Building.

It is said that night she attended a party to celebrate the successful gubernatorial campaign of Samuel Jones Tilden. Others maintain it was created much earlier in the 1860s by a bartender named Black who worked in a saloon on Broadway. In 2005 it was served garnished with two cherries as a 9/11 tribute.

Elizabeth Taylor, *Butterfield 8*

BUTTERFIELD 8 (1960)
Directed by Daniel Mann

Starring Elizabeth Taylor, Laurence Harvey, Eddie Fisher and Dina Merrill

Elizabeth Taylor apparently hated starring in this feature, based on the novel of the same name by John O'Hara, though she was contracted to it for her then standard fee of $125,000. Despite this, the role enabled her to win her first Academy Award for Best Actress, after four unsuccessful nominations. In the movie she plays Gloria Wandrous, a model and hedonistic party girl who falls for Western Liggett (Laurence Harvey), an emotionally distant man, who comes from a working class background and has married into money. Gloria and Weston bond over their lack of self-confidence and frustration at their lives, gradually their secrets as their fondness for drinking. As the story enfolds they fall in love, and the drama enfolds around whether Gloria can commit to one man and whether Weston will leave his wife Emily (Dina Merril).

Their stormy relationship ultimately shatters the lives of those around them, ending in tragedy for Gloria.

MADRAS

2 Shots Vodka
3 Shots Cranberry Juice
2 Shots Freshly Squeezed Orange Juice

Shake all ingredients in an ice-filled shaker and strain into a glass filled with ice.

MAE WEST MARTINI

2 Shots Vodka
½ Shot Amaretto Liqueur
1½ Shots Cranberry Juice
Dash Melon Liqueur

Shake all ingredients in an ice-filled shaker and strain into a chilled Martini glass.

MAIDEN'S BLUSH

2 Shots Gin
4 Dashes Orange Curacao
3 Dashes Grenadine
1 Dash Freshly Squeezed Lemon Juice

Shake all ingredients in an ice-filled shaker and strain into a chilled glass.

MAIDEN'S PRAYER

1½ Shots Gin
1 Shot Cointreau or Triple Sec
½ Shot Freshly Squeezed Orange Juice
½ Shot Freshly Squeezed Lemon Juice

Shake all ingredients in an ice-filled shaker and strain into a chilled glass.

MARTINEZ

1½ Shots Gin
1½ Shots Sweet Vermouth
Dash Cointreau or Triple Sec

Stir all ingredients with ice and strain into a chilled glass.

MARY PICKFORD

2 Shots Rum
2 Shots Pineapple Juice
¼ Shot Grenadine
Dash Marashino

Shake ingredients in an ice-filled shaker and strain into a chilled glass.

MAI TAI

1 Shot Demerara Rum
Freshly Squeezed Lemon Juice
Freshly Squeezed Lime Juice
Orange Curacao
Apricot Brandy
Orgeat Syrup
Angostura Bitters
Pineapple Juice
2 Mint Leaves
Slice of Pineapple
Sprig of Mint

Pour the rum and large dashes of lemon juice, lime juice and orgeat syrup into a cocktail shaker filled with cracked ice. Add small shots of apricot brandy and orange curacao, two dashes of Angostura bitters, a large measure of pineapple juice and two mint leaves. Shake the mixture sharply; pour into a rocks glass. Garnish with a slice of pineapple and a sprig of mint.

MARGARITA

1 Shot Tequila
½ Shot Freshly Squeezed Lime Juice
½ Shot Triple Sec or Cointreau

Rub the rim of a Margarita glass with a wedge of lime and dip the rim into the salt. Place all the ingredients into a cocktail shaker filled with ice. Shake well and strain into the glass. For the perfect Margarita liquidize sea salt to make it finer. Rimming just half the glass gives the option of enjoying the cocktail with salt or without.

Although many theories as to who invented the Margarita are in circulation today, there is one regarded more highly than the rest. In 1948 Margaret Sames held a glamorous party at her house in Acapulco, Mexico. It is said that she began playing at the bar with different ingredients for something to liven up the occasion and stumbled across the combination that then became the Margarita.

After the party she completely forgot about it, until flying home to San Antonio from Acapulco she noticed a bar selling 'Margarita's Drink', a cocktail exactly the same as the one she had mixed at the party.

Clark Gable and Constance Bennett, *After Office Hours*

AFTER OFFICE HOURS (1935)
Directed by Robert Z. Leonard

Starring Clark Gable and Constance Bennett

Socialite Constance Bennett gets a job as a reporter on a big-city newspaper. Soon she and put upon editor, Clark Gable, are up to their necks in a murder mystery when the wife in a major divorce case is killed. The finger of suspicion falls on Bennett's boyfriend and he is accused of the crime. More interested in Bennett than the story, Gable tracks down the murderer and free the boyfriend who courteously steps aside, allowing Gable and Bennett, who, of course, have loved each other right from the start, to go and get married.

Time Out said that it was a typical standard depression era plot, with Gable 'overdoing the brashness as a working newspaperman who resents the socialite, Bennett he assumes to be shirking when she joins the paper's staff. Their love-hate affair, conducted in pretty flat wisecracks, comes to a head when a friend of hers is murdered and he tracks down the killer. Fine Charles Rosher camerawork, otherwise unremarkable'.

While Channel 4 said that 'Gable is the tough newspaper editor (was there any other kind in mid-30s Hollywood?). With a glamorous socialite (Bennett) who wants a job on his paper, he gets to solve a murder. The victim is another society woman and the killer turns out to be her husband. Not, then, terribly original as a story, even to the romantic end when editor and would-be journalist marry. But efficiently directed by Leonard, and the stars are eminently watchable'.

MAYFAIR

2 Shots Gin
1 Shot Apricot Brandy
1 Shot Freshly Squeezed Orange Juice
2 Cloves

Muddle the cloves in a shaker and add the remaining ingredients. Shake with ice and strain into a chilled glass.

MERRY WIDOW

1½ Shots Gin
1½ Shots Dry Vermouth
2 Dashes Absinthe
2 Dashes Benedictine
3 Dashes Angostura Bitters

Stir all ingredients in an ice-filled shaker and strain into a chilled glass.

MILANO

1 Shot Vodka
1 Shot Campari
1 Shot Sweet Vermouth

Stir all ingredients with ice and strain into a glass filled with ice.

MILLIONAIRE COCKTAIL

1 Shot Sloe Gin
1 Shot Apricot Brandy
1 Shot Rum
¼ Shot Freshly Squeezed Lime Juice
Dash Grenadine

Shake all ingredients in an ice-filled shaker and strain
into a chilled glass.

MIMOSA

½ Shot Grand Marnier
2 Shots Freshly Squeezed Orange Juice
Champagne

Pour the ingredients into a chilled glass and stir gently.

MINT COCKTAIL

Handful Fresh Mint leaves
2 Shots Gin
1 Shot Dry White Wine
¼ Shot Crème de Menthe
¼ Shot Sugar Syrup

Muddle the mint in a shaker. Add the other ingredients,
shake with ice and strain into a chilled glass.

MINT COLLINS

2 Shots Gin
1 Shot Freshly Squeezed Lime Juice
¼ Shot Sugar Syrup
Handful Fresh Mint Leaves
Soda

Muddle the mint leaves in the shaker. Add the lime juice, gin and sugar syrup and shake with ice. Strain into a glass filled with ice. Top with soda.

MINT FIZZ

2 Shots Gin
1 Shot Freshly Squeezed Lime Juice
½ Shot Sugar Syrup
Handful Fresh Mint Leaves
Soda

Muddle the mint in the base of a shaker. Add the gin, lime juice and sugar syrup. Shake with ice and strain into a glass filled with ice. Top up with soda.

MINT JULEP

1 Shot Bourbon or Whisky
5 Sprigs of Fresh Mint Leaves
Sugar Syrup
Soda (or Water)

Lightly muddle the mint leaves and sugar together with the spirit in the base of a shaker until the sugar has dissolved and the flavour of the mint has been extracted. Add the other ingredients, shake and strain into a glass filled with crushed ice and stir. Garnish with a mint sprig and serve with straws.

The secret is to serve it ice cold. If possible, put the shaker in the fridge with the mint and spirit in advance. It is important to only bruise the mint and not to crush them, since crushing the leaves will release the bitter juices.

The name Julep is originally from the Arabic 'julab' meaning rosewater. It was soon absorbed into Western drinking culture, originally served in Julep cups, and soon became a firm favourite in the Southern States where it has been drunk at 4th July festivities ever since. In its earliest incarnations it was made with brandy, rum or whisky, but by the turn of the last century whisky had become the norm. It was brought across the Atlantic by Frederick Marryat, a writer, who would be woken every morning by a slave brandishing the drink.

MOJITO

1 Shot Light White Rum
¼ Shot Freshly Squeezed Lime Juice
Dash of Sugar Syrup
Fresh Mint Leaves
Soda

Place mint leaves into a Collins glass and add rum. Muddle just enough to bruise the leaves. Add the ice, lime juice and sugar syrup. Top up with soda, churn and stir. Serve with straws.

The home of the Mojito is Cuba and the Bodeguita del Medio bar in Havana is universally credited with having invented the Mojito, regularly and famously patronised by the likes of Ernest Hemmingway.

Legend has it that the first Mojito was actually mixed centuries earlier by a pirate named Richard Drake, who introduced the drink to Cuba when sailing the high seas hunting for treasure in the Caribbean and South Americas. It is said he used unrefined rum or aguardiente and named the drink 'El Draque', the dragon, after his onetime commander Sir Francis Drake.

MONKEY GLAND

2 Shots Gin
¼ Shot Absinthe
1 Shot Grenadine
1½ Shots Freshly Squeezed Orange Juice

Shake all ingredients in an ice-filled shaker and strain into a chilled glass.

MONZA

2 Shots Vodka
2 Shots Campari
2 Shots Apple Juice
¼ Shot Sugar Syrup
Juice of 1 Passion Fruit

Shake all ingredients in an ice-filled shaker and strain into an ice-filled glass.

MOONSHINE

1½ Shots Gin
1 Shot Dry Vermouth
½ Shot Maraschino
Dash Absinthe

Shake all ingredients with ice and strain into a chilled glass.

MULE'S HIND LEG

1 Shot Benedictine
1 Shot Calvados
1 Shot Gin
Dash Applejack
Dash Maple Syrup
Dash Apricot Brandy

Shake all ingredients in an ice-filled shaker and strain into a chilled Martini glass.

MULLED WINE

2 Shots Red Wine
Teaspoon Grand Marnier
Teaspoon Freshly Squeezed Lemon Juice
5 Cloves
Pinch Nutmeg
Pinch Cinnamon
Hot Water

Warm the ingredients in a saucepan. Pour into a warmed toddy glass.

MOSCOW MULE

1 Shot Vodka
½ Shot Freshly Squeezed Lime Juice
¼ Shot Sugar surup
Ginger Beer
Lime Wedge

Shake the vodka, lime juice and sugar syrup with ice and strain into an ice-filled glass. Top up with ginger beer and garnish with a lime wedge.

The classic combination of vodka and ginger beer was the brain child of two men over a drink at New York's Chatham Bar in 1941. Jack Morgan was launching his own ginger beer, while John G. Martin had bought the trademark brand of Smirnoff Vodka for a small distribution company in Conneticut named Hublein. In deciding to combine forces and mix the two ingredients together, they created a lasting cocktail great.

The drink was initially advertised with a promotional gimic, when special Moscow Mule mugs engraved with a kicking mule were sold alongside the Vodka. If you can find one nowadays, they are a collector's item.

Jack Lemmon, *The Apartment*

THE APARTMENT (1960)
Directed by Billy Wilder

Starring Jack Lemmon, Shirley MacLaine and Fred MacMurray

C. C. Baxter (Lemmon) is an insurance worker in New York and lives a sedentary life. His flat is regularly commandeered by four different company managers for each of their adulterous affairs. He fails to stand up to them and instead tries to coordinate each of their requirements. He longs to get the attention of the elevator operator Fran Kubelik (MacLaine). Because of the amount of women coming and going from his apartment, Baxter's neighbours think he is a predatory womaniser. To protect his bosses he keeps the truth to himself.

To reward Baxter for his forbearance the managers write flattering reports about him but the personnel director Mr. Sheldrake (Fred MacMurray) grows suspicious. Mr. Sheldrake allows Baxter's promotion to go ahead but only if he can use his apartment for his extramarital excursions. Buoyed by his promotion, Baxter asks Miss Kubelik out. She acquiesces but stands him up. On Christmas Eve, Baxter is surprised to discover her in his bed having taken an overdose. Mr. Sheldrake is using the flat that night. She comes round and explains she has been having an affair with Mr Sheldrake. She attempted suicide when the ghastly reality of the affair hit home.

Kubelik stays in the apartment to recuperate. Mrs Sheldrake finds out about the affair and Mr Sheldrake moves out and continues to see Kubelik while also enjoying the single life. Sheldrake demands the apartment for New Year's Eve, and Baxter quits his job. Kubelik, realising Baxter loves her leaves Sheldrake on New Year's Eve to see Baxter. Both unemployed they play gin rummy. Baxter tells her he loves her to which she replies 'Shut up and deal.'

OLD CHAPPIE

4 Shots Beer
½ Shot Freshly Squeezed Lime Juice
Dash Angostura Bitters

Pour the ingredients over crushed ice in a 12-oz glass. Stir and serve with a straw.

OLD FASHIONED

50ml Bourbon
1 White Sugar Cube
Orange Bitters
Orange Zest

Place the sugar cube into a rocks glass and add the bourbon. Mix together with a spoon. Add ice throughout the process, stirring continuously until the sugar has dissolved. Add a dash of orange bitters and serve with a strip of orange zest.

OLD PAL

1 Shot Bourbon
1 Shot Dry Vermouth
1 Shot Campari

Mix togetherwith ice and strain into a glass filled with ice.

OPAL

2 Shots Gin
½ Shot Cointreau or Triple Sec
1 Shot Freshly Squeezed Orange Juice
¼ Shot Sugar Syrup

Shake all ingrdients in an ice-filled shaker and strain into a chilled Martini glass.

OPENING SHOT

1 Shot Bourbon
½ Shot Sweet Vermouth
Dash Grenadine

Shake all ingredients in an ice-filled shaker. Strain into a glass filled with ice.

OPERA

2 Shots Gin
1 Shots Dubonnet
1 Shot Maraschino

Shake all ingredients in an ice-filled shaker. Strain into a chilled Martini glass.

ORANGE BLOOM

2 Shots Gin
1 Shot Cointreau or Triple Sec
1 Shot Sweet Vermouth

Shake all ingredients in an ice-filled shaker and strain into a chilled glass.

ORANGE MARTINI

2 Shots Gin
2 Shots Dry Vermouth
2 Shots Sweet Vermouth
1 Shot Orange Bitters
1 Shot Freshly Squeezed Orange Juice
Rind of One Orange

Muddle the orange rind in the base of a shaker. Add the gin, vermouth, orange juice and orange bitters and shake with ice. Strain into a chilled Martini glass.

PADDY

1 Shot Irish Whisky
1 Shot Dry Vermouth
Dash Angostura Bitters

Shake all ingredients in an ice-filled shaker and strain into a chilled glass.

PAISLEY MARTINI

2 Shots Gin
½ Shot Dry Vermouth
¼ Shot Whisky

Stir all ingredients with ice and strain into a a chilled glass.

PARADISE

1 Shot Gin
1 Shot Freshly Squeezed Orange Juice
½ Shot Apricot Brandy
Dash Freshly Squeezed Lemon Juice

Shake all ingredients in an ice-filled shaker and strain into an ice-filled Martini glass.

PARISIEN BLONDE

1 Shot Fresh Double Cream
1 Shot Curacao
1 Shot Rum

Shake all ingredients in an ice-filled shaker and strain into an ice-filled Martini glass.

PARK AVENUE

2 Shots Gin
½ Shot Grand Marnier
½ Shot Sweet Vermouth
1 Shot Pineapple Juice

Shake all ingredients in an ice-filled shaker and strain into a chilled glass.

PHEASANT RUNNER

Despite its exotic name, few hard-core drinkers would be likely to rush for the pick-me-up offered by the Pheasant Run in St Charles, Illinois.

The thought of combining beer, tomato juice and vodka is certainly not immediately attractive, but for those who feel so awful that there is no hope, the idea that anything could be better than nothing might prevail.

1 Shot Vodka
2 Shots Tomato Juice
5 Shots Beer

Mix together and serve.

PIMM'S CUP

1 Shot Pimm's No 1 Cup
Lemonade or 7-up
Cucumber
Strawberry
Fresh Mint Leaves

Pour Pimm's over ice into a glass part-filled with ice. Add the fruit and fill the glass with more ice. Then add the lemonade. Finish off with a sprig of mint. Serve with a straw.

When James Pimm began trading in shellfish in 1823 in the city of London he could not have foreseen the impact he would have on summer al fresco drinking. Gradually his business expanded and in 1840 at his Oyster Warehouse at number 3 Poultry he first served his unique concoction.

However, as with many cocktails, there are some sceptics who dispute the validity of the story. Some experts hold that James Pimm was not the true inventor of the drink and that it was his successor, Samuel Morey, who devised a recipe in the 1860s based on gin and flavoured with a range of herbs and botanical ingredients including quinine. The sceptics maintain that it was only named after Pimm in his honour.

However it began, Pimms grew in popularity until 1906, when it was formed into a company by Sir Horatio David Davies and then took off in the 1920s.

Bette Davis and Paul Henreid, *Now Voyager*

NOW, VOYAGER (1960)
Directed by Irving Rapper

Starring Bette Davis, Paul Henreid, Claude Rains and
Gladys Cooper

Charlotte Vale (Davis) is a fat, unsightly, withdrawn spinster
whose life is controlled by her bullying mother (Cooper).
Lisa, Charlotte's sister-in-law thinks that Charlotte could
have a nervous breakdown and introduces her to psychiatrist
Dr. Jaquith (Rains), who suggests she go to a sanatorium.

Out of the clutches of a mother Charlotte comes out of
her shell and decides to delay returning home and go on a
cruise. It is here that she meets devoted father Jeremiah
Duvaux Durrance (Henreid), who is travelling with friends.
Jeremiah is in a miserable marriage with a wife who has
stopped him from pursuing his dream job as an architecture.
Charlotte and Jeremiah are stranded in Rio and miss their
ship. Although they both fall in love they resign not to see
each other again.

Back at home Charlotte's family are shocked at the vivid
improvement in Charlotte's demeanour and character.
Charlotte resists her mother's attempts at controlling her and
becomes engaged to an affluent widower, but when she
accidentally encounters Jerry, she breaks it off the
engagement, which leads her to argue with her mother,
causing the old lady to die from a heart attack. She returns
to the sanatorium, where she meets Jerry's depressed
daughter, Tina. She takes her under her wing, and once they
both improve she takes her home with her. Jerry chooses to
leave Tina with Charlotte, but his relationship with
Charlotte can never be.

PLANTER'S PUNCH

1½ Shots Myers Punch Rum
½ Shot Freshly Squeezed Lime Juice
1 Shot Sugar Syrup
3 Dashes Angostura Bitters
Soda
Lime Wedge

Shake all the ingredients apart from the soda with ice in a shaker and then strain into a Highball glass filled with ice. Top up with soda and garnish with a lime wedge.

It was Fred L. Myers who first thought of what is now known as the 'Old Plantation formula' in the late nineteenth century. This recipe follows the traditional rum punch proportions of one sour (lime), two sweet (sugar), three strong (rum) and four diluted (soda).

The word 'Punch' originally derives from the Hindi word for five, 'panch', and the Persian, 'panj'. It had been drunk on the Indian subcontinent for centuries where it was made with the pure spirit, arak, before being introduced into Europe in the seventeenth century where it was often diluted with tea.

The basis of a good punch is to sucessfully balance citrus, sugar, water and alcohol – in other words, to combine sweet with sour, spirit and dilution. Spices and herbs can add fragrance and piquancy to the mix, and warmth or chill depending on whether the punch is hot or cold.

GUYS AND DOLLS (1955)
Directed by Joseph L. Mankiewicz

Starring Marlon Brando, Jean Simmons and Frank Sinatra

Gambler, Nathan Detroit (Sinatra) has to arrange an unlicensed crap game and avoid detection by police Lieutenant Brannigan (Robert Keith). The usual venues are ruled out due to Brannigan's crack down. However Nathan does find someone willing to host the game but only if he pays $1000 up front. Meanwhile Nathan's fiancée, Miss Adelaide (Blaine) wants him to marry her and start going straight.

Nathan meets Sky Masterson (Brando), a man who will bet on practically everything. Nathan bets him $1000 that he can't get Sergeant Sarah Brown (Simmons), a sister at the Save a Soul Mission to go to Havana with him. Sarah's Mission is under threat of closure because it's not busy enough, so Sky offers to help get sinners into the Mission if she will go with to Havana. Sarah reluctantly agrees.

Meanwhile Sky and Sarah fall in love and return to Broadway to discover Nathan has held his game in the empty Mission, but it has been broken up by the police.

Sky still has to provide sinners to the Mission. He lies to Nathan saying he lost the original bet and gives him £1000. Nathan is now hosting his game in a sewer. One of the gangsters is refusing to let the game end until he recovers his losses. Sky asks to join the game saying if he wins all the gamblers have to go to a prayer meeting at the mission.

Sky wins the bet and just as the Mission is about to close the gamblers arrive and confess their sins. Sarah makes up with Sky and they, along with Adelaide and Nathan, get married.

PINA COLADA

1 Shot Golden Rum
2 Shots Coconut Cream
¼ Shot Double Cream
6 Shots Pineapple Juice
Slice of Pineapple

Pour all the ingredients into a blender, add one scoop of crushed ice and blend on a high speed for one minute. Too much ice will spoil the creamy effect and make for a too watery drink. Pour into a large Hurricane glass, garnish with a slice of pineapple and serve with straws.

The origins of the Pina Colada are hotly contested. No fewer than three Puerto Rican bartenders have laid claim to its invention in 1954, two of whom, Ramon Marrero Perez and Ricardo Garcia, worked at the Caribe Hilton hotel's Beachcomber Bar in San Juan. The other claimant is Ramon Portas Mingot who says he created it in 1963 at the Barrachina Bar in Old San Juan.

Pina Colada, meaning 'strained pineapple' should be made with a high quality coconut cream, a syrup of coconut juice and sugar created by another Puerto Rican, named Don Ramon Lopez-Irizarry.

PINK GIN

1 Shot Gin
Angostura Bitters
2 shots Chilled mineral water

Add a few drops of angostura bitters to a martini glass, roll around, then shake out. Add water, gin and serve.

Pink gin has always been a favourite of the Royal Navy, along with rum, which was served as a daily ration right up until the 1970s. Pink gin was always mixed with healthy ingredients to make them more palatable and often with the traditional herbal Angostura Bitters, for stomach upsets and to drive away disease.

PINK HOUND

2 Shots Gin
2 Shots Pink Grapefruit Juice
¼ Shot Sugar Syrup

Shake all ingredients with ice and strain into a chilled Martini glass.

Marilyn Monroe and Tony Curtis, *Some Like it Hot*

SOME LIKE IT HOT   (1959)
Directed by Billy Wilder

Starring Marilyn Monroe, Tony Curtis and Jack Lemmon.

The screenplay was adapted from a story by Robert
Thoeren and Michael Logan. The film was supposed to be
in full colour, but after had to be changed to black and
white because of a noticeable 'green tint' surrounding the
heavy make-up worn by Curtis and Lemmon.

Two musicians who have fallen on hard times, Joe and
Jerry (Curtis and Lemmon), witness a mob related massacre
on St Valentine's day in 1929. They are spotted by the Chicago
based gangsters whose leader goes by the name of 'Spats'
(Raft). The pair escape and go on the run. The only jobs
available to them are in an all-girl band headed to Florida.

Joe and Jerry masquerade as women, going by the names
of Josephine and Geraldine, although Jerry later switches his
alias to Daphne, sign up with the band and board a train.
Joe and Jerry are both attracted to Sugar Kane (Monroe), the
band's vocalist, who also plays the ukulele player. They
attempt to win her over but have to balance this with
sustaining their disguises.

The mobsters turn up at the hotel that the band are
staying in and it's not long before Spats sees Joe and Jerry.
A chase ensues but Jerry, Joe, Sugar, and Osgood manage
to escape to the millionaire's yacht. Sugar tells Joe she loves
him and not his alter ego and Osgood is undeterred by
Jerry's revelation that he is, in fact, a man.

PRAIRIE OYSTER

1 Shot Cognac
1 Egg Yolk
1 Barspoon Malt Vinegar
2 Dashes of Tabasco Sauce
1 Barspoon Worcestershire sauce
Salt and Pepper

Place the egg yolk, unbroken into a Margarita glass. Gently pour in the rest of the ingredients without breaking the yolk. Drink it down in one – and pray.

The Prairie Oyster is a regular remedy that will be offered by most barmen. It tastes as unpleasant as one of the stories about the origin of its name. 'Prairie oysters' in the cattle-raising areas of the United States was the local term for calves' testicles, after the cattle had been castrated and their redundant organs had been fried for breakfast. Whether the breakfast dish was named after the drink or the drink after the dish is uncertain. There is no doubt that the egg floating in the glass does look like a disembodied eyeball. Not one for the squeamish!

There are many variations on the Prairie Oyster. At its most basic, it is non-alcoholic, but this particular recipe includes port, for its hair of the dog status. In France, port is widely used to settle upset stomachs, so its inclusion in this drink may just allow you to keep the lot down.

PRINCESS

1 Shot Dry Vermouth
1 Shot Dubonnet
1 Shot Cointreau or Triple Sec

Shake ingredients in an ice-filled shaker and strain into a glass filled with ice.

PUSSYFOOT COCKTAIL

½ Shot Freshly Squeezed Lime Juice
½ Shot Freshly Squeezed Lemon Juice
½ Shot Freshly Squeezed Orange Juice
Dash of Grenadine
Stemmed Cherry

Shake all of the ingredients in a cocktail shaker filled with ice. Strain into a rocks glass. Garnish with a stemmed cherry.

PULP FICTION

2 Shots Cognac
2 Shots Apple Juice
Lemonade

Pour ingredients into a glass filled with ice.

Audrey Hepburn, *Breakfast at Tiffanys*

RAGING BULL

1 Shot Sambuca
1 Shot Kahlua Coffee Liqueur
1 Shot Tequila

Layer the ingredients carefully in a shot glass.

RAMOS GIN FIZZ

1 Shot Gin
1 Shot Freshly Squeezed Lemon Juice
Dash of Sugar Syrup
Dash of Fresh Single Cream
Dash of Egg White
3 Dashes Orange Flower Water
Soda

Shake all of the ingredients, except the soda, in a cocktail shaker filled with ice. Strain into a Highball glass and garnish with a lemon slice. Top up with soda, if desired. A perfect Fizz is made using charged water from a siphon, but when none is available it is perfectly acceptable to use soda.

A Fizz is almost the same as a Collins, but in theory a Collins should be served in a glass that takes 14 ounces of liquid whereas a Fizz is shorter, and should be served in an 8-ounce glass. The most important difference is that, whereas a Collins is served in a glass filled with ice, a Fizz should never be served with ice.

The Ramos Gin Fizz was devised in 1888 by Henry C. Ramos at the Imperial Cabinet Bar in New Orleans. Today The Fairmont in New Orleans retains the copyright of the Ramos Gin Fizz name.

RASPBERRY MARTINI

6 Fresh Raspberries
2 Shots Gin
1 Shot Creme de Framboise
2 Dashes Orange Bitters

Middle the raspberries in the base of a shaker. Add the remaining ingredients, shake with ice and strain into a chilled Martini glass.

RASPUTIN

2 Shots Cranberry Juice
2 Shots Grapefruit Juice
2 Shots Raspberry Vodka

Shake all ingredients with ice and strain into a glass filled with ice.

RATTLESNAKE

2 Shots Bourbon
Dash Absinthe
½ Fresh Egg White
¼ Shot Freshly Squeezed Lemon Juice
¼ Shot Sugar Syrup

Shake all ingredients with ice and strain into a chilled Martini glass. Harry Craddock said of this cocktail ' it will either cure a rattlesnake bite, or kill rattlesnakes, or make you see them.'

REMEMBER THE MAIN

1 Shot Absinthe
2 Shots Bourbon
¾ Shot Cherry Brandy
¾ Shot Sweet Vermouth

Pour the Absinthe into a glass filled with ice and set to one side. Pour the other ingredients into a shaker filled with ice and stir. Discard the Absinthe and ice and strain the remaining ingredients into the Absinthe-rinsed glass.

RED SNAPPER

A variation on a Bloody Mary. Made with gin, not vodka, it's said to have been a favourite of John Jacob Astor, served by Parisian barman Fernand Petiot who worked at the King Cole Bar in New York's St Regis Hotel.

3 Shots Tomato Juice
Dash Freshly Squeezed Lemon Juice
1 Shot Gin
Pinch Celery Salt
2 Dashes Worcestershire Sauce
2 Dashes Tabasco sauce
Freshly Ground Black Pepper

Fill a highball glass with ice-cubes, then pour in the tomato and lemon juices. Add the gin, celery salt and sauces and stir. Add a quick twist of black pepper. Garnish with a wedge of lime on the rim, and a stalk of celery, if requested. Serve with a stirrer.

REMSEN COOLER

2½ Shots Whisky
Top up with Soda

Pour the ingredients into a glass filled with ice and serve with straws.

RESOLUTE

2 Shots Gin
1 Shot Apricot Brandy
½ Shot Freshly Squeezed Lemon Juice

Shake all ingredients in an ice-filled shaker and strain into a chilled Martini glass.

RICKEY

1 Shot Gin
¼ Shot Freshly Squeezed Lime Juice
¼ Shot Sugar Syrup
Soda
Lime Wedge

Shake the first three ingredients with ice and strain into an ice-filled glass. Top up with soda, and garnish with a lime wedge.

Named in honour of Colonel Joe Rickey, the Rickey cocktail is believed to have been first devised at the Shomaker's restaurant in Washington around the turn of the twentieth century. It is usually made with gin, but you can also make it with vodka or even apricot brandy for an Apricot Rickey. The Rickey is not to be confused with the Collins which is made with lemon juice, whereas the Rickey is made with lime juice and is normally served in a shorter glass.

RITZ REVIVER

A standard restorative for those whose excesses the night before have left them within striking distance of the Paris Ritz.

Twist of Orange Peel
⅔ Shot Fernet Branca
⅔ Shot Crème de Menthe
Dash Angostura bitters

Rub the rim of a cocktail glass with the orange peel. Shake the remaining ingredients in a cocktail shaker filled with ice. Strain into a cocktail glass. Drop in the twist of orange peel, and serve.

ROB ROY

1 Shot Scotch Whisky
1 Shot Sweet Vermouth
4 drops Angostura Bitters
Orange Zest
Maraschino Cherry

Pour the whisky, vermouth and bitters into an ice-filled mixing glass. Stir until the mixture is chilled and blended, then strain into a frosted Martini glass. Garnish with a Maraschino cherry and a strip of orange zest.

SANGRITA

Serves 10

6 Shots Tequila
1 litre or 35 fl oz Tomato Juice
450ml or 16 fl oz Freshly Squeezed Orange Juice
5 Teaspoons Runny Honey
90ml or 3 fl oz Freshly Squeezed Lime Juice
1 Chilli, Finely Chopped
2 Teaspoons Finely Chopped White Onion
Pinch Salt and Freshly Ground Black Pepper
10 Drops Worcestershire Sauce

Pour all ingredients into a mixing bowl; stir well. Chill for two hours, then strain into a large pitcher. Serve in wine glasses.

SANGRIA

1 Shot Red Wine
1 Shot Freshly Squeezed Orange Juice
2 Shots Cognac
1 Shot Schnapps

Shake all ingredients in an ice-filled shaker and strain into a glass filled with ice.

Gene Kelly, *On the Town*

ON THE TOWN (1949)
Directed by Stanley Donen

Starring Gene Kelly, Frank Sinatra, Betty Garrett, Ann Miller, Jules Munshin and Vera-Ellen

On the Town is adapted from the Broadway musical of the same name. However much of Bernstein's music was cut and replaced with new compositions from Edens. Gene Kelly insisted that much of the film was shot on location in New York City, including scenes at the American Museum of Natural History, the Brooklyn Bridge, and Rockefeller Center.

The movie won an Academy Award for Best Music, Scoring of a Musical Picture, and was nominated for a Golden Globe Award for Best Cinematography. Comden and Green picked up the Writers Guild of America Award for Best Written American Musical.

Three sailors, Gabey (Gene Kelly), Chip (Frank Sinatra), and Ozzie (Jules Munshin) arrive in New York on 24 hours shore leave determined to have a fun time and find some girls. Gabey falls in love with a picture of Ivy Smith (Vera-Ellen) the 'Miss Turnstiles' for the month of June and vows to find her. Chip tries to fend off the attention an ardent lady taxi driver (Garret) and Ozzie meets a beautiful anthropologist (Miller) who thinks he is a shining example of a 'prehistoric' man. Gabey continues his search for Ivy, who he still thinks is a successful debutant and is unaware that she is, in fact, a humble dancer. All three couples eventually meet on top of the Empire State building but Ivy must leave to go to work. After another set of adventures they all meet again and share a kiss on the pier, just as a new crew of sailors heads out into the city for their leave.

SAZERAC

1 Shot Bourbon
1 Shot Cognac
Small Dash of Pernod
¼ Shot Sugar Syrup
Peychaud Bitters
Soda
Twist of Lemon

Add the dash of Pernod to an ice-filled glass. Top up with water and leave to stand. Then shake the Bourbon, Cognac, sugar and Bitters with ice. Discard the contents of the glass and strain the contents of the shaker into the glass. Garnish with a twist of lemon.

The brand name of Sazerac is owned by the Sazerac Company and licensed to the Sazerac Bar at the Fairmont Hotel in New Orleans, but perhaps the most interesting story belongs to the Sazerac's unique ingredient, Peychaud Bitters, a mixture that dates back to the eighteenth century. The American Aromatic Bitter Cordial, as it was then known, was devised by Antoine Amadee Peychaud at his Apothecary in New Orleans in 1834 and was soon offered mixed with brandy and other spirits in bars across New Orleans. Leon Lamothe, the bartender of one of them, the Sazerac Coffee House, at 13 Exchange Alley, is said to have conceived the original Sazerac, using the Bitters, sugar and Cognac.

Hard times were in store for both chemist and bar.

Peychaud later sold his apothecary business and along with it, the recipe and brand of the Bitters. Cognac became hard to obtain during the years of the American Civil War and the bar, under the new ownership of Thomas H. Handy, altered the cocktail recipe, substituting Maryland Club rye whisky with a dash of cognac and a splash of absinthe until it was banned in the States in 1912.

SCARLETT O'HARA

1 Shot Southern Comfort
½ Shot Cranberry Juice
½ Shot Freshly Squeezed Lime Juice

Shake all ingredients with ice and strain into a chilled Martini glass.

The Scarlett O'Hara was created in 1939 in honour of the heroine of *Gone with the Wind*. Using as its base the newly available Southern Comfort, the cocktail is widely attributed with putting the liqueur on the map.

Clark Gable and Vivien Leigh, *Gone with the Wind*

GONE WITH THE WIND (1939)
Directed by Victor Fleming

Starring Clark Gable, Leslie Howard, Olivia de Havilland
and Vivien Leigh

Adapted from the novel by Margaret Mitchell's this epic
movie tells a story of the Civil War and its aftermath from a
white Southern viewpoint. It received ten Academy Awards,
a record that stood for twenty years.

At Twelve Oaks, Scarlett O'Hara (Leigh) notices that she is
being admired by a handsome but roguish visitor, Rhett Butler
(Gable), who had been disowned by his Charleston family.

Scarlett is in love with Ashley Wilkes, a neighbour, but he
intends to marry Scarlett's friend Melanie Hamilton. When
war is declared, Scarlett must deal with death, destruction
and ruin, Atlanta burning, the Union Army carrying off
everything from her beloved Tara, the carpetbaggers who
arrive after the South's defeat. But at the beginning of
hostilities Scarlett agrees to marry Melanie's brother
Charles. She is quickly widowed when Charles, now in the
army dies of measles and pneumonia.

After the war, Scarlett marries Frank Kennedy, a successful
business man, but he is killed when he and some others attack
a shanty town to try and get rid of the people who live there.

Then Rhett turns up again and this time Scarlett agrees to
marry him. It is a stormy relationship because of her obsession
with Ashley and finally Rhett decides to leave her. She
implores him to stay, telling him she loves him. He replies
coldly: 'Frankly my dear, I don't give a damn'.

SCOTCH MIST

1 Shot Scotch Whisky
Ice
Lemon Zest

Pour the whisky into a cocktail shaker filled with ice. Shake sharply and strain into a small wine glass filled with crushed ice. Garnish with a strip of lemon zest.

SCREWDRIVER

1 Shot Vodka
Fresh Orange Juice
Slice of Orange

Pour the vodka into a Highball glass filled with ice. Top up with orange juice and garnish with a slice of orange.

SEA BREEZE

1 Shot Vodka
1½ Shots Cranberry Juice
Freshly queezed Grapefruit Juice
Lime Wedge

Shake all the ingredients with ice and strain into an ice-filled glass. Garnish with a lime wedge.

SENSATION

3 Dashes Maraschino
3 Sprigs Mint
1 Shot Freshly Squeezed Lemon Juice
2 Dashes Absinthe

Shake all ingredients in a shaker filled with ice and strain into a chilled Martini glass..

SEVENTH HEAVEN

2 Shots Gin
1 Shot Freshly Squeezed Orange Juice
½ Shot Maraschino
Dash Angostura Bitters

Shake all ingredients in a shaker filled with ice and strain into a chilled Martini glass.

SHIRLEY TEMPLE

Grenadine
Ginger Ale
Maraschino Cherry

Pour the ginger ale into a Highball glass filled with ice. Add the Grenadine to taste and stir. Garnish with a cherry.

SIDECAR

1 Shot Cognac
1 Shot Cointreau or Triple Sec
1 Shot Freshly Squeezed Lemon Juice

As the Sidecar was invented in Paris during the First World War it seems unsurprising it was named after the motorcycle sidecar in which its inventor was taken to the bistro where the drink was conceived, Harry's New York Bar at 5 rue Danou. However, in Harry's own book he gives the credit to MacGarry of Buck's Club in London.

SHOWBIZ

2 Shots Vocdka
1 Shot Crème de Cassis
2 Shots Grapefruit Juice

Shake all ingredients in an ice-filled shaker and strain into a chilled Martini glass.

BELOVED INFIDEL (1959)
Directed by Henry King

Starring Gregory Peck, Deborah Kerr and Eddie Albert

This 20th Century Fox picture is based on the life of F. Scott Fitzgerald and was based on a memoir by Sheilah Graham and Gerold Frank.

It follows the wild, drunken and turbulent relationship of F Scott Fitzgerald (Peck) and Sheilah Graham: Towards the end of his life, Fitzgerald is forced to work for a Hollywood studio in order to pay his booze bills and his daughter's school fees. He's also attempting to write another novel. Graham (Kerr) a British chorus girl turned gossip columnist and would-be novelist works as his aid and tries to keep him off the drink for long enough to complete his work.

The pair bicker and fight despite being in love and Fitzgerald dies of a heart attack before he can compete his final novel.

Gregory Peck and Deborah Kerr, *Beloved Infidel*

SILVER FIZZ

2 Shots Gin
1 Shot Lemon Juice
½ Shot Sugar Syrup
½ Fresh Egg White
Top up with Soda

Shake the first four ingredients in an ice-filled shaker.
Top up with soda.

SILVER MARTINI

2 Shots Gin
2 Shots Dry Vermouth
Dash Marashino Liqueur
2 Dashes Orange Bitters

Sahke all ingredients in an ice-filled shaker and strain
into a chilled Martini glass.

SLOE MOTION

1 Shot Sloe Gin
Champagne

Pour the sloe gin into a chilled flute glass and top up
with champagne.

SINGAPORE SLING

1 Shot Cognac
½ Shot Freshly Squeezed Lemon Juice
½ Shot Cointreau or Triple Sec
½ Shot Chilled Mineral Water

Pour the ingredients into a shaker with ice and strain into an ice-filled glass.Garnish with a slice of lemon and a stemmed cherry, and serve with straws.

It is well known that the Singapore Sling was created by Ngiam Tong Boon at the Long Bar in Raffles Hotel, Singapore, between 1911 and 1915, though the debate rages as to the actual ingredients and, indeed, the name. At the time Singapore was known as Straits Settlements so it is likely that Boon's original drink was called the Straits Sling and that the name subsequently altered sometime between 1922 and 1930. Even the Raffles Hotel itself is uncertain as to the original ingredients.

In *The Fine Art of Mixing Drink*s David Embury writes that 'Essentially the Sidecar is nothing but a Daiquiri with brandy in the place of rum and Cointreau in the place of sugar syrup'.

SNAKEBITE

1 Shot Lager
1 Shot Cider

Pour lager into a tall glass and top up with cider.

SNOWBALL

2 Shots Advocaat
1 Shot Fino Sherry
1 Shot Lime Cordial
Top up with Lemonade

Shake the advoaat, sherry and lime cordial in an ice-filled shaker and strain into a glass filled with ice.

SOUTH PACIFIC

Flesh of 1 Passion Fruit
1 Shot Vodka
1 Shot Pineapple Juice
1 Shot Freshly Squeezed Lime Juice
Dash Lychee Liqueur if available

Shake all ingredients in a shaker filled with ice and strain into a chilled Martini glass.

STANLEY

½ Shot Freshly Squeezed Lemon Juice
½ Shot Grenadine
1 Shot Gin
1 Shot Rum

Shake all ingredients in a shaker filled with ice. Strain into a chilled Martini glass.

STINGER

1 Shot Brandy
½ Shot White Crème de Menthe

Pour the brandy and crème de menthe into a cocktail shaker filled with ice. Shake sharply and strain into a frosted Martini glass.

STOMACH REVIVER

1 Shot Fernet Branca
1 Shot Brandy
3 Dashes Angostura Bitters

Pour all ingredients into a cocktail shaker filled with ice. Shake. Strain into a shot glass, then knock it back and breathe a sigh of relief.

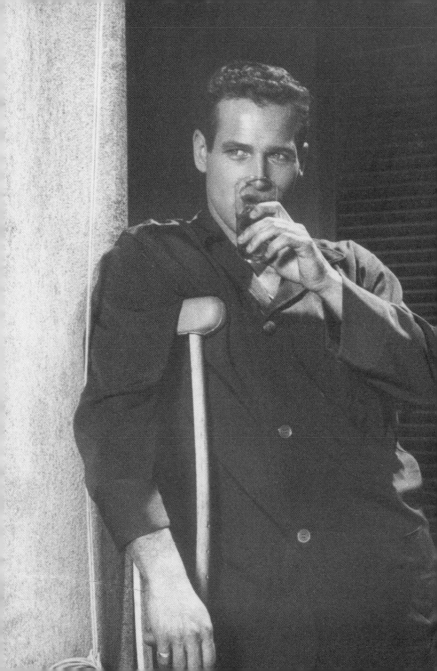

CAT ON A HOT TIN ROOF (1958)
Directed by Richard Brooks

Starring Paul Newman, Elizabeth Taylor and Burl Ives.

Adapted from the Tennesee Williams' play by Richard Brooks and James, *Cat on a Hot Tin Roof* concerns Mississippi plantation owner Big Daddy Pollitt (Ives), who doesn't know he has terminal cancer and only a few days left to live, because his family and doctors decline to tell him. He worries about the strained and childless marriage of his favoured alcoholic son Brick (Newman) and he hates his second son, Gooper, (Jack Carson) for his greed and ambition over Big Daddy's money. He confronts Brick about his stubbornness but is refused an answer.

Brick's wife, Maggie (Taylor) is beautiful and desirable and tries unsuccessfully to coax her husband away from the bottle, while alternately enticing him and taunting him about his obsession with his deceased best friend, Skipper, who has committed suicide. The steamy tensions reach a climax when the truth of Big Daddy's health is revealed. He and Brick manage to resolve their differences and Maggie finally manages to make her affections for Brick understood. The film concludes with the couple kissing.

Due to strict censorship in the late 1950s all the references in the original play, to homosexuality and four-letter words were deleted, watered down, or obscured, and the ending was considerably changed

The film received Academy Award nominations for Best Picture, Best Director, Best Actor, Best Actress, Best Cinematography and Best Adapted Screenplay.

SUFFERING BASTARD

Angostura Bitters
¼ Shot Gin
¼ Shot Brandy
1 Teaspoon Freshly Squeezed Lime Juice
Cold Ginger Ale

Swirl the bitters around a Highball glass and toss the excess. Half-fill the glass with ice and add the gin, brandy, lime juice and ginger ale. Garnish with slices of lime, cucumber and orange. Add a sprig of fresh mint on the rim.

SYMPATHY

1 Whole Egg
1 Shot Freshly Squeezed Lemon Juice
½ Shot Sugar Syrup
1 Shot Brandewign
Soda to taste

Pour all ingredients, except the soda, into a cocktail shaker and shake vigorously. Strain into a glass filled with ice. Top up with soda.

TANGO MARTINI

½ Shot Gin
½ Shot Sweet Vermouth
½ Shot Dry Vermouth
½ Shot Cointreau or Triple Sec
1 Shot Freshly Squeezed Orange Juice

Shake all ingredients in an ice-filled shaker and strain into a chilled Martini glass.

TEQUILA SLAMMER

1 Shot Tequila
1 Shot Champagne

Pour tequila into a shot glass and layer the champagne on top. Hold and cover the glass with the top of the hand. Pick it up and slam it down firmly, then drink while still fizzing.

TATANKA

2 Shots Vodka
2½ Shots Apple Juice

Shake ingredients in an ice-filled shaker and strain into a glass filled with ice.

TEQUILA SUNRISE

1 Shot Tequila
Freshly Squeezed Orange Juice
½ Shot Grenadine

Pour the Tequila into a Highball glass filled with ice, top up with orange juice and add a sunken float of grenadine. Garnish with a slice of orange and serve with a straw.

Tequila is fermented from the juice of the blue agave cactus. It is an ancient spirit, formulated centuries ago by the Aztecs.

THOMAS ABERCROMBIE

This is a classic hangover remedy that combines both an antacid with a hair of the dog. Its single failing is the call for golden Tequila, which is going to contain more congeners than the clear type. It is named, by the way, after the man whose research uncovered the formula.

2 Alka Selzer tablets
1 double shot of José Cuervo Tequila Gold

Drop the tablets into the liquor and allow to fizz for four seconds before drinking.

TOKYO BLOODY MARY

1 Shot Saké
5 Shots Tomato Juice
½ Shot Fresh Lemon Juice
8 Dashes Tabasco Sauce
4 Dashes Worcestershire Sauce
4 dashes Medium Sherry
Pinch of Celery Salt
Pinch of Black Pepper

Pour all the ingredients into cocktail shaker filled with ice. Shake. Strain into a highball glass filled with ice. Garnish with a stick of celery. Serve.

TOM AND JERRY

1 Shot Dark Rum
⅔ Shot Brandy
1 Egg, Separated
1 Barspoon Sugar
Boiling Water
Ground Nutmeg

Beat the egg white and yolk separately, then mix them together in a heat-resistant wine glass. Add remaining ingredients to the egg mixture and top it up with boiling water. Sprinkle with ground nutmeg.

TOM COLLINS

1 Shot London Dry Gin
Fresh Lemon Juice
Sugar Syrup
Soda
Slice of Lemon

Pour the gin, a small shot of lemon juice and a dash of sugar syrup into a Highball glass filled with ice. Top up with soda, stir, and garnish with a slice of lemon.

TRILBY

1 Shot Whisky
1 Shot Parfait Amour
1 Shot Sweet Vermouth
2 Dashes Orange Bitters
Dash Absinthe

Stir all ingredients in a shaker filled with ice. Strain into a chilled Martini glass.

TRINITY

1 Shot Whisky
1 Shot Dry Vermouth
¼ Shot Crème de Menthe Liqueur
¼ Shot Apricot Brandy
Dash Orange Bitters

Stir in an ice-filled shaker. Strain into a chilled Martini glass.

TROPIC

2 Shots Dry White Wine
1 Shot Benedictine
2 Shots Freshly Squeezed Lemon Juice
2 Shots Freshly Squeezed Grapefruit Juice

Shake all ingredients in a shaker filled with ice and strain into a tall glass filled with ice.

TULIP

1 Shot Calvados
1 Shot Apricot Brandy
1 Shot Sweet Vermouth
½ Shot Freshly Squeezed Lemon Juice

Shake all ingredients in a shaker filled with ice and strain into a chilled Martini glass.

TYPHOON

2 Shots Gin
2 Shots Sambuca
½ Shot Rose's Lime Cordial

Stir all ingredients with ice and strain into an ice-filled glass.

UMBONGO

Flesh of 1 Passion Fruit
1 Shot Vodka
2 Shots Freshly Squeezed Orange Juice
Ginger Ale

Shake first three ingredients in an ice-filled shaker. Pour into an ice-filled glass and top up with ginger ale.

UNION JACK

1 Shot Grenadine
1 Shot Maraschino
1½ Shots Green Chartreuse.

Layer ingredients into a chilled glass.

VAMPIRE

A popular drink in Mexico – so popular, in fact, that it is frequently described as Mexico's national drink. It combines a variety of flavours, of orange, tomato juice, spices, honey and onion. It doesn't sound promising, but if it is made and left to settle overnight, it is surprisingly drinkable, especially if served well-chilled. As it can be made in advance, the number of ingredients is not a deterrent to making it.

The variety of spices in the drink is capable of bringing to life even the most jaded taste bud. The drink is rich in vitamins, as it contains tomatoes, orange juice, lime and chilli. The honey and onion provide calories, some in the form of a rapidly absorbed sugar, the rest as a complex carbohydrate so that there will be a lasting benefit.

75ml or about 2½ fl oz Tomato Juice
30ml or 1 fl oz Fresh Orange Juice
30ml or 1 fl oz Silver Tequila
1 Teaspoon Clear Honey
10ml or about ⅓ fl oz Fresh Lime Juice
Half a Slice of Onion, Finely Chopped
A Few Slices Fresh Red-hot Chilli
A Few Drops Worcestershire Sauce
Salt, to taste

Pour the ingredients into an ice-filled shaker. Shake well to release the flavour of the chilli. Strain into a highball glass filled with ice. Garnish with a wedge of lime on the rim.

VESPER MARTINI

3 shots Plymouth Gin
1 shot Vodka
Half a shot Dry Vermouth

Shake all ingredients with ice and fine strain into a chilled Martini glass.

The Vesper Martini is 007's original 'shaken not stirred' Martini as chronicled in the first James Bond novel, Casino Royale.

Many bartenders believe a Martini should be stirred and not shaken, some saying that shaking might 'bruise' the gin. However, a Vesper is always shaken, as it aerates the drink and makes it colder, giving it a slightly cloudy appearance. Shaking can leave minute shards of ice on the surface of the cocktail, so always strain when pouring out.

VODKA MARTINI

1 Shot Vodka
¼ Shot Dry Vermouth
1 Green Olive or Lemon Zest

Add a couple of drops of vermouth into a mixing glass filled. Stir and strain out excess vermouth, leaving a coating on the ice. Add more ice to the vodka and stir again. Strain into a chilled martini glass. Garnish with either a strip of lemon zest or an olive.

CASINO ROYALE   (2006)
Directed by Martin Campbell

Starring Daniel Craig, Eva Green, Mads Mikkelsen, Judi
Dench and Jeffrey Wright

Casino Royale is the twenty-first film in the James Bond
series and the first to star Daniel Craig as Bond. It is based
on the 1953 novel of the same name by Ian Fleming.

The film is set at the beginning of James Bond's career as
Agent 007, just as he is earning his famous licence to kill. He
prevents a terrorist attack at Miami International Airport,
and it is here that he falls for Vesper Lynd (Green), a beautiful
treasury agent assigned to supply the money he needs to take
part in a high-stakes poker tournament planned by the villain
Le Chiffre (Mikkelsen). The film's story arc continues in the
22nd James Bond film, Quantum of Solace.

In his first mission as 007, Bond pursues an international bomb-maker named Mollaka (Sebastien Foucan)
in Madagascar. After a chase across the city, Bond kills his
target and blows up a part of the embassy to facilitate his
escape. He gets hold of Mollaka's mobile phone and
discovers that it has received an SMS from Alex Dimitrios,
an associate of Le Chiffre in the Bahamas. Bond travels
there, wins Dimitrios's Aston Martin DB5 in a poker game,
and later kills him. The culmination of the film is a high-
stakes poker game at Casino Royal in Montenegro and a
fight in a collapsing building in Venice where Lynd is
revealed to be a traitor.

Daniel Craig, *Casino Royale*

WAKE –UP CALL

⅔ Shot Vodka
½ Shot Cointreau or Triple Sec
¼ Shot Freshly Squeezed Lemon Juice
2 Shots Tomato Juice
Tabasco Sauce
Pinch Celery Salt
Pinch Castor Sugar
Champagne

Pour all the ingredients, except the Champagne, into a cocktail shaker filled with ice. Shake. Pour into a highball glass filled about three-quarters with ice. Top up with Champagne. Stir. Garnish with a wedge of lime.

WHISKY MAC

1 Shot Scotch Whisky
1 Shot Stone's Green Ginger Wine

Pour the whisky and ginger wine over ice into a rocks glass. Stir and serve.

Edward Arnold and Constance Cummings, *Remember Last Night*

REMEMBER LAST NIGHT (1935)
Directed by James Whale

Starring Edward Arnold, Constance Cummings and Robert Young

A madcap comedy based on the novel *The Hangover Murders.*

A wealthy group of socialites celebrate the six month anniversary of their friends Tony (Young) and Carlotta (Cummings) with a debauched party that winds up in a restaurant. They are unaware that the owner of the restaurant has hatched a plan with the chauffer of the party's host, Vic, to kidnap Vic. The next morning Tony and Carlotta awake to find Vic is dead and his wife Bette missing. Due to the amount of alcohol consumed, no one can remember a single thing that happened the night before. In fact Tony and Carlotta are still drunk while the district attorney, Danny Harrison (Arnold) attempts to solve the crime.

Evidence begins to point suspicion at Tony, who rings a hypnotist to assist people in recovering their memories. However the hypnotists is murdered and the corpses begin to stack up. Tony gets to the truth of the matter, the murder is solved and Danny persuades Tony and Carlotta to stop become tea total. They agree and drink a toast to it.

WHISKEY SOUR

½ Shot Bourbon
¼ Shot Freshly Squeezed Lemon Juice
¼ Shot Sugar Syrup
3 Dashes Angostura Bitters
Splash of Egg White

Shake all the ingredients in a shaker with ice and strain into an ice-filled glass. Garnish with a cherry and an orange slice.

The 'sour' in sours is derived either from the tartness of the lime or lemon juice. Whiskey Sour is way ahead of other sours in terms of its pupularity and is sometimes made with a small amount of egg white to make it more palatable.

VALENCIA

½ Shot Freshly Squeezed Orange Juice
½ Shot Apricot Brandy
Champagne

Pour the orange juice and apricot brandy into a chilled flute glass and top up with champagne.

WHITE SWAN

An attractive name for a drink based on sherry, honey and egg yolk. It follows the scientific principle of combining sugars, a taste of alcohol and the fat and protein of egg yolk. It was invented by Joe Familoe of the Three Swans Pub at Forest Hills Inn, Long Island, New York. The drink is a short, down-in-one-shot type. To deal with the dehydration, orange juice to follow is probably best.

1 Shot Sherry
Teaspoon Runny Honey
1 Fresh Egg Yolk
Milk
Freshly Grated Nutmeg

Mix the first three ingredients well and add them to a tumbler of cold milk. Sprinkle with fresh nutmeg.

Claudette Colbert, *It Happened One Night*

IT HAPPENED ONE NIGHT (1934)
Directed by Frank Capra

Starring Clark Gable, Claudette Colbert and Walter Connolly

Socialite (Colbert) is attempting to escape her authoritarian father's influence and falls in love with a roguish reporter. The plot was based on the story *Night Bus* by Samuel Hopkins Adams.

It was the first film ever to win all five of the main Academy Awards (Best Picture, Director, Actor, Actress, and Screenplay), not equalled until *One Flew Over the Cuckoo's Nest* (1975). The film was remade in 1956 as a musical comedy, *You Can't Run Away from It*, starring Jack Lemmon and June Allyson.

The plot has heiress Ellen 'Ellie' Andrews marrying a fortune-hunter against the wishes of her exceptionally wealthy father (Connolly). He grabs her back before the marriage can be consummated, but then she runs away. While on a bus to New York City, she meets fellow passenger Peter Warne (Gable), an out-of-work newspaper reporter. He recognizes her and gives her an ultimatum: if she gives him an exclusive on her story, he will lend a hand in reuniting her with her husband, if not, he will inform her father where she is and pick up a reward. She feels she has no choice but to agree.

There follows a series of coincidences and confusions which see Peter and Ellie lose touch with each other. She goes home and her father agrees she can return to her husband. But her father has learned what happened between her and Peter and encourages her to go to him. Ellie's marriage is annulled and all ends happily.

WHITE LADY

1 Shot Gin
Fresh Lemon Juice
Cointreau or Triple Sec
Egg White

Mix together the gin, a large dash of lemon juice, a dash of Triple Sec, and the egg white. Shake in a cocktail shaker and strain into a frosted Martini glass.

To make a Pink Lady add a dash of Grenadine and an extra splash of gin.

At first appearance the White Lady is like a Sidecar made with gin instead of brandy. Although no one knows who invented the Sidecar, the inventor of the White Lady is well known. It was first created in 1919 by Harry MacElhone, Head Barman at Ciro's Club in London. Originally made with Creme de Menthe, Harry later changed the recipe and added gin instead.

ZOMBIE

½ Shot Light Rum
½ Shot Golden Rum
½ Shot Jamaican Rum
½ Shot Over-Proof Rum
¼ Shot Marashino LiqUeur
¼ Shot Freshly Squeezed Lime Juice
¼ Shot Freshly Squeezed Grapefruit Juice
¼ Shot Sugar Syrup
2 Dashes Angostura Bitters
2 Dashes Pernod
3 Dashes Grenadine Syrup

Blend all ingredients with crushed ice and pour into a Collins glass with three ice cubes. Finish with a pineapple wedge, orange slice, cherry and mint sprig.

The origins of the Zombie are hotly contested. The most widely held opinion is that it was invented by Don the Beachcomber at his restaurant in Hollywood in 1934. Wherever it was born, it is surely one of the great cocktails, as attested in *The Fine Art of Mixing Drinks*, whose author David Embury describes the Zombie as the 'grandfather of all pixies, and a great uncle to the gremlins'.

INDEX OF COCKTAILS

A
Absinthe
  Bunny Hug 51
  Death in the Afternoon 69
  Dixie 70
  Earthquake 75
  Fascinator 79
  Johnnie Mack 112
  London 119
  Merry Widow 129
  Monkey Gland 134
  Moonshine 134
  Rattlesnake 162
  Remember the Main 162
  Trilby 189
advocaat
  Snowball 180
Alka Selzer tablets
  Thomas Abercrombie 187
almond syrup
  Blue Bird 37
amaretto
  Brooklyn 47
  Dolce-Amaro 71
  Downhill Racer 71
  Godfather 101
  Jockey Club 112
  Mae West Martini 123
Angostura bitters
  Alamagoozlum 12
  Apple Jack 16
  Banana Cow 27
  Bourbon Smash 42
  Brandy Sour 46
  Camel 52
  Champagne Cocktail 56

  Dandy Cocktail 69
  East India Cocktail 75
  Fallen Angel 77
  Fine and Dandy 86
  Flying Scotsman 83
  Imperial 109
  Incognito 109
  Jockey Club 112
  Journalist 113
  Mai Tai 125
  Merry Widow 129
  Old Chappie 139
  Paddy 142
  Pink Gin 152
  Planter's Punch 147
  Ritz Reviver 165
  Rob Roy 165
  Stomach Reviver 181
  Suffering Bastard 185
  Whiskey Sour 201
  Zombie 206
Anis
  Hemingway 106
apple juice
  Apple Martini 16
  English Garden 76
  Hobson's Choice 106
  Monza 134
  Pulp Fiction 158
  Tatanka 186
apple Schnapps
  Apple Martini 16
applejack brandy
  Jack Collins 111
  Mule's Hind Leg 135
apples

Apple of my Eye 17
apricot brandy
    Angel Face 15
    Apricot Cocktail 17
    Charlie Chaplin 59
    Empire 76
    Fifth Avenue 86
    Hop Toad 107
    Incognito 109
    Leap Year 117
    Leave it to Me 117
    Mai Tai 125
    Mayfair 129
    Millionaire Cocktail 130
    Mule's Hind Leg 135
    Paradise 142
    Resolute 164
    Trinity 190
    Tulip 190
    Valencia 199

B
Bacardi rum
    Bacardi Cocktail 24
    Fox Trot 87
    Little Devil 118
    Little Princess 118
Bailey's Irish Cream
    E.T. 77
    Irish Flag 110
    Irish Latté 110
bananas
    Banana Cow 27
Beef Bouillon
    Bloody Bull 32
    Bullshot 48
beer
    Old Chappie 139
    Pheasant Runner 143

Benedictine
    Froupé 87
    Merry Widow 129
    Mule's Hind Leg 135
    Tropic 190
blending 7–8
Bourbon
    Apple of my Eye 17
    Back to Work 22
    Blues Cocktail 38
    Bourbon Highball 39
    Bourbon Pick-Me-Up 42
    Bourbon Smash 42
    Brooklyn 47
    Dandy Cocktail 69
    Embassy Royal 75
    Mint Julep 132
    Old Fashioned 139
    Old Pal 139
    Opening Shot 140
    Rattlesnake 162
    Remember the Main 162
    Sazerac 169
    Whiskey Sour 199
    see also whisky
Branca Menta
    Bourbon Pick-Me-Up 42
Brandewign
    Sympathy 185
brandy
    American Beauty 15
    Baltimore Eggnog 27
    Big Boy 30
    Brandy Alexander 43
    Brandy Flip 44
    Breakfast Egg Nog 47
    Cecil Pick-Me-Up 55
    Champagne Cocktail 56
    Corpse Reviver 61

East India Cocktail 75
Fizz 86
Flip 83
Fog Lifter 84
Froupé 87
Loud Speaker 119
Stinger 181
Stomach Reviver 181
Suffering Bastard 185
Tom and Jerry 188

C
Calvados
    Angel Face 15
    Apple Jack 16
    Bentley 29
    Corpse Reviver 61
    Empire 76
    Jack Collins 111
    Mule's Hind Leg 135
    Tulip 190
camomile tea
    Camomile Fizz 52
Campari
    Aura 20
    Bloodhound 31
    Campari Nobile 55
    Dolce-Amaro 71
    Milano 129
    Monza 134
    Old Pal 139
celery sticks
    Bloody Maria 34
    Bloody Mary 33–4
Champagne
    Black Velvet 30
    Champagne Cup 59
    Champagne Daisy 59
    Corpse Reviver 61

Death in the Afternoon 69
Grand Mimosa 102
Harry's Pick-Me-Up 104
Hemingway 106
Jayne Mansfield 111
Mimosa 130
Sloe Motion 178
Tequila Slammer 186
Valencia 201
Wake-Up Call 196
Champagne, Brut
    Kir Royale 114
Champagne, dry
    Bellini 23
    Buck's Fizz 51
    Cecil Pick-Me-Up 55
    Champagne Cocktail 56
Chartreuse
    Alaska 12
Chartreuse, green
    Episcopal 77
    Union Jack 191
Chartreuse, Yellow
    Alamagoozlum 12
    Champagne Daisy 59
    Episcopal 77
cherries
    Pussyfoot Cocktail 158
cherries, Maraschino
    Manhattan 120
    Rob Roy 165
    Shirley Temple 173, 175
cherry brandy
    Remember the Main 162
cherry liqueur
    Gin Sling 97
chillies
    Sangrita 166
    Vampire 192

cider
  Snakebite 180
cinnamon
  Mulled Wine 135
cinnamon sticks
  Batonnet 28
Clamato
  Bloody Caesar 32
cloves
  Mayfair 129
  Mulled Wine 135
Coca Cola
  Cuba Libre 65
  Iced Tea 108
coconut cream
  Batida de Coco 22
  Pina Colada 151
coconut milk
  Batida de Coco 22
coffee
  Irish Coffee 110
coffee, espresso
  Hot Shot 107
  Irish Latté 110
coffee liqueur
  Heaven's Above 105
  Raging Bull 160
Cognac
  Batonnet 28
  Brandy Fizz 43
  Brandy Milk Punch 44
  Brandy Sour 46
  Champagne Cup 59
  Fog Cutter 83
  Iced Tea 108
  Incognito 109
  Prairie Oyster 155
  Pulp Fiction 158
  Sangria 166

Sazerac 169
Between the Sheets 29
Sidecar 174
Singapore Sling 179
Cointreau
  Big Boy 30
  Cosmopolitan 64
  Dandy Cocktail 69
  Fine and Dandy 86
  Iced Tea 108
  Little Devil 118
  Loud Speaker 119
  Maiden's Prayer 124
  Margarita 126
  Martinez 124
  Opal 140
  Orange Bloom 141
  Princess 158
  Between the Sheets 29
  Sidecar 174
  Singapore Sling 179
  Tango Martini 186
  Wake-Up Call 198
  White Lady 205
cranberry juice
  Bourbon Smash 42
  Cosmopolitan 64
  Cranberry Collins 64
  Madras 123
  Mae West Martini 123
  Rasputin 161
  Scarlett O'Hara 170
  Sea Breeze 173, 175
cream, double
  Baltimore Eggnog 27
  Barbary Coast 28
  Bourbon Milk Punch 39
  Brandy Alexander 43
  Brandy Flip 44

Brandy Milk Punch 44
Fifth Avenue 86
Flip 83
Fog Lifter 84
Hot Shot 107
Parisien Blonde 142
Pina Colada 151
cream, fresh
Angel's Tip 15
Belmont 29
Irish Coffee 110
Ramos Gin Fizz 160
cream, single
Hair of the Dog 102
crème de cacao
Angel's Tip 15
Barbary Coast 28
Fifth Avenue 86
crème de cacao, dark
Brandy Alexander 43
Heaven's Above 105
crème de cacao, white
Brandy Alexander 43
crème de cassis
Ballet Russe 24
El Diablo 76
Kir Royale 114
Showbiz 175
crème de fraise
Jayne Mansfield 111
crème de framboise
Raspberry Martini 161
crème de menthe
American Beauty 15
The Apothecary 19
Heart Starter 105
Hurricane 107
Irish Flag 110
Mint Cocktail 130

Ritz Reviver 165
Trinity 190
crème de menthe, white
The Assassin 19
Corpse Reviver 61
Fallen Angel 77
Stinger 181
cucumber
Pimm's Cup 144
Curaçao
Blue Bird 37
Parisien Blonde 142

D
Demerara rum
Mai Tai 125
Drambuie
Embassy Royal 75
Dubonnet
Appetiser 16
Aviator 18
Bentley 29
Dandy Cocktail 69
Dubonnet cocktail 70
Jackson 111
Opera 140
Princess 158

E
egg whites
Brandy Sour 46
Ramos Gin Fizz 160
Rattlesnake 162
Silver Fizz 178
Whiskey Sour 201
White Lady 205
egg yolks
Blues Cocktail 38
Brandy Flip 44

Cecil Pick-Me-Up 55
Prairie Oyster 155
White Swan 200
eggs
    Baltimore Eggnog 27
    Breakfast Egg Nog 47
    Fog Lifter 84
    Sympathy 185
    Tom and Jerry 188
elderflower cordial
    English Garden 76

F
Fernet Branca
    The Apothecary 19
    The Assassin 19
    Blood Transfusion 31
    Corpse Reviver 61
    Fernet Branca Cocktail 79
    Hanky Panky 104
    Heart Starter 105
    Ritz Reviver 165
    Stomach Reviver 181
Fino Sherry
    Snowball 180

G
Galliano
    Bourbon Milk Punch 39
    Hot Shot 107
    Jumping Jack Flash 113
gin
    Alaska 12
    Angel Face 15
    Appetiser 16
    Apricot Cocktail 17
    Atta Boy Cocktail 18
    Aviation Cocktail 18
    Aviator 18

Barbary Coast 28
Belmont 29
Blue Bird 37
Bradford 46
Bunny Hug 51
Dixie 70
Dry Martini 72
Dubonnet cocktail 70
Earthquake 75
Empire 76
English Garden 76
Fallen Angel 77
Fascinator 79
Fernet Branca Cocktail 79
Fine and Dandy 86
Fizz 86
Flip 83
Fog Cutter 83
Fog Horn 84
Franklin Martin 88
Gibson 90
Gimlet 93
Gin & Tonic 98
Gin and It 97
Gin Daisy 97
Gin Sling 97
Hanky Panky 104
Hurricane 107
Ideal 108
Imperial 109
Jackson 111
Jockey Club 112
John Collins 112
Journalist 113
Jupiter Martini 114
Leap Year 117
Leave it to Me 117
Little Devil 118
London 119

Loud Speaker 119
Maiden's Blush 123
Maiden's Prayer 124
Martinez 124
Mayfair 129
Merry Widow 129
Mint Cocktail 130
Mint Collins 131
Mint Fizz 131
Monkey Gland 134
Moonshine 134
Mule's Hind Leg 135
Opal 139, 140
Opera 140
Orange Bloom 141
Orange Martini 141
Paisley Martini 141
Paradise 142
Park Avenue 143
Pink Gin 152
Pink Hound 152
Ramos Gin Fizz 160
Raspberry Martini 161
Red Snapper 163
Resolute 164
Rickey 164
Silver Fizz 178
Silver Martini 178
Stanley 181
Suffering Bastard 185
Tango Martini 186
Tom Collins 189
Typhoon 191
Vesper Martini 193
White Lady 202 203
ginger ale
    Bourbon Highball 39
    Fog Horn 84
    Shirley Temple 173, 175

Suffering Bastard 185
Umbongo 191
ginger beer
    Dark 'n' Stormy 69
    El Diablo 76
    Moscow Mule 136
ginger wine
    Whisky Mac 196
gommé syrup
    Blues Cocktail 38
Grand Marnier
    Alamagoozlum 12
    Champagne Cup 59
    Gloom Chaser 101
    Grand Mimosa 102
    Irish Flag 110
    Leap Year 117
    Leave it to Me 117
    Mimosa 130
    Mulled Wine 135
    Park Avenue 143
grapefruit juice
    Bloodhound 31
    Ideal 108
    Lima Sour 118
    Pink Hound 152
    Rasputin 161
    Sea Breeze 173, 175
    Showbiz 175
    Tropic 190
    Tulip 190
    Zombie 204
grenadine
    American Beauty 15
    Atta Boy Cocktail 18
    Bacardi Cocktail 24
    Belmont 29
    Champagne Daisy 59
    Clipper Cocktail 60

211

Gin Daisy 97
Gloom Chaser 101
Harry's Pick-Me-Up 104
Hobson's Choice 106
Leap Year 117
Leave it to Me 117
Maiden's Blush 123
Mary Pickford 124
Millionaire Cocktail 130
Monkey Gland 134
Opening Shot 140
Pussyfoot Cocktail 158
Shirley Temple 173, 175
Stanley 181
Tequila Sunrise 187
Union Jack 191
Zombie 204
Guiness
Black Velvet 30

H
honey
Aura 20
Blue Blazer 37
Cold Comfort 60
Hair of the Dog 102
Honey Bee 106
Sangrita 166
Vampire 192
White Swan 202
horseradish sauce
Bloody Mary 33–4

I
ice 8–9
Scotch Mist 173
ingredients, basic 9–10

J

Jonge Jenever
Alamagoozlum 12
Collins 60

L
lager
Snakebite 180
layering 8
lemon, bitter
Campari Nobile 55
lemon juice
Apricot Cocktail 17
Aura 20
Aviation Cocktail 18
Bloody Bull 32
Bloody Caesar 32
Bloody Maria 34
Bloody Mary 33–4
Blue Bird 37
Bourbon Pick-Me-Up 42
Brandy Fizz 43
Brandy Sour 46
Bullshot 48
Camel 52
Champagne Daisy 59
Charlie Chaplin 59
Collins 60
Corpse Reviver 61
Doctor 71
Fallen Angel 77
Fine and Dandy 86
Fizz 86
Gin Daisy 97
Gin Sling 97
Gloom Chaser 101
Harry's Pick-Me-Up 104
Honey Bee 106
Hop Toad 107
Hurricane 107

Iced Tea 108
Ink Street 109
Jack Collins 111
Jockey Club 112
John Collins 112
Journalist 113
Leave it to Me 117
Little Devil 118
Loud Speaker 119
Mai Tai 125
Maiden's Blush 123
Maiden's Prayer 124
Mulled Wine 135
Paradise 142
Pussyfoot Cocktail 158
Ramos Gin Fizz 160
Rattlesnake 162
Red Snapper 163
Resolute 164
Between the Sheets 29
Sidecar 174
Silver Fizz 178
Singapore Sling 179
Stanley 181
Sympathy 185
Tokyo Bloody Mary 188
Tom Collins 189
Tropic 190
Tulip 190
Wake-Up Call 196
Whiskey Sour 299
White Lady 203
lemon peel
    Blue Blazer 37
lemon slice
    Tom Collins 189
lemon twist
    Bourbon Highball 39
    Sazerac 169

lemon zest
    Dry Martini 72
    Scotch Mist 173
    Vodka Martini 197
lemonade
    Lemon Pie 117
    Pimm's Cup 144
    Pulp Fiction 158
    Snowball 180
lime cordial
    Fog Horn 84
    Gimlet 93
    Snowball 180
    Typhoon 191
lime juice
    Bacardi Cocktail 24
    Ballet Russe 24
    Blood Transfusion 31
    Bourbon Smash 42
    Cold Comfort 60
    Cosmopolitan 64
    Cuba Libre 65
    Cuban Special 65
    Daiquiri 66
    Dark 'n' Stormy 69
    El Diablo 76
    English Garden 76
    Fog Cutter 83
    Fox Trot 87
    Hobson's Choice 106
    Lima Sour 118
    Mai Tai 125
    Margarita 126
    Millionaire Cocktail 130
    Mint Collins 131
    Mint Fizz 131
    Mojito 133
    Moscow Mule 136
    Old Chappie 139

Planter's Punch 147
Pussyfoot Cocktail 158
Rickey 164
Sangrita 166
Scarlett O'Hara 170
South Pacific 180
Suffering Bastard 185
Vampire 192
Zombie 204
lime wedges
    Bullshot 48
    Gimlet 93
    Moscow Mule 136
    Planter's Punch 147
    Rickey 164
    Sea Breeze 173, 175
Limoncello
    Campari Nobile 55
lychee liqueur
    South Pacific 180

M
Madeira
    Baltimore Eggnog 27
    Blues Cocktail 38
maple syrup
    Mule's Hind Leg 135
Maraschino juice
    Champagne Cup 59
Marashino liqueur
    Aviation Cocktail 18
    Diplomat 70
    Ideal 108
    Imperial 109
    Lima Sour 118
    Mary Pickford 124
    Moonshine 134
    Opera 140
    Silver Martini 178

Union Jack 191
    Zombie 204
Martini, dry
    Dixie 70
measuring shots 9
melon liqueur
    E.T. 77
    Mae West Martini 123
milk
    Aura 20
    Baltimore Eggnog 27
    Banana Cow 27
    Bourbon Milk Punch 39
    Brandy Alexander 43
    Brandy Milk Punch 44
    Breakfast Egg Nog 47
    Irish Latté 110
    White Swan 202
mint
    Apple of my Eye 17
    Bourbon Pick-Me-Up 42
    Bourbon Smash 42
    Campari Nobile 55
    Fascinator 79
    Mai Tai 125
    Mint Cocktail 130
    Mint Collins 131
    Mint Fizz 131
    Mint Julep 132
    Mojito 133
    Pimm's Cup 144
mixing 7–8
muddling 8
Myers Punch Rum
    Planter's Punch 147

N
nutmeg
    Brandy Alexander 43

Breakfast Egg Nog 47
Mulled Wine 135
Tom and Jerry 188
White Swan 202

O
olives 10
  Dry Martini 72
  Franklin Martin 88
  Vodka Martini 193
onions
  Vampire 192
onions, cocktail
  Gibson 90
  Sangrita 166
orange bitters
  Alaska 12
  Bradford 46
  Jackson 111
  Jockey Club 112
  London 119
  Manhattan 120
  Old Fashioned 139
  Orange Martini 141
  Raspberry Martini 161
  Silver Martini 178
  Trilby 189
  Trinity 190
orange Curaçao
  Breakfast Egg Nog 47
  East India Cocktail 75
  Fox Trot 87
  Gloom Chaser 101
  Johnnie Mack 112
  Mai Tai 125
  Maiden's Blush 123
orange flower water
  Ramos Gin Fizz 160
orange juice

American Beauty 15
Appetiser 16
Apricot Cocktail 17
Aura 20
Back to Work 22
Buck's Fizz 51
Campari Nobile 55
Cranberry Collins 64
Embassy Royal 75
Fog Cutter 83
Fuzzy Navel 87
Grand Mimosa 102
Hobson's Choice 106
Iced Tea 108
Ink Street 109
Jumping Jack Flash 113
Jupiter Martini 114
Madras 123
Maiden's Prayer 124
Mayfair 129
Mimosa 130
Monkey Gland 134
Opal 140
Orange Martini 141
Paradise 142
Pussyfoot Cocktail 158
Sangria 166
Sangrita 166
Screwdriver 174
Tango Martini 186
Tequila Sunrise 187
Umbongo 191
Valencia 199
Vampire 192
orange peel
  Ritz Reviver 165
orange rind
  Orange Martini 141
orange slices

Screwdriver 174
orange twist
    Campari Nobile 55
orange zest
    Manhattan 120
    Old Fashioned 139
    Rob Roy 165
orgeat syrup
    Mai Tai 125
Ouzo
    Camel 52

P
Parfait Amour
    Brazen Martini 46
    Joan Bennett 113
    Jupiter Martini 114
    Trilby 189
passion fruit
    Monza 134
    South Pacific 180
    Umbongo 191
peach juice
    Bellini 23
Pernod
    Corpse Reviver 61
    Fog Lifter 84
    Heart Starter 105
    Sazerac 169
    Zombie 206
Peychaud Bitters
    Sazerac 169
Pimm's
    Pimm's Cup 144
pineapple juice
    Cuban Special 65
    Downhill Racer 71
    East India Cocktail 75
    Heaven's Above 105

Joan Bennett 113
Jumping Jack Flash 113
Mary Pickford 124
Park Avenue 143
Pina Colada 151
South Pacific 180
pineapple slices
    Mai Tai 125
    Pina Colada 151
Pisco brandy
    Lima Sour 118
port
    American Beauty 15
    The Assassin 19
presentation 10
Punsch, Swedish
    Doctor 71
Punt e Mes
    The Apothecary 19

R
raspberries
    Bourbon Smash 42
    Campari Nobile 55
    Raspberry Martini 161
raspberry juice
    Campari Nobile 55
rum
    Baltimore Eggnog 27
    Cold Comfort 60
    Cuban Special 65
    Dark 'n' Stormy 69
    Fog Cutter 83
    Iced Tea 108
    Joan Bennett 113
    Mary Pickford 124
    Millionaire Cocktail 130
    Parisien Blonde 142
    Stanley 181

see also Bacardi rum
rum, dark
    Tom and Jerry 188
rum, golden
    Daiquiri 66
    Doctor 71
    Downhill Racer 71
    Heaven's Above 105
    Pina Colada 151
    Zombie 206
rum, Jamaican
    Zombie 206
rum, light
    Aura 20
    Zombie 206
rum, white
    Alamagoozlum 12
    Banana Cow 27
    Clipper Cocktail 60
    Cuba Libre 65
    Honey Bee 106
    Jayne Mansfield 111
    Mojito 133
    Between the Sheets 29
rye whiskey
    Back to Work 22

S
Sagatiba Cachaca
    Batida de Coco 22
saké
    Tokyo Bloody Mary 188
Sambuca
    Raging Bull 160
    Typhoon 191
Schnapps
    Sangria 166
Schnapps, peach
    Fuzzy Navel 87

Scotch whisky
    Blue Blazer 37
    Godfather 101
    Scotch Mist 173
    Whisky Mac 196
shaking 7–8
sherry
    Blood Transfusion 31
    White Swan 202
sherry, dry
    Alaska 12
sherry, medium
    Tokyo Bloody Mary 188
Sirop de Citron
    Big Boy 30
sloe gin
    Charlie Chaplin 59
    Johnnie Mack 112
    Millionaire Cocktail 130
    Sloe Motion 178
soda
    Brandy Fizz 43
    Camel 52
    Camomile Fizz 52
    Collins 60
    Cranberry Collins 64
    Fizz 86
    Gin Sling 97
    Jack Collins 111
    John Collins 112
    Mint Collins 131
    Mint Fizz 131
    Mint Julep 132
    Mojito 133
    Planter's Punch 147
    Ramos Gin Fizz 160
    Remsen Cooler 163
    Rickey 164
    Sazerac 169

Silver Fizz 178
Sympathy 185
Tom Collins 189
Southern Comfort
    Scarlett O'Hara 170
strawberries
    Jayne Mansfield 111
    Pimm's Cup 144
strawberry liqueur *see* crème de fraise
sugar cubes
    Champagne Cocktail 56
    Old Fashioned 139

T
Tabasco sauce
    Back to Work 22
    Bloody Caesar 32
    Bloody Maria 34
    Bloody Mary 33–4
    Bullshot 48
    Prairie Oyster 155
    Red Snapper 163
    Tokyo Bloody Mary 188
    Wake-Up Call 198
tea, cold
    Iced Tea 108
Tequila
    Bloody Maria 34
    El Diablo 76
    Margarita 126
    Raging Bull 160
    Sangrita 166
    Tequila Slammer 186
    Tequila Sunrise 187
    Thomas Abercrombie 187
    Vampire 192
tomato juice
    Aura 20

Back to Work 22
Blood Transfusion 31
Bloody Bull 32
Bloody Maria 34
Bloody Mary 33–4
Pheasant Runner 143
Red Snapper 163
Sangrita 166
Tokyo Bloody Mary 188
Vampire 192
Wake-Up Call 196
tonic water
    Gin & Tonic 98
Triple Sec
    Cosmopolitan 64
    Dandy Cocktail 69
    Iced Tea 108
    Little Devil 118
    Maiden's Prayer 124
    Margarita 126
    Martinez 124
    Opal 140
    Orange Bloom 141
    Between the Sheets 29
    Sidecar 174
    Singapore Sling 179
    Tango Martini 186
    White Lady 205

V
vermouth
    American Beauty 15
    Apple Jack 16
    Atta Boy Cocktail 18
    Corpse Reviver 61
vermouth, dry
    Aviator 18
    Bradford 46
    Brooklyn 47

Clipper Cocktail 60
Diplomat 70
Dolce-Amaro 71
Dry Martini 72
Franklin Martin 88
Gibson 90
Imperial 109
Incognito 109
Journalist 113
Jupiter Martini 114
Leap Year 117
Leave it to Me 117
Little Princess 118
Merry Widow 129
Moonshine 134
Old Pal 139
Orange Martini 141
Paddy 142
Paisley Martini 141
Princess 158
Silver Martini 178
Tango Martini 186
Trinity 190
Vesper Martini 193
Vodka Martini 195
vermouth, red
    Embassy Royal 75
vermouth, sweet
    Aviator 18
    Diplomat 70
    Fascinator 79
    Fernet Branca Cocktail 79
    Flying Scotsman 83
    Froupé 87
    Gin and It 97
    Hanky Panky 104
    Ideal 108
    Journalist 113
    Manhattan 120

Martinez 124
Milano 129
Opening Shot 140
Orange Bloom 141
Orange Martini 141
Park Avenue 143
Remember the Main 162
Rob Roy 165
Tango Martini 186
Trilby 189
vinegar, malt
    Prairie Oyster 155
vodka
    Apple Martini 16
    Aura 20
    Ballet Russe 24
    Blood Transfusion 31
    Bloodhound 31
    Bloody Bull 32
    Bloody Caesar 32
    Bloody Mary 33–4
    Brazen Martini 46
    Bullshot 48
    Camomile Fizz 52
    Campari Nobile 55
    Cosmopolitan 64
    Cranberry Collins 64
    E.T. 77
    Fizz 86
    Madras 123
    Mae West Martini 123
    Milano 129
    Monza 134
    Moscow Mule 136
    Pheasant Runner 143
    Screwdriver 174
    Sea Breeze 173, 175
    Showbiz 175
    South Pacific 180

Tatanka 186
Umbongo 191
Vesper Martini 193
Vodka Martini 193
Wake-Up Call 196
vodka, raspberry
  Rasputin 161

W
whisky
  Barbary Coast 28
  Blues Cocktail 38
  Bourbon Milk Punch 39
  Bunny Hug 51
  Earthquake 75
  Fizz 86
  Flip 83
  Flying Scotsman 83
  Hair of the Dog 102
  Hurricane 107
  Ink Street 109
  Jumping Jack Flash 113
  Lemon Pie 117
  Manhattan 120
  Paisley Martini 141
  Remsen Cooler 163
  Rob Roy 165
  Trilby 189
  Trinity 190
      see also Bourbon; rye
whiskey; Scotch
whisky, Irish
  Irish Coffee 110
  Paddy 142
wine, red
  Mulled Wine 135
  Sangria 166
wine, white
  Batonnet 28

Mint Cocktail 130
Tropic 190
Worcestershire sauce
  Aura 20
  Blood Transfusion 31
  Bloody Bull 32
  Bloody Caesar 32
  Bloody Maria 34
  Bloody Mary 33–4
  Bullshot 48
  Prairie Oyster 155
  Red Snapper 163
  Sangrita 166
  Tokyo Bloody Mary 188
  Vampire 192

INDEX OF FILMS

A

After Office Hours (1935) 128
Albert, Eddie 177
All about Eve (1950) 92
Apartment, The 138
Armstrong, Louis 14
Arnold, Edward 197

B

Bacall, Lauren 36
Baxter, Anne 92
Beloved Infidel (1959) 177
Bennett, Constance 128
Bergman, Ingrid 58
Big Sleep, The (1946) 36
Bitter Victory (1958) 54
Blaine, Vivian 150
Bogart, Humphrey 36, 58, 63
Born to Dance (1936) 96
Brando, Marlon 150
Brook, Albert 100
Brooks, Richard 184
Brown, Joe E. 154
Burton, Richard 54, 96
Bushell, Anthony 54, 96
Butterfield (1960) 122

C

Campbell, Martin 196
Capra, Frank 204
Caron, Leslie 26
Casablanca (1942) 58
Casino Royale (2006) 193
Cat on a Hot Tin Roof (1958) 184
Chandler, Raymond 36

Cheadle, Don 100
Chevalier, Maurice 26
Clooney, George 100
Colbert, Claudette 201
Connolly, Walter 204
Cooper, Gladys 146
Coward, Noel 68
Craig, Daniel 193
Crawford, Joan 50
Cromwell, John 63
Crosby, Bing 14
Cukor, George 116
Cummings, Constance 197
Curtis, Tony 154
Curtiz, Michael 58

D

Davis, Bette 92, 146
de Havilland, Olivia 172
Dead Reckoning (1947) 63
Del Ruth, Roy 96
Dench, Judi 196
Donen, Stanley 168

E

Ellen, Vera 168

F

Farina, Dennis 100
Fisher, Eddie 122
Fleming, Victor 172

G

Gable, Clark 128, 172, 204
Garrett, Betty 168
Garson, Greer 88

Gigi (1958) 26
Gingold, Hermione 26
Gone with the Wind (1939) 172
Grant, Cary 116
Green, Eva 196
Guinness, Alec 68
Guys and Dolls (1955) 150
Guzman, Luis 100

H
Harvey, Laurence 122
Hawks, Howard 36
Hemmingway, Ernest 66
Henreid, Paul 58, 146
Hepburn, Katharine 116
High Society (1956) 14
Holm, Celeste 14, 92
How to Murder your Wife (1965) 41
Howard, Leslie 172

I
It Happened One Night (1934) 202
Ives, Burl 68, 184

J
Jourdan, Louis 26
Jurgens, Curt 54, 96

K
Kaye, Stubby 150
Keaton, Michael 100
Kelly, Gene 168
Kelly, Grace 14
Kerr, Deborah 177
King, Henry 177
Kovacs, Ernie 68

L
La Cava, Gregory 74
Leigh, Vivien 172
Lemmon, Jack 41, 138, 154
Leonard, Robert Z. 128
Lombard, Carole 74
Lopez, Jennifer 100
Loy, Myrna 82
Lund, John 14

M
MacLaine, Shirley 138
McLeod, Norman Z. 88
Mankiewicz, Joseph L. 92, 150
Mann, Daniel 122
Merrill, Dina 122
Merrill, Gary 92
Mikkelsen, Mads 196
Miller, Ann 168
Miller, David 50
Minnelli, Vincente 26
Monroe, Marilyn 92, 154
Munshin, Jules 168
My Man Godfrey (1936) 74

N
Newman, Paul 184
Now, Voyager (1960) 146

O
O'Brien, Pat 154
O'Hara, Maureen 68
On the Town (1949) 168
Our Man in Havana (1959) 68
Out of Sight (1998) 100

P
Palance, Jack 50
Peck, Gregory 177